CURIOUS ENCOUNTERS: VOYAGING, COLLECTING, AND MAKING KNOWLEDGE IN THE LONG EIGHTEENTH CENTURY

THE UCLA CLARK MEMORIAL LIBRARY SERIES

CURIOUS ENCOUNTERS

VOYAGING, COLLECTING, AND MAKING KNOWLEDGE IN THE LONG EIGHTEENTH CENTURY

Edited by Adriana Craciun and Mary Terrall

Published by the University of Toronto Press in association with the UCLA Center for Seventeenth- and Eighteenth-Century Studies and the William Andrews Clark Memorial Library utorontopress.com

ISBN 978-1-4875-0367-3

Library and Archives Canada Cataloguing in Publication

Curious encounters : voyaging, collecting, and making knowledge in the long eighteenth century / edited by Adriana Craciun and Mary Terrall.

(UCLA Clark Memorial Library series ; 26)
Includes bibliographical references and index.
ISBN 978-1-4875-0367-3 (hardcover)

1. Civilization, Modern – 18th century. 2. Civilization, Western – 18th century. 3. Eighteenth century. 4. Collectors and collecting – History – 18th century. 5. Curiosity – History – 18th century. 6. Discoveries in geography – History – 18th century. I. Craciun, Adriana, 1967–, editor II. Terrall, Mary, editor III. Series: UCLA Clark Memorial Library series ; 26

CB411.C87 2019 909.7 C2018-904971-5

This book has been published with the help of a grant from the UCLA Center for Seventeenth- and Eighteenth-Century Studies.

University of Toronto Press acknowledges the financial assistance to its publishing program of the Canada Council for the Arts and the Ontario Arts Council, an agency of the Government of Ontario.

Canada Council for the Arts Conseil des Arts du Canada

Funded by the Government of Canada Financé par le gouvernement du Canada

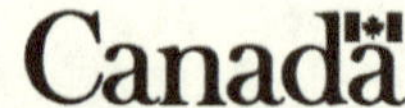

Contents

Illustrations

Acknowledgments

The editors wish to thank the staff of the UCLA Center for Seventeenth- and Eighteenth-Century Studies and the William Andrews Clark Memorial Library for their generous assistance and support of the year-long series of conferences on "Explorations, Encounters, and the Circulation of Knowledge" that inspired the publication of this volume. We are also grateful to all the participants in our conferences, speakers and audience members, who made these events so intellectually fruitful. We would especially like to acknowledge the participation of our three postdoctoral fellows for 2014–15: Matthew Goldmark, Eric Otremba, and Elizabeth Montañez Sanabria.

CURIOUS ENCOUNTERS: VOYAGING, COLLECTING, AND MAKING KNOWLEDGE IN THE LONG EIGHTEENTH CENTURY

Figure 0.1 "First Communication with the Natives of Prince Regents Bay, Drawn by John Sackheouse [*sic*]." Lithograph printed in John Ross, *A Voyage of Discovery* (1819). Courtesy of the John Carter Brown Library at Brown University.

Introduction

ADRIANA CRACIUN AND MARY TERRALL

> If historical facts are launched by historians with creative freedom, that license to make History is hedged about by two limitations: discipline and discovery. Historians are bound by the poetics of their particular kind of history, and the only past they can recover is the relics of it they find.
>
> – Greg Dening, *History's Anthropology: The Death of William Gooch*

Our histories of global exploration and encounter in the long eighteenth century are often drawn from the scientific voyages of discovery and their richly illustrated books, like John Ross's *A Voyage of Discovery* (1819). Ross voyaged in the Enlightenment tradition of Bougainville and Cook, who had returned to Europe in ships laden with knowledge in the form of diverse natural and artificial curiosities, innovative images, observations, even people. These global voyages transformed European systems of knowledge and aesthetics, while the missionary, military, and commercial interests that often followed their tracks profoundly affected indigenous people the world over.

Ross failed to find the Northwest Passage through the High Arctic, but he made his claim to original discovery in his encounter with an Inuit group previously unknown to Europeans. Ross, a Scotsman, claimed credit for discovering the Inughuit of Qaanaaq in northern Greenland, and named them "Arctic Highlanders." The Inughuit "exist in a corner of the world by far the most secluded which has yet to be discovered," wrote Ross, and had "until the moment of our arrival, believed themselves to be the only inhabitants of the universe."[1] Spending several days meeting with the Inughuit on the ice and aboard his ship, Ross described their "astonishment" (94), "terror and amazement" (85) upon seeing the

British ships, weapons, and scientific instruments – all set pieces within the "encounter genre" of Enlightenment exploration.[2] Ross's conventional version of the meaning of these encounters, and of the isolation of the "Arctic Highlanders" as the literal location of the mythic *Ultima Thule*, are partial stories that have become iconic examples of European exploration and encounter. They are the "relics" of our disciplined histories, as Greg Dening would say.

But, as Nicholas Thomas has pointed out, "knowing was never a one-way activity."[3] Inuit stories and Inuit images of these encounters allow us to imagine otherwise, to consider what Greenlanders may have discovered in their encounters with these "peculiar floating samples"[4] of Britain. Accompanying Ross's expedition was an indigenous Greenlander known to the British as John Sacheuse (aka Zacheus), who orchestrated the first contact with the Inughuit.[5] Converted by Moravian missionaries in Disko Bay, Sacheuse voluntarily boarded a whaler for Edinburgh in 1816, and lived the rest of his extraordinary and brief life traversing the borders of several cultures. In Edinburgh, Sacheuse had met two leading figures in the arts and sciences: Alexander Nasmyth, the leading landscape painter of the age, and Sir Basil Hall, a naval captain and brother to the president of the Royal Society of Edinburgh. He studied painting in Nasmyth's prestigious school and accompanied Ross as a paid interpreter on board the *Isabella*. We know that the *Isabella* was searching for the Northwest Passage, but what was Sacheuse searching for?

Sacheuse returned to Edinburgh with Ross and immediately began preparing for another expedition, Parry's 1819 search for the Northwest Passage: "he looked forward with the utmost keenness and anxiety to the sailing of the expedition ... being perfectly aware, at the same time, of his own value upon the occasion." Before the ship sailed, Sacheuse died quite suddenly of "inflammation" in February 1819, aged twenty-two, and our research confirms that he was buried in the prestigious Canongate Kirkyard on the Royal Mile in Edinburgh. The location of his grave remained unknown until now and thus no marker in Canongate memorializes Sacheuse among the dead buried there.[6] Sacheuse's death was followed by the dispersal of his belongings to family in Denmark, the ethnographic collections of British museums, and probably private art collections. The erasure of his grave and career in the capital of the Scottish Enlightenment reminds us of the dangers "of overstating ... encounters and equivalencies," as Coll Thrush warns, "drawing our attention to the unequal power relations of empire"[7] that continue to reinscribe histories in uneven ways.

Sacheuse made several paintings while on board the *Isabella*, and one of them survives in the form of a coloured lithograph, offering us a glimpse of his perspective: "First Communication with the Natives of Prince Regents Bay, Drawn by John Sackheouse [*sic*]" (Figure 0.1).[8] This image enjoyed pride of place in the official voyage publication at a time when visual knowledge was one of the most highly valued commodities collected on long-distance expeditions. Whereas Ross stressed priority, discovery, and the otherness of the Inughuit in his narrative, Sacheuse focused in on encounter and exchange. "Everything in the picture tells of a meeting," writes one of the few art historical accounts of Sacheuse's work.[9] As one of the earliest known Inuit artists trained in European practices, Sacheuse combined "Inuit traditions for visual storytelling with European representational techniques to arrive at a synthesis that testifies to the ways in which [he] himself lived and moved in both cultures."[10]

Sacheuse had devised a novel, hybrid technique suited for a singular "first communication." And even more significantly, he placed himself at the centre of the encounter in what appears to be the first extant Inuit self-portrait. Having given the Inughuit mirrors, Sacheuse then pictured them in the act of self-reflection, a carefully drawn Inuk's face smiling in the mirror. These fleeting glimpses of Inuit self-reflection and storytelling appear in an image otherwise devoted to ceremonies of possession – Ross's title, the associated map, and the narrative all rename Qaanaaq as Prince Regents Bay, and the people as Arctic Highlanders. Sacheuse evidently called them the Northmen.[11]

In his prose account, Ross described how Sacheuse had made the initial overtures to the Inughuit, persisting in difficult meetings over several days because the two Greenlandic dialects spoken were initially mutually incomprehensible. Sacheuse then led Ross and Parry, captains of the *Isabella* and *Alexander*, to meet the Inughuit, whom he shows exchanging narwhal tusks for knives. Sacheuse actually depicted three distinct encounters in "First Communication": an initial meeting between himself and the Inughuit in the distance; his second meeting, this time wearing a naval uniform (holding the shirt), with the Inughuit, who see themselves in the mirror he has given them; and in the foreground Captains Parry and Ross exchanging gifts with two Greenlanders. The series of three meetings is unusual in Western encounter pictures and suggests a temporal progression, with "the figures positioned closer to the foreground not only growing in size but representing events that occurred closer to the present."[12] Sacheuse's lively vision of plural encounters reflects one of this volume's central tenets, that "[c]onquest, exploration, voyages of discovery are about the meeting up of histories, not merely a pushing-out 'across space.'"[13]

As lead intermediary, Sacheuse devised an innovative composition for imagining and representing their encounters, and pictured himself as a central figure wearing British naval clothing. He included the conventional elements of this genre of history painting – the ships at anchor with their prominent ensigns, the submissive posture and astonished faces of the Native people. But he also shows us two sources of European astonishment in the Arctic: the sublime icescape surrounding the bay, and the Inuk on the sledge commanding his dogs without hands or reins, using only his voice and whip, as Ross had marvelled in his account (102). European amazement at the technical skill and arts of indigenous people was a common feature of Pacific and Arctic exploration accounts, and "First Communication" highlights this, creating a subtle symmetry of wonder. Sacheuse's art may have been included in the book by Ross as a kind of "converted artifact"– "evidence of Inuit 'improvement' according to the British – but it is simultaneously an inscription (and part of a larger cultural exchange) that may have signified something completely different to its maker."[14] As his obituary noted, Sacheuse "never expressed any of that idiotic surprise which savages sometimes evince, on seeing any thing very different from what they had been accustomed to."[15] A patronizing compliment, but one that gives us a glimpse of a worldly and self-assured young man who could hold his own in European salons, naval ships, and ice floe encounters.

Sacheuse produced other shipboard drawings, now lost: a self-portrait with a broken arm, a drawing of Inughuit aboard the *Isabella* interacting with the crew and instruments, another encounter picture featuring himself planting a flag on the ice in an effort to attract the attention of the Inughuit.[16] Sacheuse's art, like his extraordinary life, left few traces, but these are intriguing and merit our attention. We do not know how much freedom Sacheuse enjoyed over the formal composition of "First Communication," over the depiction of the Inughuit, or how representative this brief catalogue of images was in its repeated motif of self-representation. But we can recognize with Miles Ogborn that "[t]o make a representation was always to take a position."[17]

What had initially appeared as a stolidly imperial vision of the discovery of an exotic and "unknown" people in Ross's official account has revealed a rich archive of encounters, with meanings as diverse as their participants, places, and media. Naval voyagers like Ross and Parry saw themselves as pushing out into empty spaces, driven by scientific curiosity and sometimes by a desire for conquest. But their partial visions should not frame our inquiries, lest we repeat the imperial histories that cast Europeans as history's mobile agents of global change and indigenous peoples as "firmly situated in place and culturally coherent."[18] Sacheuse was converted by missionaries, had family in Denmark, travelled aboard a British whaling ship, and joined a naval expedition of geographical discovery bound for North America and, beyond that, the Pacific. He probably spoke two European and two Greenlandic languages, was highly skilled with kayak and harpoon, and had started to study with artists and men of science in the Edinburgh Enlightenment. How might his perspective help us see "both sides"? An even more intriguing question, one that Nicholas Thomas broached regarding Pacific Island voyagers: How did voyagers like Sacheuse come to share a cosmopolitanism and curiosity that too often we consider exclusively European?[19]

Sacheuse was a singular figure, but he helps us to see the larger world in which these explorers ventured. For Ross and the Admiralty, Northwest Greenland was a remote outpost that might be absorbed into an expanding British empire. But Sacheuse was inspired by the possibilities of connecting Inuit communities across great distances, a common feature of Inuit sociality, with its long-distance travel and xenophilia. The Inughuit were hardly as isolated as the British believed; indeed, historically they descended from a much larger circumpolar Arctic civilization that had enjoyed long-range contact with European, North American, and Asian cultures in previous centuries.[20]

Thanks to the popularity of books like Ross's, however, "[t]he Inuit became the thrilling archetype of an aboriginal population that was truly *ab origine*: they were the only people who had ever occupied this region of the world" and "they had lived there since time immemorial."[21] This perspective on the "Arctic Highlanders" is, as archaeologist Robert McGhee argues, "truly obsolete" (129), and we can see that by attending to the complexities of Sacheuse's relations to the multivalent ways of voyaging long distances in his time – in kayaks, whalers, sledges, and naval warships, as well as in stories, pictures, and carvings.

As Michael Bravo writes in this volume about a different long-distance indigenous voyage, we need to rethink what counts as "Native travel," "exploration" and "migration." James Cook had begun to do this in 1774 when he realized the astonishing distances that Polynesians had travelled to colonize Oceania's islands: "It is extraordinary that the same nation should have spread themselves over all the isles of this Vast Ocean … which is almost one-fourth part of the circumference of the globe."[22]

Cook wrote this in Rapanui (Easter Island), which he considered the most isolated community on earth. But rather than seeing just the periphery of the present, Cook also glimpsed a different spatial vision on Rapanui, a vision grounded in cultural and linguistic affinities that connected people across a "sea of islands"[23] in ways Europeans were only beginning to imagine.

Global historians, anthropologists, postcolonial scholars, and geographers have also asked this: In what places and times, for what purposes, and with what transformative effects have cultures around the world pursued exploration more broadly conceived? Felipe Fernández-Armesto begins his global history of exploration with the "great divergence" at the origins of human history, the large-scale migrations of "trail finders" from Africa that fanned out across the globe more than one hundred thousand years ago.[24] Keeping in mind the existence of this vast historical and geographical scale of exploration, a scale that Cook had begun to recognize in the 1780s, we focus on the long eighteenth century in part because long-distance voyages were central to this era of European expansion and global connection. European encounters on the global stage remained "sporadic and unpredictable" during this time, as Miles Ogborn has written in a different context: "It was uncertain whether [encounters] would produce spectacular successes or equally spectacular failures ... No one on any side of these encounters knew what was going to happen next."[25] By the nineteenth century, however, "[e]ncounters had become routines," with modern systems of slavery, commercial trading, and colonial government often determining the possible outcomes.[26] The dynamic artefacts of encounters in the eighteenth century, from the material culture collected to the narratives composed, frame our collective inquiry in this volume precisely because they remained in flux.

Discussions of eighteenth-century exploration and explorers have until recently been figured through discourses of discovery like those of Ross and Cook. Such grand narratives of discovery have given way across historical disciplines to more nuanced investigations of "discovery events," entanglement, and encounter. As Simon Schaffer argues in an important essay on Enlightenment voyages of scientific discovery, "culturally defined communities matter to the establishment of discovery events."[27] Rather than describing the heroes and villains of discovery and exploration as if these are self-evident and transhistorically stable entities, we untangle the often complex cross-cultural forces that made discovery events legible as such. Registering credit and priority, financing inquiries, disseminating or suppressing results, displaying prestige, pursuing sociable exchange and violent usurpation – all are examples of how different communities shape our stories of what counts as discovery, why and where, and by whom. Sacheuse, who inhabited radically different societies, stands as important reminder that voyagers often belonged to multiple communities that spanned cultures, languages, and even oceans.

We began to pursue such questions collectively through the "Material Cultures of Knowledge" Research Group at the University of California in 2012; this culminated in a series of four conferences at UCLA's William Andrews Clark Library in 2014 and 2015: "Collections in Flux" and the year-long series on "Explorations, Encounters, and the Circulation of Knowledge." We invited historians of art, science, and literature, as well as museum curators, geographers, and anthropologists, to think about the instabilities and multi-directional communications entailed in various kinds of encounters and explorations. We sought to challenge assumptions about how metropolitan centres relate to distant peripheries, focusing particularly on dynamic collections, diverse discovery events and agents, and hybrid textual forms.

One of our goals in this collection has been to restore some degree of symmetry to our understanding of encounters and explorations by embracing multiple perspectives. To that end we have pursued diverse agents of historical change, both human and inanimate: commodities, curiosities, texts, and specimens moved through their own global circuits of knowledge and power. Following the circulation of things, as recently explored in the volume *The Material Cultures of Enlightenment Arts and Sciences*, can reframe our histories of the Enlightenment and its divisions of knowledge.[28] Like those of European and indigenous people, the travels of natural and artificial curiosities were unpredictable, and in the essays in this volume, they illuminate new geographies of knowledge and power.

In chapter 1, Markman Ellis destabilizes the encounter of Britons with China through the medium of tea, by imagining the agency of inanimate things. Ellis tells the story of "how tea discovered Britain" in the early eighteenth century. A few decades later, botanists like Linnaeus tended to erase the much longer history of Chinese knowledge of tea. But earlier in the British acculturation of tea, the plant itself was imagined to be the exotic agent of sociability and civilization, one that, as Ellis shows, played a visible role in Britain's self-identity as a polite and sociable nation. The new story of the transformation of *Camellia sinensis* into the quintessentially British drink varies across media – from printed essays and voyage accounts, to paintings and verse. The travels of tea – across space, aesthetic traditions, and domains of knowledge – exemplify the social life of things that shaped the "exotic genealogies"[29] of the European Enlightenment.

One of the most remarkable long-distance travellers of the early modern era was the Ottoman Evliya Çelebi. As Donna Landry shows in chapter 2, the legendary Sufi cosmopolitan Evliya has been neglected in European exploration studies, but deserves to be better known for the ways in which he instantiates "Ottoman modes of exploration, as well as theories of imperial management" distinct from those of Western voyagers. For starters, Evliya travelled on horseback, not aboard ships as European long-distance voyagers typically did. As a technology of travel and a form of intimacy, travel with horses produced distinctive relationships to the people, places, and animals encountered along the route. As Landry argues, for the Sufi explorer Evliya, horses were companions as well as essential allies in hostile encounters. Evliya produced a ten-volume account of his travels in manuscript, and in Landry's discussion of his erudite and cosmopolitan approach to the exotic West, we see the value of "provincializing Europe"[30] in our accounts of the Enlightenment and of exploration.

At the same time, indigenous long-distance voyagers can help provincialize heroic European voyages. As guides, interpreters, way finders, and mapmakers, indigenous people have been significant players in European exploration, sometimes in subordinated roles celebrated by European powers as signs of indigenous acceptance of European benevolence or reciprocity.[31] The high-ranking Raiatean priest Tupaia joined the *Endeavour* and played a critical role in Cook's explorations by sharing his oceanic and ethnographic knowledge, famously materialized in "Tupaia's chart" of the South Pacific islands unknown to the British. The naturalist Joseph Banks famously joked in his shipboard journal that he was tempted "to keep him [Tupaia] as a curiosity." But Banks also admired Tupaia as a social equal and as a "most proper man" who had visited seventy Pacific islands, far more than the British ships would ever explore. As Nicholas Thomas has shown, Tupaia's motivations for voyaging had much to do with the political turmoil of his life in exile on Tahiti, but also were driven by an insatiable curiosity: "He was ready to discover new paths, new *taio* [friends], and new temples." Cook treated Tupaia with the respect owed to his high social rank and expertise, but he also bristled at appearing to share command at times – theirs was a complex alliance that was shaped as much by Tupaia's political ambition, will, and curiosity as it was by Cook's geographical quest.

Tupaia was unique but he was not alone – "by the end of the eighteenth century, dozens certainly and maybe hundreds of [Pacific] Islanders had joined traders, whalers and other ships" on long-distance voyages. Pacific voyagers were also "avidly curious about other Polynesian places" and "were excited about the potential of political practices that were akin but distinct, by new rites that might be imported, by unfamiliar and prestigious objects, by the scope for new sorts of trade."[32] In other words, indigenous voyagers encountered by European explorers were not simply travelling from the imperial periphery to the European centre, and we should not reorient their travels and histories as though they began with or centred on European contact or priorities.

Michael Bravo in chapter 3, "Indigenous Voyaging, Authorship, and Discovery," illustrates this central thread by showing the myriad interests and perspectives of a group of Inuit during an 1811 missionary voyage to Ungava Bay in the Arctic. As Bravo argues, "guide" was a problematic term to apply to indigenous people who joined European voyages of exploration, for it could obscure or even erase their complex intentions. Bravo's "social history of travel as a cross-cultural phenomenon" focuses on the intriguing Arctic voyage of a ship chartered by a Moravian evangelical missionary who acknowledged a converted Inuit elder as "captain" of the enterprise. A predominantly Inuit crew sailed the ship in pursuit of a combination of missionary, geographical, and trading goals.

Instead of reinscribing this story as one of European geographical discovery or missionary conquest facilitated by Native guides, Bravo reveals the complex entanglements of numerous Inuit and Moravian perspectives. Christian Inuit and an unconverted shaman travelled with missionaries, experiencing icescapes through divergent spiritual traditions and often sharing common purposes. By introducing this hybrid voyage into our histories of exploration, Bravo points out the inadequacies of our taxonomies of exploration and encounter. The Inuit travellers were driven by xenophilia, spiritual purpose, a love of travel, and curiosity about other Inuit communities; the Moravians (unlike contemporary naval explorers) were respectful of local knowledge and technology among the people they hoped to convert and bring to trade. Was this a voyage of geographical discovery? a missionary expedition? an expansion of commercial and imperial power? an instance of Native travel for spiritual ends? In pursuing such questions, the essays in this volume restore questions of cross-cultural encounter and agency to our understanding of long-distance voyaging, no longer taking for granted, as in Bravo's essay, what distinguishes "native travel" from "exploration."

Replacing grand narratives of discovery with accumulated episodes of encounter – entailing exchanges, negotiations, and translations as well as violence and co-optation – requires finding ways to bring non-European, and non-literate, voices into audible range. As scholars looking back across the centuries, we must read the traces of encounters through surviving archives and artefacts, such as the paintings of Sacheuse. These traces are not always easy to decipher or to interpret, or even to identify. In each case, local circumstances and contingencies set limits on what we can know, through the mediation of diverse archives, about the negotiations and translations necessary for making knowledge about nature, societies, and cultures.

Collections of natural history specimens and other artefacts are one fruitful site for retrieving at least some elements of the exchanges and negotiations that brought objects together into European cabinets. The ubiquity of collections of all types in eighteenth-century Western Europe – in cities and provinces, in private homes and medical schools and botanical gardens – is a familiar theme in eighteenth-century studies. Collectors included the scientific and literary elite, nobles of robe and sword, government officials, and financiers, descending down the social scale to physicians, merchants, and apothecaries. Thousands upon thousands of stones and fossils, stuffed birds and mounted butterflies, animal skeletons and shells, plant materials and medical remedies, preserved reptiles and human body parts, filled cases and cabinets alongside weapons, clothing, and ceremonial objects from distant lands. How did these accumulated items mediate between nature and viewers, metropole and colony, Europe and the rest of the world? By juxtaposing objects from everywhere, such collections made visible not only the relations among natural or manufactured things, and the connections of resources to markets, but also the social relations underpinning these global exchanges of objects.

While such connections could be displayed in the labels and stories attached to items in collections, the knowledge and skills of the people who had collected specimens for their masters or for the market became invisible, as did the local meanings of objects wrenched from one context and reassigned to another. Thus common American animals like armadillos and hummingbirds became wondrous when killed, dried, and transported across the ocean, even though their new owners knew almost nothing about how and where these creatures lived or what they meant to people familiar with them. The motion of collected materials across the oceans and around the globe, from their original settings to shipboard to glass display boxes, endowed them with significance and opened them up to new interpretations. The history of surviving collections of objects and their associated texts can tell us about the uses of such arrays of things, as well as the activities that made their accumulation possible.

Hans Sloane's collection, numbering in the tens of thousands of objects and forming the basis for the British Museum, has attracted a great deal of scholarly attention recently, due in part to its sheer size, but also to the remarkable number of surviving specimens of all kinds, as well as catalogues, labels, and other related materials.[33] In chapter 4, Miles Ogborn and Victoria Pickering read Sloane's collection as "a mode of encounter with the early modern world," and it is in this innovative sense that our volume reconceives of archives as dynamic contact zones.[34] Sloane himself came in contact with Caribbean plants and people as a young doctor in colonial Jamaica, returning to England with hundreds of herbarium sheets, seeds, drawings, and notes. His experience in the tropics grounded a lifetime of collecting, organizing, and displaying. Visitors, and readers of Sloane's massive book on the natural history of Jamaica, came face to face with Caribbean nature newly framed for European consumption. Thus Sloane's own experiences on the American side of the Atlantic enabled not only his collection and his authorial productions, but also the experience of his visitors, who encountered a virtual version of Jamaica (and indeed many other places) in his London townhouse. As Ogborn and Pickering show, Sloane's collections aspired to completeness though he was constantly on the verge of being overwhelmed by the incoherence and heterogeneity of his possessions.

Even a collection as "universal" as Sloane's did not necessarily make the world straightforwardly knowable. So, for example, James Petiver's collection of Chinese medicinal plants (which Sloane later incorporated into his own museum), extensive though it was, hardly made Chinese knowledge of diagnostics or therapeutics accessible to English physicians. Similarly, exotic animals like the armadillo, whose story Kathleen Murphy tells in chapter 5, were literally only the shells of living animals, extracted from their habitats and any local meanings or uses they might have had to the people familiar with them. By the time this particular animal ended up in Sloane's collection, having passed through the hands of the ship surgeon John Burnet and the collector Petiver, Burnet's efforts to acquire a living armadillo, to keep it alive on its transatlantic journey, and then to use it to enhance his own status in London – all of this was erased in the display of the dried and mounted animal skin. Even more invisible were the conditions that put Burnet in a position to acquire the animal, namely, the slave ships on which he plied his medical trade. When the transatlantic slave trade becomes a "space of natural history," or when the profits of Jamaican sugar plantations are spent – as they were by Sloane – to swell the collections viewed with admiration by learned and fashionable visitors, what does that imply about the knowledge condensed into, or erased from, the arrays of specimens in museums? Encounters in archives can be as problematic and unpredictable as those between people.

In her examination of the bark cloth collected in the South Pacific by James Cook and others (chapter 6), Billie Lythberg opens up this kind of inquiry further; she considers the swatches of bark cloth as "ethnographic fragments" that reframe the original cloths on very different scales, abstracting them from their original meanings and local uses on the Pacific islands where they were made. Across Oceania, barkcloth (*tapa*) is a collectively produced art form with great social and spiritual significance, as well as everyday uses. The extraordinary compendia of barkcloth swatches, cut and pasted into limited-edition printed books by a London bookseller, crystallized one version of the encounters of Cook and his sailors and naturalists with Pacific islanders. These books, with their brief explanations of the different kinds of cloth from different places, and occasional stories of how they were acquired, also functioned as palpable relics of Cook's voyages, memorializing and aestheticizing encounters between Europeans and Pacific Islanders. The barkcloth books are thus hybrid archives in themselves, incorporating distinct cultural forms into a novel, transcultural form and thereby transforming (and diminishing) them.

In Lythberg's exploration of the nuances of these hybrid books, we can also see the value of considering the material form of the codex book itself as a dynamic archive. As Luisa Calè has argued regarding late-eighteenth-century practices such as "extra illustration" (wherein one book is transformed by breaking its binding, adding hundreds of new pages, and often vastly expanding the format in a new bound form), we can begin to rethink all books as "unstable repositories in a dynamic order of things."[35] Thus, like cabinets and collections, books can also work as both "modes of encounter" and technologies of exploration.

Encounters and exploration necessitated new forms of knowledge on this material level (e.g., the codex and the cabinet), and also in terms of the divisions of knowledge made possible by these novel forms. Global voyages of exploration like those of Cook or La Pérouse employed an encyclopedic scale of scientific inquiry, and in the case of European encounters with Pacific Islanders and islands, this meant that the convergence of natural history, early anthropology, and indigenous knowledge generated disciplinary changes. In chapter 8, Noah Heringman reads Johann Reinhold and George Forster, the German father-and-son naturalists on Cook's second voyage, to show how debates on the age of the earth and the "age of man" converged on the *Resolution.* At stake were the seemingly unbridgeable historical scales at work in each of these emerging fields. As Heringman shows, these began to overlap as the voyagers came to understand the challenges posed to the stadial frameworks and scales of their human and natural sciences as they visited dynamic volcanic islands and their populations. The Forsters' published accounts of their global voyage would become embroiled in disputes over intellectual and authorial propriety vis-à-vis the official Admiralty publications. But as Heringman argues, their remarkable books also served as occasions for disciplinary innovation, "mapping a generative area of uncertainty between geological and species time."

Books criss-crossed great spatial, cultural, and disciplinary distances on these global voyages, generating new forms such as the barkcloth books and new disciplinary possibilities such as the Forsters' Oceanic explorations of temporal scales. As Matthew Goldmark shows in chapter 7, these novel textual forms included new forms of address between newly converted indigenous Christians and "Old Christian" authorities in early modern Latin America. Examining petitions addressed by indigenous converts to Christian authorities, Goldmark shows how standard forms employed in colonial exchanges became problematic in the hands of indigenous writers, because they "could insinuate Indigenous and Spanish similarity." Written petitions from indigenous Christians, printed catechisms designed for their use, and priests themselves were transformed as they travelled in contact zones characterized by the uneasy interplay of Native custom and church doctrine. Rather than documenting events, these novel textual forms themselves served as modes of encounter between indigenous and Iberian customs, bodies, and languages.

The essays collected here reflect a variety of approaches to our central concern with encounters and the circulation of knowledge resulting from them. Our authors have found geographies of knowledge reflected in and condensed into material form in collections, documents, books, and images. Bringing essays on widely diverging topics into conversation with one another, we hope to show how productive it can be to think across the usual historiographical, literary, and geographical boundaries.

Greg Dening reminds us, in our epigraph, that our own encounters with the past are limited by the relics we find in our archives. Those relics are many and various, though, and when held up to different lights and refracted through different lenses they can allow us to rethink familiar readings.

NOTES

1 John Ross, *A voyage of discovery, made under the orders of the Admiralty, in his Majesty's ships Isabella and Alexander for the purpose of exploring Baffin's Bay, and enquiring into the possibility of a North-West Passage* (London: John Murray, 1819), 123.

2 Michael Bravo, "The Anti-Anthropology of Highlanders and Islanders," *Studies in the History and Philosophy of Science Part A* 29 (1998): 369–89, at 370.

3 Nicholas Thomas, *Discoveries: The Voyages of Captain Cook* (London: Allen Lane, 2003).

4 Ibid.

5 John Sacheuse was the most common English version of his converted Moravian name of Hans Zaccheus (presumably named for Zaccaheus in the New Testament), but he was referred to by many different spellings, including Sackehouse, Sackhouse, Sakeouse, Zakaeus, and Sakaeus. Accounts of Sacheuse's life in Britain (and theories about his reasons for leaving Greenland) were available at the time in Ross's account, in the extensive obituary in *Blackwood's* (see n11), and in contemporary newspaper accounts.

6 The burial register for Canongate Kirk notes the death of "Sackhouse, John, Native of Davies Straits" on 14 February 1819; he is "Intered in the Area 8 feet South of Fraser ground & 4 feet from the west wall," and died of "inflammation" at age twenty-two (Old Parish Registers Records 685/3 310 255 f128). There is a large monument to the Fraser family near the current west wall of the churchyard, but many of the remaining memorials in the area are illegible; the plaque of illustrious dead at the churchyard names Adam Smith, the poet Robert Fergusson, and many others.

7 Coll Thrush, "The Iceberg and the Cathedral," *Journal of British Studies* 53 (2014): 59–79, at 64.

8 Ross discusses Sacheuse's picture in detail and insists that the lithograph is "without the slightest variation from the original, the scale only being reduced to accommodate the size of the work" (87). The original paintings have not been found.

9 Bodil Kaalund, *The Art of Greenland* (Berkeley: University of California Press, 1983), 158.

10 Ingeborg Høvik, *Arctic Images 1818–1859* (PhD diss., Art History, University of Edinburgh 2013), 237.

11 Anon., "Some Account of the Late John Sakeouse, The Esquimaux," *Blackwood's Edinburgh Magazine* (March 1819): 656–658 (probably authored by Basil Hall).

12 Høvik, *Arctic Images*, 238.

13 Doreen Massey, *for space* (London: Sage, 2005), 120.

14 Adriana Craciun, *Writing Arctic Disaster: Authorship and Exploration* (Cambridge: Cambridge University Press, 2016); "converted artifact" is quoted from Nicholas Thomas, *Entangled Objects: Exchange, Material Culture, and Colonialism in the Pacific* (Cambridge, MA: Harvard University Press, 1991).

15 Anon, "Some account of the Late John Sakeouse," 658.

16 An anonymous newspaper account of the Inughuit encounters drawn from on-board witnesses notes that "we have seen some of the pictures drawn by Sackhouse, a representation of his first interview," showing him planting a flag on the ice. Another picture shows "the astonishment of the natives, upon examining the different parts of the vessel," and another shows Sacheuse himself with his arm in a sling ("The Newly Discovered Nation," *Hereford Journal*, 23 December, 1818, 4). These three images have not been located but their details correspond to the narrative of shipboard events later published by Ross. It is probable that like all shipboard artists, Sacheuse produced many drawings and that some of these have been dispersed, unidentified or misidentified, into various collections, as was the case with Tupaia's sketchbook, misidentified as the work of Joseph Banks until recently (see Keith Vincent Smith, "Tupaia's Sketchbook" *Electronic British Library Journal* [2005], http://www.bl.uk/eblj/2005articles/article10.html).

17 Miles Ogborn, *Global Lives: Britain and the World 1550–1800* (Cambridge: Cambridge University Press, 2008), 314.

18 Nicholas Thomas, *Islanders: The Pacific in the Age of Empire* (New Haven: Yale University Press, 2010), 3.

19 Ibid., 3–6.

20 Richard Vaughan, "How Isolated Were the Polar Eskimos in the Nineteenth Century?," in *Between Greenland and America: Cross-Cultural Contacts and the Environment in the Baffin Bay Area*, ed. L. Hacquebord and R. Vaughan (Groningen: University of Groningen, Arctic Centre, 1987), 95–107.

21 Robert McGhee, *The Last Imaginary Place: A Human History of the Arctic World* (Oxford: Oxford University Press, 2005), 106.

22 James Cook, *A Voyage Towards the South Pole* (London: Strahan and Cadell, 1777), 290.

23 Epeli Hau'ofa, "Our Sea of Islands," *The Contemporary Pacific* 6 (1994): 147–61.

24 Felipe Fernández-Armesto, *Pathfinders: A Global History of Exploration* (New York: W.W. Norton, 2006).

25 Ogborn, *Global Lives,* 330.

26 Ibid.

27 Simon Schaffer, "Visions of Empire: Afterword," in *Visions of Empire: Voyages, Botany, and Representations of Nature,* ed. D.P. Miller and P.H. Reill (Cambridge: Cambridge University Press, 1996), 335–52, at 336.

28 Adriana Craciun and Simon Schaffer, eds., *The Material Cultures of Enlightenment Arts and Sciences* (London: Palgrave Macmillan, 2016).

29 Simon Schaffer, "How Disciplines Look," in *Interdisciplinarity: Reconfigurations of the Social and Natural Sciences,* ed. Andrew Barry and Georgina Born (London: Routledge, 2013): 57–81; Arjun Appadurai, ed., *The Social Life of Things* (Cambridge: Cambridge University Press, 1996).

30 Dipesh Chakrabarty, *Provincializing Europe* (Princeton: Princeton University Press, 2000).

31 Felix Driver and Lowri Jones, *Hidden Histories of Exploration* (London: Royal Holloway, University of London and Royal Geographical Society, 2009).

32 Thomas, *Islanders,* 4.

33 See James Delbourgo, *Collecting the World: Hans Sloane and the Origins of the British Museum* (Cambridge, MA: Harvard University Press, 2017).

34 See James Clifford, "Museums as Contact Zones," in *Routes: Travel and Translation in the Late Twentieth Century* (Cambridge, MA: Harvard University Press, 1997).

35 Luisa Calè, "Gray's Ode and Walpole's China Tub: The Order of the Book and the Paper Lives of an Object," *Eighteenth-Century Studies* 45 (2011): 105–25.

chapter one

The British Way of Tea: Tea as an Object of Knowledge between Britain and China, 1690–1730

MARKMAN ELLIS

Tea, the hot infusion of the oxidized and prepared leaves of *Camellia sinensis*, was an extraordinary innovation when first encountered by British drinkers in the seventeenth century. There was no language to describe its flavour, almost no information about it, and few directions about how it should be consumed. Accordingly, the encounter with tea was a creative and experimental act, mediated by curiosity and habituation on the one hand and by networks of information on the other. This essay is concerned with the production of knowledge *about* tea, and the production of knowledge *by* tea, in late-seventeenth- and early-eighteenth-century Britain. It explores how tea was understood in Britain, where, before this period, it was almost entirely unknown. The discovery of tea by British consumers was a creative, culinary, scientific, and scholarly process that borrowed and transculturated some information from China and that supplemented or supplanted it with newly minted knowledge in Europe.

The chapter focuses on cultural events in this period in which tea (including knowledge about tea) was mediated between China and Britain. It provides four case studies: a commercial tract, botanical specimens, conversation paintings, and descriptive poems. These case studies point towards the decisive and sudden development, over a period of several decades, of a distinctive British approach to the consumption and understanding of tea: a "way of tea" that was not particularly Chinese but not yet wholly British. The case studies all focus on tea as commodity and event and have been chosen as means to explore different aspects of tea's early history in Britain, in a closely delimited period from 1690 to 1730. These multiple sites and kinds of encounter explore how tea was consumed, how its consumption was performed and represented, and how the cross-cultural encounter with tea functioned as an exchange of knowledge.

These documents, works of art, and objects are conventionally depicted as evidence of the "discovery" of tea in this period, by commerce, science, and culture in Britain and Europe. But tea was, of course, not "discovered" in this period, for it already had an enduring Chinese history several millennia in extent, enmeshed in complex layers of religious, horticultural, and cultural signification. In coming to the West, tea was remade, not simply as it was in China, and not without changing its host culture in Britain. In surveying the evidence presented in the case studies, this essay proposes to entertain, but also veer away from, the narrative of British "discovery," towards other forms of cross-cultural engagement, figuring complex and revisionist processes of acculturation, reinvention, and exploitation. At the end of this essay, I suggest how the discovery narrative might be revised, with tea reconfigured as an active agent of its own history.

Tea Discovers Britain

When first encountered in Europe, tea was an exotic and luxury commodity, cultivated and manufactured for consumption in their own culture by peasant artisans in China and Japan. Although tea was known by report before 1650, the first positive evidence that tea had been consumed in London is the record made in May 1657 by Samuel Hartlib, the intelligencer, in his *Ephemerides.* He based his commendation of "Herba The" on the commentaries of the Dutch physician Tulpius (Nicolaes Tulp, 1593–1674). He noted that it was "used as an Univ[ersal] Medecin in China et Jappan curing fumes indigestions stone and gout," was sourced by way of Amsterdam, was remarkably expensive, and "tastes a little bitterish."[1] As Hartlib's citation of Tulp's commentaries suggests, tea was in greater supply and better known in this period in the Netherlands, where it was noted as early as 1637 in orders issued by the directors of the Vereenigde Oost-Indische Compagnie.[2] In London, advertisements in newspapers from September 1658 announced that "[t]hat Excellent, and by all Physitians approved, *China* Drink, called by the *Chineans, Teha,* by other nations *Tay alias Tea*" was available for public sale at the "*Sultaness-head,* a *Cophee-house,* in *Sweeting's* Rents by the Royal Exchange, *London.*"[3] However, tea remained relatively rare and exotic in London throughout the Restoration. Despite tea's growing association with elite court circles and high-status women, the English East India Company imported little of it; early consumers relied on supplies sourced in the secondary trade from Amsterdam. Tea sociability was a conspicuous aspect of Dutch influence on British social life, reinforced by the Revolution of 1688 and the accession to the throne of William and Mary.

Between 1690 and 1760, tea consumption in Britain was transformed from a rare and elite event to an almost universal quotidian habit. Tea became increasingly widely available for reasons that reflect both supply (such as the East India Company's interest in and capacity for importing the commodity and the large quantities smuggled from European markets) and demand (the rising curiosity and thirst for cheap tea on the London market). In this way, tea became closely associated with the British way of life, transcending distinctions of social class, national geography, and cultural background. By the 1820s, commentators were identifying the British as "a tea-drinking nation."[4] Tea had become a defining symbol of British identity in a period when all tea came from China (tea from British India was first sold in London in 1839 but was not a large presence on the market until the 1870s).

When British merchants and consumers first encountered tea in the late seventeenth century, it was recognized as an exotic, luxury, herbal, and sanative commodity sourced from China. There was a lively debate among Dutch physicians and medical writers as to the effects of tea on human physiology and on the causes of those effects; contributors to that debate included Nicolaes Tulp or Tulpius (1593–1674), Willem Pies or Piso (1611–1678), Cornelis Bontekoe (1640–1685), and Steven Blankaart (1650–1704), among others.[5] But among these writers there was little recognition of Chinese knowledge of tea, or of the sophistication and history of that knowledge; nor was there any recognition that tea represented a complex and processed commodity. In being made anew in European science, tea became a simple botanical specimen, divorced from its context in China, where it was the product of sophisticated agricultural processes and commercial interests and part of a complex religious and cultural history.[6] Transculturation, for tea, was first an act of *de*culturation.

British consumers became habituated to tea and developed their own customs for its consumption, largely in isolation from Chinese authorities. Taking tea was rule-governed, but there was little public agreement about those rules, and at first there were no conduct manuals for performance at the tea table. Tea required acculturation to become legible. By the middle of the eighteenth century at least, a distinctive British method and ceremony of tea consumption had emerged, and this made specific demands on Chinese producers, who began to retrofit tea to suit British taste priorities.

In the first two or three decades of the eighteenth century, a number of writers and painters considered the emerging ceremonies of tea taking in Britain, scripting what might be called, with some irony, the "British way of tea." Such a phrase suggests that the sociable event of taking tea in Britain was codified and ritualized in this period, somewhat like Japanese *chanoyu*, the "Way of Tea" or tea ceremony (though, of course, almost nothing like it in practice).[7] *Chanoyu* is a "highly formalized sociocultural activity" related to the consumption of powdered green tea (matcha), which evolved in Japan in the early Tokugawa period (1603–1827). Recent research suggests that though *chanoyu* presents itself today as a cultural formation of great antiquity, its codes, participants, and social functions underwent very significant renovation in Meiji-era Japan (1868–1912).[8] Similarly, the British way of tea is a ritual whose practice is much debated and whose forms in popular culture are highly codified, despite their historical emergence in the relatively recent past.

Making and remaking knowledge about tea, between China and Britain, describes an active cultural process. Preparing and consuming tea was a practical skill in Britain, as was the social performance of the tea table: both were different and distinct from their equivalent formations in China. As such, Pierre Bourdieu's term "habitus" suggests itself as a useful way to describe the relation between the embodied experience of the individual tea drinker within the social structure.[9] Habitus describes a deep structure that generates both thought and behaviour, an acquired set of behaviours or habits whose achievement allows the subject to participate appropriately in society. Bourdieu's notion of habitus is structured and structuring, allowing for transformation and change, as for example tea-taking practice evolves in response to the dialogue between past practices and cultural innovations. The habitus of early-eighteenth-century British tea consumption would describe both the classifying and perceptual structures developed for tea in this period (how to understand tea), as well as the generative structures of practical actions (how to take tea), and both coincide in the formation of a "way of tea." The invocation of the term "habitus" here emphasizes how tea consumption has an acquired, performative, and ritualized aspect, that these behaviours were new and innovative, and that they can be read in and through culture and its outputs in this period.

Before pursuing this further, the historiography of tea is worth noting. The late seventeenth century (1660–99) saw a vigorous debate on coffee and coffee-houses in English, with more than thirty distinct tracts, satires, and verses published on coffee.[10] The same cannot be said of tea, even though tea was also available in the period. However, in the opening decades of the eighteenth century (1700–40) there was a decisive expansion in discourse on tea. This was inaugurated by John Ovington's *Essay upon the Nature and Qualities of Tea* in 1699, described below, and for the next three or four decades, there continued an important series of scientific and literary texts, the latter in verse as well as in prose, that debated and discussed tea, its properties and manifestations, and the cultures of its consumption.[11] This burst of activity was a distinctively British phenomenon, not matched in Continental Europe, and was broadly coincident with the very significant increase in tea sales and consumption in Britain in these years.

John Ovington and the Discovery of Chinese Tea Knowledge in the 1690s

The first significant English attempt to rectify British ignorance about tea was the research and publications of the clergyman John Ovington (1658–1731). As an East India Company chaplain, Ovington had spent two and a half years in the English Factory in Surat, a prosperous port city in Gujarat, India, between 1689 and 1692. After he returned to London in 1693 he published an account of his travels, titled *A Voyage to Suratt in the Year 1689* (1696), which included some discussion of Chinese tea, derived from knowledge that he admitted was from secondary sources. Primary among these sources were his encounters with the Bania (or Bannians as he knew them), a Gujarati caste or community of merchants and traders who operated an extensive commercial system offering banking, intermediation, moneylending, and financial services for both English factors and their Indian counterparts. The principal trade of Surat was silk and spices, for which the Bania maintained extensive trading contacts with China. Through them, Ovington also had direct contact with the embassy of a Chinese "mandarine" to the Muslim court at Surat. Ovington noted the love of tea among the Bania, the Chinese official's retinue, and Surat's Dutch merchants. Tea was, he said, "a common Drink with all the inhabitants of *India*, as well *Europeans* as Natives; and by the *Dutch* is used as such a standing Entertainment, that the Tea-Pot's seldom off the Fire, or unimploy'd." Ovington observed that tea was "agreeable" despite the heat of the climate and that it was also an effective remedy, "prevailing against the Headach, Gravel, and Griping in the Guts." As Ovington advertised, all tea in this period, whether encountered in India or in Britain, was sourced from China, and even in Surat it was an expensive and exotic imported commodity.

Ovington was the first British authority to recognize that tea came in a number of distinct kinds and preparations: he specified two forms of green tea, *bing* and *singlo*, and one "red" tea, *bohea*. In his account he gave some further information about the shrub from which tea was harvested and the manner in which it was prepared. "The Leaf is first green, but is made crisp and dry by frying twice, or oftner, in a Pan; and as often as it is taken off the Fire it is roll'd with the Hand upon a Table, till it curls."[12] This was all new information in London, and valuable to the East India Company as well as to natural philosophers and common consumers.

Ovington's report of the high regard for these varieties of tea among the Bania, Dutch, and Chinese was soon after confirmed in a publication by the French mathematician Louis le Comte (1655–1728). Le Comte, who was a "Corresponding Member" of the Académie des Sciences (the French Academy of Sciences), had travelled to China as part of a Jesuit mission to Beijing. He contended that tea drinking compensated for poor water quality, a problem that was solved by drinking hot water. "Because warm Water is unpalatable and nauseous," he went on, the Chinese "bethought themselves of putting some Leaves of a Tree to it, to give it a Gusto, Those of Tea seemed to be the best, and so they frequently make use of it."[13] While travelling in "*Fokien*" (Fujian), Le Comte witnessed tea under cultivation, though he was unable to study the plant in detail. In his *Memoirs and Observations*, published in Paris in 1696 and translated into English in 1697, he offered a brief survey of Chinese medical opinion on its properties, although his own experiments, he said, "evince that its Virtue is not so Universal as People imagine." Like Ovington, Le Comte offered a tripartite typology for the multiple varieties of processed leaves. The most common, he said, "hath no particular Name, because it is gather'd hand over head in different Territories and Soils." He described this accordingly: "It is good, the Infusion is reddish, the Taste faint and somewhat bitter: The People use it indifferently at all hours of the day, and it is their most usual drink." Le Comte then identified two superior types of leaf, used by "Persons of Quality" and named after their place of origin. "*Thee Soumlo*" he described as a green tea with a fleeting "pleasant" taste and a scent "a little of Violets"; while "*Thee Voüi*" generated a "delicious" infusion "inclining to black."[14] Le Comte's *soumlo* equates with Ovington's *singlo*; *voüi* with his *bohea*.

In 1699, Ovington consolidated his renown as the tea expert in London by publishing an octavo pamphlet titled *An Essay upon the Nature and Qualities of Tea* (Figure 1.1).[15] This was an innovative attempt to

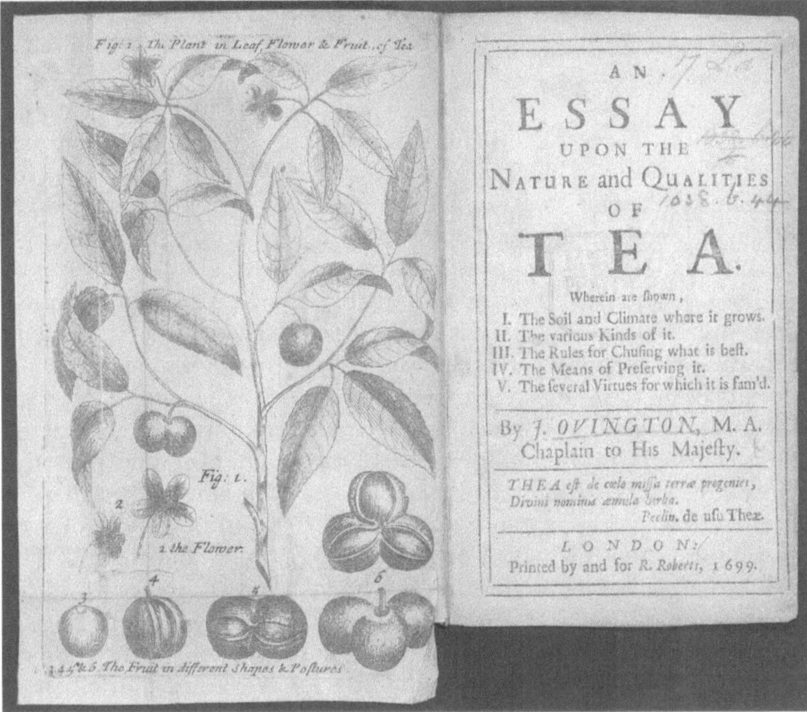

AN
ESSAY
UPON THE
NATURE and QUALITIES
OF
TEA.
Wherein are shown,
I. The Soil and Climate where it grows.
II. The various Kinds of it.
III. The Rules for Chusing what is best.
IV. The Means of Preserving it.
V. The several Virtues for which it is fam'd.
By J. OVINGTON, M. A.
Chaplain to His Majesty.
THEA est de cœlo missa terræ progenies,
Divini nominis æmula herba.
Pechlin. de usu Theæ.
LONDON:
Printed by and for R. Roberts, 1699.

Figure 1.1 John Ovington, Title page and frontispiece, *An Essay upon the Nature and Qualities of Tea* (London: Printed by and for R. Roberts, 1699). Beinecke Rare Book and Manuscript Library, Yale University, New Haven CT.

methodize all English knowledge of tea by combining the available commercial, natural-philosophical, and medical information. It no doubt served a selfish purpose too, in that Ovington was seeking favour and patronage within the East India Company and the royal court. Ovington dedicated his work to Henrietta van Ouwerkerk, Countess of Grantham (d. 1724), who was known for her love of Oriental fashions. Ovington's address flatters her:

> 'Tis from Your innate Goodness only, and that condescending Temper which is so remarkable in You, that this Foreign Leaf dares presume to court Your Favour, and hope for a welcome Entertainment. For where can a Stranger, that was always bred among a People the most polite of any in the

> World, expect a kind Reception with more Assurance, than from a Person, whose Conversation is adorn'd with all that Civility that even China it self can boast of?[16]

Among the fawning and flattery conventional to a prefatory address, Ovington figures not himself but tea as the active agent in his story. Tea itself is a "tender leaf" courting the favour of the countess, personified as a stranger long-bred among a polite and civilized people, now seeking a "kind Reception" among people who are similarly polite and civilized – or whose politeness and civilization might be judged by their openness to tea. For Ovington, tea itself is civilized and civilizing: there is nothing barbarous or corrupting about its approach to the British palate.

In his *Essay*, Ovington reinforced the view that tea came in different kinds, for which he proposed aesthetic descriptions and value judgments. This was innovative, for the dominant medicalized discourse on tea mostly described the sanative *effects* of tea drinking, rather than its taste, flavour, and appearance. Recent research on the history of taste has proposed that the act of tasting is both cultural and natural. The "natural" aspect of taste refers to how the make-up of food or drink (its combination of chemical compounds) is tasted through a physiological interaction with taste buds on the tongue. In the case of tea, these effects are wrought mainly by what are now understood as comparatively small quantities of caffeine (3 to 4 per cent), tannins, and a great number of other alkaloids and essential oils, L-theanine especially.[17] Although tea manufacturing may have changed since the early eighteenth century, it is thought that the neurophysiology of the tasting process has not. However, as Steve Shapin has argued, taste also has a cultural aspect, constructed through "networks of expectations and understandings about how things should taste, with frameworks relating taste both to the nature of aliments and to bodily consequences, and with the available vocabularies for talking about them and describing them to others." In this way, he argues, taste is "temporally and culturally variable."[18]

The qualities Ovington admired about tea were that it was green and refined. Regarding its greenness, Ovington commented on "the remarkable Ingenuity of the *Chinese*, to prepare the *Leaves* with so much Art to make them still continue *green*, notwithstanding all the Length of Time they have been dried." The aim of tea storage and tea preparation, Ovington concluded, was "to preserve the *spirit* and *Verdure*" of the tea. "Verdure" was a word that summarized both the colour and taste of tea, both its fresh greenness and its vegetable aromas. The quality of being refined was partly produced by cultivation – the tender leaf was, he said, "planted in the most refin'd Earth, and carefully defended from all Injuries of the Air, from all excessive Colds and Heats, and every thing that may be apt to offend the tender Leaf" – but was also a mark of its sophistication and delicacy.

Having noted that there were these different kinds of tea, which he again called "Bohea," "Singlo," and "Bing," Ovington then described how they differed in appearance and taste. *Bohea,* he noted, "generally tinges the Water brown, or of a reddish Colour." He added that it improved with age and that in both ways this made it distinct from other teas. *Singlo,* he continued, has a "*blewish green Colour,* which tastes very crisp when it is chaw'd [chewed], and afterwards looks green upon the Hand, and infuses a pale Greenness into the Water. The Flavor of it is fresh and fine, lively and pleasant ... For the *fragrant Smell,* the *green Colour,* and the *bitterish sweet Taste,* are the distinguishing Characters of the Goodness of this kind of *Tea.*" *Bing,* or Imperial, he said, is "a *large loose Leaf,*" the "finest Sort of it looks both green to the Eye, and is crisp in the Mouth, and the Smell of it is very pleasant, which inhances the Price of it here in *England;* and 'tis highly esteem'd likewise in *China,* being sold there at three times the Price of the other two."[19] Ovington's description identified several connoisseurial factors that could enhance price, including refinement, preparation, and maturation. Learning to make judgments about tea, to discern types and identify flavour preferences, was a significant part of the development of the British way of tea as habitus. These distinctions were related to, but distinct from, those made in China.

After Ovington's essay was published, British consumers became more adept at describing tea's different types. In the 1690s, tea merchants were content to describe their best wares as simply "extraordinary superfine Thea";[20] a decade later, East India Company sales had begun to specify different parcels of "Fine Singlo Tea" and "Bohee Tea"[21] and to note the difference between "Green Tea" and "Bohea Tea."[22] By 1712, company sales were registering tea in five categories: *bohea, pekoe, bing, congou,* and *singlo,* kinds that dominated the trade for the rest of the century.[23] The growth of a language of connoisseurship for tea in English reflected its subtle and nuanced flavour landscapes; as such, tea sought out more sophisticated customers and rewarded them with refined knowledge. These distinctions between teas of different manufacture and origin, and of increasingly complex varieties of flavour, aroma, and appearance, reflected a growing sophistication in the market for tea as well as greater curiosity about kinds of tea, and modes of description and appreciation – although these English tea kinds bore no direct relation to Chinese taxonomies.

Specimens of Botanical Knowledge

As knowledge about tea began to sophisticate itself, the commodity became a matter of scientific curiosity, with physicians struggling to comprehend and describe its sanative effects. Botanists who sought to describe tea without field experience found it difficult to describe and classify. Travellers' accounts, for example, allowed the Swiss herbalist Gaspard Bauhin (1560–1624) to locate tea, "a herb [that grows] in Japan," within the umbelliferous plants in his botanical classification.[24] Although no European botanist had the opportunity to observe any specimens of tea, the commodity itself provided some information, especially as crates of tea occasionally included stray twigs, flowers, and seeds. This incomplete evidence, tied to the non-specialist and fragmentary information recorded by travellers, was all that was available to European botanists.

It was not until the 1690s that a European with botanical knowledge encountered tea under cultivation. The German naturalist and physician Engelbert Kaempfer spent two years in Japan between 1690 and 1692, attached to the Dutch VOC factory at Nagasaki, returning to Amsterdam in 1693. But on his return, Kaempfer was very slow to disseminate his findings. His description of tea, "Theae Japonensis Historia," was eventually published in his *Amoenitatum Exoticarum*, published in the German university town of Lemgo, Westphalia, in 1712.[25] His herbarium and manuscripts were subsequently purchased by Sir Hans Sloane. Kaempfer's specimen of a tea branch, dated 1692, preserved in the Sloane Herbarium in London, is the oldest botanical specimen of tea known today, and as such is identified as the lectotype of the species.[26]

Sloane's botanical collection began with specimens he had gathered himself in Jamaica in the 1680s; later, as his herbarium developed – primarily by purchase and gift – he collected specimens from around the globe, especially exotic plants from Africa, Asia, and the Americas that had utility in trade or medicine. In addition to pressed specimens, mounted in the herbarium's folio volumes, Sloane collected seeds and fruits, preserving them in small boxes in the collection known as his Vegetable Substances (see Ogborn and Pickering in this collection). Both the Herbarium and the Vegetable Substances (in the Darwin Centre at the Natural History Museum in London) are the product of Sloane's activities as a master collector at the nexus of a network of botanical field agents, who included physicians, clergymen, sea captains, and merchants.[27]

Among this group was James Cuninghame (d. 1709), a Scottish ship's surgeon who twice travelled to China: first on an abortive private voyage to Amoy (Xiamen) in 1698, and again on a New East India Company voyage to establish an English factory at Chusan (Zhoushan) in 1700. Richard Coulton has demonstrated that Cuninghame was the first British natural philosopher to examine Chinese plants in their native habitat.[28] Cuninghame recognized that tea had appeal to his friends at home in London's medical and botanical circles and to men of trade in the East India Company. Botany mediated both commercial relationships and intellectual and cultural exchanges with China. Cuninghame's interest in tea was prompted in part by the intervention of an associate of Sloane, the natural historian James Petiver (c. 1665–1718). In 1698, on hearing he was going to China, Petiver wrote to Cuninghame with a list of about eighty species he should search for, including "Thea or Cha." Botanical inquiry served as a supplement to commercial exchange. Petiver suggested that Cuninghame "inquire what variety their is of it & wherin the Bohe Tea differs from the common" or green tea.[29] During his first voyage to China in 1698, Cuninghame made field notes about tea cultivation at "Emuy" (Xiamen) and "Colonshu" (Gulangyu) in Fujian Province, China. Cunninghame identified specimens of "Tea, Planta floribus et foliis serratis Urticus subtus albicantibus" ("Tea, a flowering plant, with leaves serrated like nettles and whiteish underneath"); he also collected seeds from "Flores Tea Singlôo" ("the flowers of Singlo Tea").[30] In addition to specimens of the tea bush, Cuninghame collected images produced by local artists during his stay, which he exhibited to the Royal Society on 25 October 1699 following his return to London.[31]

On one of his two voyages to China, Cuninghame also collected a sample of tea itself, which was subsequently preserved in the Vegetable Substances (Figure 1.2).[32] "Vegetable Substance 857" comprises a small box, about six inches long, covered in black fabric. Visible through the glass lid is an ounce or two of dried leaves, curled and brittle, mottled with hues of green and brown. On opening, the leaves emit the faint ghost of a grassy, vegetable odour. Half-buried in this tiny heap are two slips of paper, inscribed in dark-brown ink by an eighteenth-century hand: one declares that this Vegetable Substance is "A sort of tea from China"; the other provides its classifying number: "857." This is not simply a botanical specimen of the tea plant, *Camellia sinsensis*; rather, it is a sample of a consumer commodity as prepared for the Chinese domestic market: a

Figure 1.2 "A Sort of Tea from China," c. 1699, Sloane Herbarium. Sloane Vegetable Substances 857, Natural History Museum, London. © The Trustees of the Natural History Museum, London.

specimen of tea leaves, probably the kind Ovington identifies as *bing*. As such, the sample is a manufactured commodity, having been subjected to many diverse industrial processes to ready it for the market and for consumption, and as such embedded in complex Chinese cultural and religious formations. In the Ming-era system for processing green teas, for example, the raw tea leaves underwent an elaborate three-stage process in which they were wilted and denatured by either stir-frying, steaming, or being exposed to the sun; they were then rolled by hand before being dried by stir-frying, baking, or drying in the sun, so as to preserve and create the desired taste profile of the variety of tea product.[33] As was his practice when collecting botanical specimens, Cuninghame made some observations about how the tea bush was carefully cultivated by Chinese farmers, as well as some notes about the complex commercial and manufacturing culture in which the plants were embedded. In doing so, he reordered Chinese knowledge about tea, privileging botanical and horticultural observation and demoting Chinese knowledge of tea's properties, meaning, and religious significance. Botany had divorced the plant from its contextual culture and joined it to a botanical culture.[34]

As Sloane, Petiver, and Cuninghame all knew from the retail market in Britain, tea came in multiple forms: two kinds of "green" and one of "red" – *bing*, *singlo*, and *bohea*. On his second voyage to China in 1700, Cuninghame returned to Petiver's question concerning this variety. While at Zhoushan (Chusan) for twelve months from October 1700, he was able to observe tea under cultivation in its natural habitat, following its annual cycle of agricultural practices, from cultivation to harvest and preparation for market. Zhoushan was an island port-city frequented by European and other merchants, which had some "Manufactories," among which, he observed, "they make some Tea, but chiefly for their own use."[35] Writing to Sloane about Zhoushan life and natural history, he declared:

> The 3 Sorts of Tea commonly carryd to England are all from the same plant, only the Season of the Year & the Soyl makes the difference. The Bohe (or Voüi, so calld of Mountains in the Province of Fokien, where it is chiefly made) is the very first bud gathred in the beginning of March, & dryd in the shade. The Bing Tea is the second growth in April: & Singlô the last in May & June, both dryd a little in Tatches or Pans over the fire. The Tea Shrub being an Evergreen is in Flower from October to Januarie, & the Seed is ripe in September & October following, so that one may gather both flowers and seed at the same time.[36]

Cuninghame's letter describing tea and its manufacturing processes was received by Sloane in 1702; it gained almost immediate notice by being read at the Royal Society and then was published in *Philosophical Transactions,* the most significant scientific journal of the period in English.[37] Cuninghame's deployment of tea nomenclature – noting as alternative terms *bohea* and *voüi* – suggests that he was aware of both Ovington and Le Comte as authorities on tea varietals. But he also concluded (correctly) that all tea came from one plant and differed only in "the Season of the Year & the Soyl" in which it was cultivated. This conclusion relied in part on information gathered from farmers and merchants in Zhoushan, but also on Cuninghame's own observation of the tea processing industry in China. He further indicated that he was aware of the role played by different methods of preparation in creating the varieties of tea on the market in London: *bohea* was "dryd in the shade" to allow full fermentation, which caused the leaves to go dark, whereas *singlo* and *bing* were "both dryd a little in Tatches or Pans over the fire" so as to arrest oxidation and preserve the verdure and greenness of the leaves.

Cuninghame's botanical declaration concerning the specific origins of various leaf teas shipped to Europe could not have been clearer: they "are all from the same plant." Besides appearing in the *Philosophical Transactions,* this claim was quoted verbatim in the second edition of Ovington's *Essay upon the Nature and Qualities of Tea* (1705) – indeed, this addition was the only significant change in the reissue.[38] Coulton, however, shows that despite Cuninghame's clarity, and the fame of publication in *Philosophical Transactions,* his conclusion was largely ignored in European botanical circles. The experience of consuming two markedly different types of tea – green and *bohea* – persistently militated against an acceptance that they were derived from one species of shrub. Botanists continued to identify two kinds of tea plant producing the two kinds of tea.

In 1759 the English natural historian John Hill identified what he claimed was a genuine botanical distinction. From specimens in his herbal, Hill observed "among my CHINA Plants, two Specimens under the name of Tea, which differ obviously." One he recorded as *bohea,* noting that it has "shorter and darker Leaves, and in each Flower six Petals"; the other as green tea, which has "longer and paler Leaves, and in every Flower nine Petals."[39] Hill's distinction was both fictitious and adventitious, for it could be clearly articulated in the sexual system of binomial botanical classification championed by the Swedish botanist Carl von Linné (1707–1778). Linnaeus was interested in the effect of plants on human physiology, and researched a wide variety of vegetable substances, including exotic hot beverages such as tea, coffee, and chocolate. He made repeated and unsuccessful attempts to cultivate the tea bush in the botanical gardens at Uppsala, in northern Sweden. With his student Pehr Cornellius Tillæus, Linnaeus wrote a dissertation on tea, published in December 1765, titled *Potus Theae* (The Tea Drink). Partly on the basis of Hill's ascription, he outlined two separate species, *Theæ Bohea* and *Theæ viridi.*[40] Linnaeus's authority within the contemporary scientific world led to the widespread acceptance of the two names, and the rationale behind them, even though specimens of the plant might have been examined in numerous botanical collections by this time.[41] It was not until the 1840s, and the research of Robert Fortune, that the idea that tea, or *Camellia sinensis,* was a single species was widely accepted in botanical circles.

European botanical research, whether undertaken by an engaged amateur such as Ovington, or by more sophisticated observers such as Cuninghame, Hill, and Linnaeus, described an encounter with tea that effectively removed the plant and the commodity from its Chinese or Japanese context. Botanists ignored the enduring history of the empirical study of plants as it had been undertaken in the Confucian tradition in China and Japan, although – as some historians of science have noted – this research was available in considerable detail, extent, sophistication, and insight.[42] Severed from this wider context, botany could "discover" tea by encountering the plant as if it was *terra incognita* and treating it as if it was *terra nullius.* Although Le Comte and Kaempfer both recorded some brief Confucian myths of origin, neither Ovington nor Cuninghame took any interest in such knowledge, treating it as just stories. Ovington and Cuninghame both began to sketch the outline of Chinese cultivation and manufacturing processes, although these had little impact in London. The British merchant and the natural philosopher extended their purview out into the wider world, making sense of it through the skilful application of their different kinds of expert knowledge. The accounts shape themselves as discovery narratives, testifying to the cultural power of commercial enterprise and the European Enlightenment: both used systems of knowledge that claimed to be adequate to the problem of discovery, even when confronted by confusing evidence.

The Tea Table in Conversation Paintings and Invention Poems

In the first decades of the eighteenth century the quantity of tea imported by the East India Company to Britain increased rapidly. Where they had previously imported irregular and comparatively small parcels of tea, after 1697 significant quantities were ordered and imported, reaching one million pounds weight in 1723. Increasing tea consumption in London in turn created cultural information about the commodity, notably in relation to the domestic scene of the tea table and enculturated British practices such as the tea party. Although they established ties with the tea performance in China, new creative representations and ideations of tea in Britain were novel formations in British cultural practice. Tea made itself known in London through complex processes of acculturation that adapted both the commodity and the consumer.[43]

At the centre of the British way of tea in this period was the sociable encounter of the tea table. Reflection on the British practice of taking tea was established in the early eighteenth century through a series of literary and visual properties, which elaborated new and complex notions surrounding tea consumption, encapsulated in the idea of the tea table and the tea party. The tea table was constructed as a space for the heterosocial but feminocentric sociability of the tea party, which was conventionally located in the private space of the home, yet linked to or embedded in public discourse through the semi-permeable membrane of conversation (variously figured as debate, gossip, discussion, chat) and print culture (variously identified as essays, literature, newspapers, poetry). This was a literary and artistic construction, promoted by some and satirized by others, in which distinct views of conversation and sociability were central: it was also a social practice, a historical event repeated on numerous occasions beyond the reach of evidence.

Richard Collins's conversation painting *The Tea Party* (1727) depicts a family taking tea, gathered around a rectangular wooden table: a woman, her husband, and two daughters (Figure 1.3). The family is prosperous, and the painting is serious about advertising their wealth. On the table there is a silver pear-shaped teapot, sitting on a silver stand above a spirit lamp, alongside an octagonal covered jug for hot water, a matching tea canister, a sugar bowl with cover, a pair of sugar tongs, a spoon boat with three teaspoons, and a slops or waste bowl.[44] The woman is dressed in a lustrous black silk gown, fabric spilling out behind her, with a gold apron, and delicate lace cuffs, handkerchief, and cap. Her husband shows his leisured relaxation by wearing a loose red gown over an unbuttoned shirt, with a soft turban-like cap known as a banyan, proclaiming his status as a gentleman at leisure at home. Sheltering under an arm of each parent is a child, dressed with loose hair and plain clothes. Though it is prepared in silver dishes, the family consumes the tea in fine blue-and-white china cups and saucers. Both parents are drinking tea, as is the elder daughter,

Figure 1.3 Richard Collins (active 1726–32), *The Tea Party*, c. 1727. Oil on canvas. The Goldsmiths' Hall, London.

who is dressed in a blue gown with a white lace panel. As was typical of the period, the cups do not have handles, and when full of scalding tea are held in various ways between the thumb and forefinger by the rim and base. The only member of the family not drinking tea is the younger daughter, dressed in a plain white gown. She is eating a piece of bread and butter – the sole dairy product on show, for there is no milk or cream. The family's spaniel puppy plays on a stool in the foreground.

Tea drinking is the occasion for this family portrait, but the polite domestic event of drinking tea is embedded in a wider circle of social and cultural connections. The family is shown performing their successful achievement of the role of a prosperous family in the middle stations of life. This painting depicts at least three Chinese commodities with significant retail presence in London: silk, porcelain, and tea. The silk and porcelain make a lustrous show of themselves; the tea itself is less visible. Conversation-piece paintings like this one give a sense of how the quotidian sociable activity of tea drinking was meaningful in the polite culture of eighteenth-century Britain and further reiterate the conversation with China. A tea party was not simply an event in which a refreshing hot beverage was consumed, although it was that. Rather, a tea party became part of an elaborate performance in which the tea joined with human actors, the props of the tea equipage, and the stage of the tea table, in a performance whose meaning exceeded its parts. Each item in the performance was itself a status symbol, and the whole event accrued complex social scripts, each of which was legible within status competition. The art historian Marcia Pointon has concluded that "[t]ea drinking is a paradigmatic case of a cultural phenomenon in which economics and performativity are inextricably bound up with representation and self-presentation."[45] The tea party performance was a highly mediated one, an event around which numerous writers, satirists, essayists, and painters battled to establish and contest scripts and tropes.

Scripting a British "way of tea" was a long and complex process, and literary texts established some innovative ways of rethinking tea in British culture in the period 1690–1730. These publications give evidence about the manner in which tea was consumed in the period, as well as what was valued about the dry tea commodity, the hot beverage prepared from it, and the social event of its service. These publications associate tea with polite manners, with female sociability, and with conversation and gossip. These characteristics made tea, this Asian leaf grown half a world away, an appropriate vehicle to celebrate distinctly British modes of polite sociability.

One of the earliest extended poems on tea in English was *Panacea: A Poem Upon Tea* by Nahum Tate, published in 1701. This is a substantial thirty-six-page mock-heroic "invention" poem that accounts for tea and the tea trade in Britain by offering complex mythological origin narratives for both.[46] It begins with a section in which tea is recommended as an appropriate beverage for intellectually inclined people, with a stanza addressing how tea reforms and improves statesmen, lawyers, physicians, natural philosophers, scholars, musicians, and painters. For each of these kinds of men – the sons of muses – tea is proposed as a palliative and an inspiration: "carousing in tea," Tate says, is like supping from the Castalian Spring, the magical fountain at Delphi that metaphorically inspired the poets of ancient Rome.

The two cantos of Tate's poem give different accounts of the origin of tea. The first relates a tale borrowed from ancient Chinese history that Tate adapted from Le Comte's *Memoirs of China* (translated in 1697).[47]

In this tale, tea is gifted to the Chinese nation by Confucius as a pacific remedy to a wounded body politic, which is suffering after the decadent depredations of a corrupt emperor. In his second canto, Tate transculturates the tea mythology, inventing an imaginary contest among the gods of the classical Roman pantheon as to which among them should be tea's patron. Meeting in a sociable encounter on Mount Olympus, the goddesses advance in series to claim their right to tea: Juno, for example, as queen of the gods, claims tea as the "Queen of Plants," and Minerva, goddess of wisdom and the arts, claims it as the reward of scholars and the inspiration of the arts. Venus, Cynthia, Thetis, Salus, and Somnus all make their claims, before the contest ends when Jove elevates tea itself to the status of a goddess.[48] Tate's neoclassicizing imaginary renders tea in a polite and elevated mode appropriate to its high-status social coding. Another important early tea poem, Peter Motteux's *A Poem in Praise of Tea*, published in 1712, takes a similar neoclassical turn, depicting a banquet at which the gods prefer to carouse in tea rather than Bacchus's wine and in doing so restore themselves to health, liberty, and peace.[49] Both Tate and Motteux see tea as a transformational drink: consuming it has the power to render men and women more polite and peaceful – which makes it, as Motteux argues in an explicitly Whiggish mode, the drink of choice in a modern and commercial nation.

Conclusion

The case studies considered in this essay, focusing on commercial tracts, botanical collections, conversation paintings, and invention poems, have examined how tea and its consumption in Britain was represented in a range of cultural forms. Curiosity about tea, whether scientific, commercial, or artistic, was encouraged by the acknowledgment that tea was both expensive and highly valued in China. Knowledge of tea in Britain, as noted in each case study, variously recognized and interrogated ideas of Chinese civilization along with associated notions of civility and politeness. In this way, discourse on tea in Britain took place alongside the wider Enlightenment encounter with Chinese philosophy, religion, and history.[50] And although little specific knowledge about tea was shared between China and Britain, tea itself produced its own information, especially about how it should be consumed, in the emergent habitus of tea. The tea table and its equipage expressed one aspect of the habitus of tea, a set of physical parameters by which tea drinkers might play the game of tea. Alongside those material objects, cultural behaviours – both stated and unstated – regulated the performance of tea taking.

Tate's and Motteux's poems invite the reader to consider tea as a reforming agent in British society: it has the power to render society more polite and peaceful. The dedication to Ovington's 1699 *Essay*, addressed to the Countess of Grantham, does something similar when it refigures tea as a polite ambassador, a tender leaf seeking a kind reception among similarly refined people. These stories of tea's encounter with Britain revise the discovery narrative: these are not stories of empire, discovery, and enlightenment. Instead, tea has discovered Britain and the discovery narrative has been inverted. In this way it is possible to propose a retelling of tea's history in Britain, with tea as an active agent of its appropriation, rather than the passive specimen or commodity of British and European scientists and merchants. This retelling would record that in the sixteenth century, tea discovered a new host, the European in China, who was a merchant, missionary, or natural philosopher. To these people, tea appealed through its curious psychoactive and sanative effects on the human body. As such it appeared to Europeans as a powerful addition to the pharmacopeia, recommending itself as a medicine, not a food. It was a sudorific, an anti-scorbutic, an emetic, a cure for hangovers, and a lengthener of life – some even described it as a panacea, a universal medicine. Although dissimulating itself as a simple material commodity, tea had the potential to transform those subjected to its influence. In the early eighteenth century, as it came more commonly into use, tea appropriated to itself a special relationship with women – both with the social life of women in the higher echelons of society, and with the idea of femininity itself. It also aligned itself with the pacific arts of conversation and polite sociability, so central to the rise of the urban and commercial middle classes in eighteenth-century Britain. Tea subtly insinuated itself into British culture, not by force, but in symbiosis with the gentle arts of civility and politeness. If tea effectively remade itself in Britain, it also remade Britain as it did so.

ACKNOWLEDGMENTS

In preparing this essay I am grateful for the advice and assistance of Rebecca Beasley, Ted Binnema, Richard Coulton, Adriana Craciun, Ben Dew, Richard Hamblyn, Matthew Mauger, Miles Ogborn, Katrina O'Loughlin, Victoria Pickering, Annicka Windahl Pontén, and Mary

Terrall. The research for this essay reflects on conclusions drawn in, and research undertaken for, Markman Ellis, Richard Coulton, and Matthew Mauger, *Empire of Tea: The Asian Leaf That Conquered the World* (London: Reaktion, 2015).

NOTES

1 Samuel Hartlib, *Ephemerides*, 29/6/12b. Hartlib transcribed a section of Nicolaes Tulp, "Descriptio Herbæ Theê, ex Tulpii lib. 4": "Observ. 59" about "Herba Theê Indiæ Orientali" [42/4/5A-6B], from Nicolaes Tulp, *Observationes medicæ. Edition Ed. nova, libro quarto auctior, et emendatior* (Amsterdam, 1652).

2 George Schlegel, "First Introduction of Tea into Holland," *T'oung Pao*, Second Series, 1, no. 5 (1900): 468–72; J.R. ter Molen, *Thema thee: de geschiedenis van de thee en het theegebruik in Nederland* (Rotterdam: Museum Boymans-van Beuningen, 1978).

3 *Mercurius Politicus*, no. 435, Thursday, 23 September 1658, 887.

4 "The Tea Trade," *The New Annual Register, or General Repository of History, Politics, and Literature, for the Year 1824* (London, 1825), 515.

5 Harold J. Cook, *Matters of Exchange: Commerce, Medicine, and Science in the Dutch Golden Age* (New Haven: Yale University Press, 2007), 220–2, 293–8; and Richard Coulton, "The Natural Philosophy of Tea," in Markman Ellis, Richard Coulton, and Matthew Mauger, *Empire of Tea: The Asian Leaf That Conquered the World* (London: Reaktion, 2015), 93–114.

6 The best guide to this is H.T. Huang, *Science and Civilisation in China*, Vol. 6: *Biology and Biological Technology. Part 5, Fermentations and Food Science* (Cambridge: Cambridge University Press, 2000), 503–70. See also James Benn, *Tea in China: A Religious and Cultural History* (Honolulu: University of Hawai'i Press, 2015).

7 Paul H. Varley and Isao Kumakura, *Tea In Japan: Essays On the History of Chanoyu* (Honolulu: University of Hawai'i Press, 1989).

8 Taka Oshikiri, "Gathering for Tea in Late-Meiji Tokyo," *Japan Forum* 25, no. 1 (2013): 24–41, at 24.

9 Habitus is defined variously in Pierre Bourdieu, *Outline of a Theory of Practice*, trans. Richard Nice (Cambridge: Cambridge University Press, 1977), 5, 72; and *The Logic of Practice* (Cambridge: Polity Press, 1990), 53.

10 These are surveyed in Markman Ellis, *Eighteenth Century Coffee-House Culture*, 4 vols. (London: Pickering & Chatto, 2006).

11 Markman Ellis, Richard Coulton, Matthew Mauger, and Ben Dew, eds., *Tea and the Tea-Table in Eighteenth-Century England* (London: Pickering & Chatto, 2010).

12 John Ovington, *A Voyage to Suratt, in the Year, 1689. Giving a Large Account of that City and its Inhabitants, and of the English Factory there* (London, 1696), 309.

13 Louis le Comte, *Memoirs and observations typographical, physical, mathematical, mechanical, natural, civil, and ecclesiastical, made in a late journey through the empire of China* (London: Printed for Benj. Tooke at the Middle Temple Gate, and Sam. Buckley at the Dolphin over against St Dunstans Church in Fleetstreet. 1697), 112.

14 Le Comte, *Memoirs and Observations*, 228–9.

15 John Ovington, *An Essay upon the Nature and Qualities of Tea. Wherein are shown, I. The soil and climate where it grows. II. The various kinds of it. III. The rules for chusing what is best. IV. The means of preserving it. V. The several virtues for which it is fam'd* (London, 1699).

16 Ibid., sig. A2.

17 "VII. Flavor of Tea," *Food Reviews International* 11, no. 3 (1995): 477–525.

18 Steven Shapin, *Changing Tastes: How Foods Tasted in the Early Modern Period and How They Taste Now*, The Hans Rausing Lecture 2011, Salvia Småskrifter, no. 14 (Uppsala: Tryck Wikströms, 2011), 7–8.

19 Ovington, *An Essay upon Tea*, 9–14.

20 *Collection for Improvement of Husbandry and Trade* 7: 156, 26 July 1695.

21 *London Gazette*, 22 August 1700.

22 *Post Man and the Historical Account*, 15 April 1707.

23 *British Mercury*, Wednesday, 1 October 1712.

24 Gaspard Bauhin, *Pinax Theatri Botanici* (Basel: Sumptibus & typis Ludovici Regis, 1623), 147.

25 Engelbert Kaempfer, *Amoenitatum exoticarum politico-physico-medicarum fasciculi* (Lemgoviæ: Typis & impensis Henrici Wilhelmi Meyeri, Aulæ Lippiacæ typographi, 1712), 13th chapter of the 2nd book, 605ff; mentioned also in fifth book, 817.

26 Detlef Haberland, *Engelbert Kaempfer 1651–1716: A Biography*, trans. Peter Hogg (London: The British Library, 1996), 94–7; C.E. Jarvis, F.R. Barrie, D.M. Allan, and J.L. Reveal, eds., *A List of Linnaean Generic Names and Their Types*, vol. 127 (Königstein: Published for the International Association for Plant Taxonomy by Koeltz Scientific Books, 1993), 93.

27 James Delbourgo, "Collecting Hans Sloane," in *From Books to Bezoars: Sir Hans Sloane and his Collections*, ed. Michael Hunter, Alison Walker, and Arthur MacGregor (London: British Library Publishing, 2012), 9–23.

28 Coulton, "The Natural Philosophy of Tea," 93–114.

29 James Petiver to James Cuninghame, [8 January 1698?], London (draft): British Library, Sloane 3333, fols 113^{r}–116^{v} (fols 113^{r-v}).

30 James Cuninghame, "Plants of China etc" (1698–99): British Library, Sloane 2376, fols 63[r], 69[r] (trans. Richard Coulton).

31 "Drawings of Chinese Plants": British Library, Additional MS 5292; James Cuninghame, "Catalogus Plantarum, quarum Icones in Chinâ delineate sunt" ("A Catalogue of Plants, of which Images were Illustrated in China"): Sloane 2376, fols 82–110; London, Royal Society, "Journal Book of the Royal Society, 1696–1702," JBO/10, 146. See also Jane Kilpatrick, *Gifts from the Garden of China: The Introduction of Traditional Chinese Garden Plants to Britain 1698–1862* (London: Frances Lincoln, 2007), 34–48.

32 "A Sort of Tea from Mr Cunningham," in Hans Sloane, "Manuscript Catalogues of Sir Hans Sloane's Collections: Vegetable and Vegetable Substances," Natural History Museum, South Kensington Botany Special Collections, Darwin Centre DC2 HCR 728. I am grateful to Richard Coulton for sharing his research on Cunningham and Sloane, and to Victoria Pickering and Charlie Jarvis for showing us this item.

33 Huang, *Science and Civilisation,* 533.

34 Kaempfer, Le Comte, and Ovington, each in his own way, do offer some situational context for understanding tea in their domestic Chinese context. But this is systematically erased by the botanical systems of collecting and taxonomy; in commercial contexts in Britain it is reduced to the vestigial exoticizing of transculturated naming practices (Bohea, Bing, Singlo).

35 Cuninghame to Sloane, 22 November 1701, British Library, Sloane 2376, fol. 92v.

36 Cuninghame to Sloane, 22 November 1701, British Library, Sloane 2376, fol. 92v; see also James Cuninghame to James Petiver, 22 November 1701, Chusan: British Library, Sloane 3321, fol. 89r.

37 James Cuninghame, "Part of Two Letters to the Publisher from Mr James Cunningham, F.R.S. and Physician to the English at Chusan in China," *Philosophical Transactions* 23 (1702–3): 1201–9.

38 Ellis et al., *Tea and the Tea-Table,* vol. 2, 17–18, 87–9.

39 John Hill, *Exotic Botany Illustrated* (London, 1759), 21–2.

40 Ibid., 22; Carl von Linné, *Potus Theae* (Uppsala, 1765), 2.

41 Annicka Windahl Pontén, "'Luxury or Beneficial Everyday Habit?': Carl Linnaeus on Coffee, Tea and Chocolate," unpublished paper delivered at "Coffee, Tea, and Chocolate: Fuelling Modernity" conference, Liverpool, June 2015; Nils-Erik Landell, *Doctor Carl Linnaeus, Physician,* trans. Silvester Mazzarella (London: I.K. Foundation, 2008).

42 Wolfgang Muntschick, "The Plants That Carry His Name: Kaempfer's Study of the Japanese Flora," in *The Furthest Goal: Engelbert Kaempfer's Encounter*

with Tokugawa Japan, ed. Beatrice Bodart-Bailey and Derek Massarella (Knoll House: Japan Library, 1995), 71–95.

43 John Berry, "Acculturation," in *Handbook of Socialization: Theory and Research*, ed. Joan Grusec and Paul Hastings (New York: Guilford Press, 2007), 543.

44 Richard Collins (active 1726–1732), *The Tea Party* (c. 1727), Goldsmiths' Hall London. See also another version, with only one child: Richard Collins, *A Family of Three Taking Tea* (c. 1727), Victoria and Albert Museum, P.9–1934

45 Marcia Pointon, *Strategies for Showing: Women, Possession, and Representation in English Visual Culture, 1665–1800* (Oxford: Oxford University Press, 1997), 28.

46 On the mock-heroic invention poem, see Ulrich Broich, *The Eighteenth-Century Mock-Heroic Poem* (Cambridge: Cambridge University Press, 1990), 78–87.

47 Le Comte, *Memoirs and Observations*, 152–7.

48 Nahum Tate, *Panacea: A Poem Upon Tea: in two canto's* (London: printed by and for J. Roberts, 1700), 18.

49 Peter Anthony Motteux, *A Poem in Praise of Tea* (London: J. Tonson, 1712).

50 J.G.A. Pocock, "Joseph de Guignes and the Discovery of Eurasia," in *Barbarians, Savages, and Empires*, vol. 4: *Barbarism and Religion* (Cambridge: Cambridge University Press, 2005), 100–4; D. E. Mungello, *The Great Encounter of China and the West, 1500–1800* (Lanham: Rowman & Littlefield, 2009).

chapter two

Evliya Çelebi, Explorer on Horseback: Knowledge Gathering by a Seventeenth-Century Ottoman

DONNA LANDRY

Why Study an Ottoman?

The longevity of the Ottoman Empire as a multicultural, multi-religious, multi-ethnic formation comparatively tolerant of difference has recently been prompting inquiries into the structures of institutions, but also the ideas and sensibilities, that enabled this staying power. Virginia Aksan proposes that studying "comparative empires" by setting the Ottomans "among their neighbours," beginning with the Habsburgs and Romanovs, might aid in the "reopening of a number of questions concerning Ottoman longevity and survival, part of ongoing discussions among Ottoman and world historians."[1] That the Ottomans conquered vast territories is self-evident; how the formation held together diverse populations for "[c]enturies of symbiosis under the banner of a multiethnic Islamic state" is less well understood.[2] Karen Barkey argues that Ottoman "longevity" was "partly the result of ingenious openness, flexibility, and willingness to negotiate": "Ottomans demonstrated their openness to the forces of the 'local' by spending much time learning, assessing, and adapting to indigenous practices," possibly even "convinc[ing] the vanquished of their conquerors' larger interest in their well-being."[3] She suggests that "Ottoman toleration emerged out of a top-down and bottom-up concern for boundaries and for peace between religious and ethnic communities," in which difference, not homogeneity, was actively valued.[4] "Alongside Islam," Barkey stresses, the Ottomans could draw upon "their Turkish-Mongolian origins" and "experience in the vast space from China to the Pontic steppes, with its various religions and different ethnicities," leading them to create "fluid boundaries in multicultural settings that would be branded open-minded even by modern standards."[5] As Dominic Lieven's comparative study shows, the early modern Ottoman Empire offered a "haven of relative peace, security and tolerance," not just to Muslims but also to Christians and Jews; as a consequence, "[t]he victory of nationalism over empire" in Ottoman as in Habsburg territory "had devastating consequences."[6] Nor should such a relative haven's existence be entirely surprising, since for the Ottomans – such as Evliya Çelebi – their lands were not conceived in Western terms of imperium, but as "the well-protected domains" of the Padishah (*memalik-i mahrusa-i şahane*), a place of safety as well as toleration for all subjects.[7] In theory, then, there were Ottoman alternatives to the violence and sectarianism wrought by what Caroline Finkel calls "the acquisitive European way of empire."[8]

In a historical moment when the Middle East appears as little more than a series of violent flashpoints, with people struggling to make sense of it, it might be worth investigating how this Ottoman longevity and comparable stability were achieved. How then might Ottoman modes of exploration, as well as theories of imperial management, have also differed? If we shift the focus of inquiry to include the Ottomans as themselves explorers, inquiring subjects, what might we learn about how the Ottomans did things differently?

The very premise of Ottoman exploration challenges the familiar claim that before the nineteenth century Muslims lacked curiosity about other peoples, and in particular, Europeans.[9] Bernard Lewis's incuriosity thesis has been powerfully contested in recent years. Nabil Matar has argued that the Ottomans "had a history of travel and cartography" that was influential in the Arab world.[10] Elsewhere Matar identifies what he calls the "searching curiosity" of Magharibi travellers to Europe with regard to European cultural institutions.[11] Ottoman maritime exploration as investigated by Palmira Brummett and Giancarlo Casale challenges what Brummett calls "Age of Discovery vintage historiography," whereby "disproportionate attention" continues to be focused on certain "conquerors and imperialists, and on certain rhetorics of conquest, in certain geographic locations, at the expense of others."[12] Disproportionate attention to Columbus's voyages to the New World has led, Brummett argues, to the Ottoman Empire not being perceived as a "protagonist" in early modern maritime history but "as something to be circumvented as the globe was to be circumnavigated."[13] Casale goes so far as to propose that the Ottomans be seen as "victors" in the "opening round" of "history's first truly global struggle for dominance" – the sixteenth-century Indian Ocean trade.[14] For our purposes the importance of the Ottomans lies in their being, significantly, a "non-Western state" whose "encounter with the outside world was experienced as a discovery precisely because it involved the same delicate interplay of political ambition, economic self-interest, and intellectual inquisitiveness characteristic of the European Age of Exploration."[15]

If "discovery," then, can be acknowledged to have been on the Ottoman agenda, along with expansion of commerce and political power, the Ottomans too will have had their explorers. The term "explorer" in English presupposes certain authorial practices and kinds of ideological freight, not least heroic individuation, that in the British case, at least, were only formalized in the nineteenth century.[16] Yet early modern voyages and imperial projects, including the Ottomans', historically preceded the coming into being of such proscriptive categories and terminology, inviting the investigation of alternatives.

An Ottoman Explorer

To speak of early modern Ottoman exploration and travel is to speak, in the first instance, of Evliya Çelebi (1611–c. 1687).[17] Istanbul-born and court-educated, Evliya Çelebi authored a ten-volume manuscript, the *Seyahatname*, or "Book of Travels," which appears in many ways to be unique in Ottoman literature. Evliya's text stands alone in its ambition and achievement.[18] The work may well be "the longest and most ambitious travel account by any writer in any language"; it is certainly a "key text for all aspects of the Ottoman Empire at the time of its greatest extension in the seventeenth century."[19] Based upon a lifetime of travel throughout the empire and beyond (from Tabriz to Vienna, from the Sea of Azov to the Sudan), the *Seyahatname* is remarkable for its playful language and amalgamation of genres, its combination of empirical knowledge-gathering, autobiography, and vivid storytelling, and its projection of anticipated readers' responses, all of which offer vital clues to characterizing a possible seventeenth-century Ottoman sensibility, or what Robert Dankoff calls an "Ottoman mentality."[20] The text bears witness to its author's engagement with the events and historical actors of his times in strikingly immediate ways, with the result that the *Seyahatname* has become "the most frequently cited source for the Ottoman seventeenth century."[21] External sources corroborate many of Evliya's claims, but there is no evidence of the text's original reception because the manuscript did not come to public attention until the early nineteenth century.[22]

"Who touches the book touches the man"[23]

Evliya's text appears remarkably personal.[24] Exploration was his life's ambition; he wore a ring inscribed "*Seyyah-ı 'alem Evliya,*" "The world traveller Evliya."[25] A significant difference from Western explorers was that Evliya's Ottoman traditions entailed an ethical obligation to fashion oneself as "a boon companion of mankind": "*nedim-i beni-adem.*"[26] That this aspiration was not merely vainglorious on Evliya's part is evidenced by the letter of recommendation written for him by the Greek Patriarch of St Catherine's Monastery in Sinai, praising him as "honourable" and "a man of peace" who desires "to investigate places, cities, and the races of men, having no evil intention in his heart to do injury to or to harm anyone."[27] The product of a privileged Ottoman upbringing, Evliya as a Sufi dervish is nevertheless a frequent critic of the Ottoman system, especially its bloody excesses and tendency towards oppression when ideals of justice are ignored.[28] Evliya is at once representative of *an* Ottoman sensibility of his times, and not a "representative Ottoman" *tout court*;[29] he is not an uncritical apologist for empire. His explorations frequently take him to political hotspots or war zones, but, imbued as he is with his own version of Ottoman inclusivity and ideals of toleration, he often writes as if he were the empire's conscience as well as its chief foreign correspondent.

Born in 1611 in Istanbul, Evliya was the son of the palace goldsmith and a tribeswoman from Abkhazia (who was related to the future grand vizier Melek Ahmed Paşa). The name "Evliya" means "the friends [Arabic: *awliya*] of God," or "saintly individuals"; "Çelebi" is "a title roughly equivalent to Gentleman or Esquire."[30] In 1623 Evliya was apprenticed to Sultan Murad IV's *imam*, Evliya Mehmed Efendi, to train as a *hafiz* – a Qur'anic reciter.[31] Perhaps Evliya "owed his name to his teacher and spiritual father."[32] Evliya learned to perform other religious offices (*imam*, prayer-leader; *muezzin*, caller-to-prayer) and, having a good voice and ready wit, would often serve as a "courtier, musician, and littérateur" during his travels.[33] He reports graduating "from the harem into the cavalry corps with a daily allowance of forty *akçe*," but he did not achieve "officer status" (the titles of "Agha or Pasha") and indeed "[a]ll his life" "avoided official appointments" that "would have limited his travel options."[34] After completing the *haj*, the pilgrimage to Mecca, in 1672, Evliya died in Cairo in 1687 or soon after, after what he claimed were fifty-one years on the road. He never married.

Reading Evliya in the light of "exploration" (as it was known to his Western European contemporaries) reveals paradoxes at every turn. For a Turk from Istanbul, Evliya travelled well beyond familiar turf, gathering new knowledge in his encyclopaedic work. But did he explore in the sense of discovering "new worlds"? Yes, because for the Ottomans, the cities of Western Europe such as Vienna were just as exotic as the empire's northern, eastern, or southern frontiers.[35] If the definition of exploration literature is that it involves "engag[ing] the indigenous populations and civilizations for their own sake to the point of studying them and compiling the results of their efforts in books we would today find invaluable," then Evliya's might be said to be one of the few Ottoman texts to qualify.[36] Evliya's "Book of Travels" is also paradoxical in its blending of empirically verifiable knowledge with literary flights of fancy, bawdy jokes, satire, and political allegory. Evliya both engages in highly idiosyncratic wordplay and goes "to great lengths to record sounds accurately"; historians and historical linguists still mine his text for its acute observations.[37] The marvels and wonders (*garîb ü acîb*) to be expected in the tradition of the *rihla*[38] jostle with geographical facts and episodes suggestive of allegorical or satirical purpose.[39]

So far as geography goes, Evliya's greatest contribution may be the map of the Nile held in the Vatican library.[40] However, the *Seyahatname* is itself replete with detailed enumerations of structures that the Ottomans have built throughout their "well-protected domains" – bridges, mosques, medreses, bathhouses, soup kitchens, caravansarais for travellers. It is also rich in natural historical detail. Of a Nile bird living in symbiosis with the crocodile, Evliya reasons: "There is a proverb that 'The magpie does not groom the calf out of love.' It picks out lice and worms from the calf's back in order to get something to eat. This bird performs a similar service for the crocodile."[41] Scientific explanations of unfamiliar phenomena are sought in the first instance, with close observation of new fauna and flora being joined with rational deduction and analogy, the whole often packaged with folk wisdom: neither the low nor the high is to be neglected. By the time Evliya is exploring Egypt, Sudan, and Ethiopia, after decades of travel, his earlier enthusiasm for hunting wild animals has given way to keen observation only. In the Sudan, Evliya's travelling party try to rescue a young elephant attacked by a bird of prey, and are later joined by eleven elephants who accompany them for seven hours, "sometimes walking in front of us, sometimes to our right or left, chasing one another, or playing, or fighting." "Though we were armed," Evliya observes, "we agreed not to shoot at them, but simply to watch."[42] Evliya keeps thinking about elephants. When the party come upon monkeys, who are "funny and clever," he reflects that "[t]he elephant is also a clever animal."[43] Evliya's animal tact, or sensitivity to and fellow-feeling for non-human species, is central to his mode of being,[44] but also to his method of exploring.

Educated Ottomans, then, far from being incurious, could burn with curiosity to see as much of the world as possible. The text of the *Seyahat-name* begins with a dream, a "sleep of wish fulfilment," as Evliya puts it, foregrounding his longing to travel. He has been asking himself how he can "get free of the pressures of father and mother, teacher and brother, and become a world traveller?"[45] "I was always on good terms with heart-wounded dervishes and glad to converse with them," he says, indicating the source of his inspiration to travel. "And when I heard a description of the seven climes and the four corners of the earth" from these wandering dervishes, "I longed to travel with all my heart and soul."[46] Thus a wandering life compelled Evliya precisely because it was *not* unknown though it would take him to unknown places. In the dream, the nineteen-year-old Evliya, surrounded in his neighbourhood mosque by saints and holy men, is granted an audience with the Prophet (itself an outrageous claim) and makes a slip of the tongue, asking for *seyahat* (travel) instead of *şefa'at* (intercession), to which the Prophet "smiled and replied, '*My intercession and my travel and my pilgrimage, may God give you health and well-being.*'"[47] Evliya's greatest desire is thereby confirmed by a prophetic dream, a slip of the tongue, and a pun. Matters worldly and spiritual are everywhere entangled, and this entanglement is at issue in the very prose of his text.

The injunction to travel is also an injunction to write, to produce a "marvellous work," a compendium of geographical knowledge that will be itself a marvel. Dankoff characterizes Evliya's style, which is unlike that of any other Ottoman text and nearly amounts to a private language, as follows: "On the one hand, he often adopts a *playful attitude.* On the other hand, he devises his own *rules* and applies them consistently."[48] This combination of playfulness with the establishing and consistent application of rules could be said to describe not only Evliya's prose style but also his method of recording and representing more broadly.

As an explorer-author, Evliya regularly relishes being a pious and thereby rule-conscious Muslim who finds himself nevertheless having to relate outrageous, scandalous, and disgraceful happenings. Sa'd ibn Abi Waqqas, the patron saint of archers, in the dream sends Evliya forth explicitly with a knowledge-gathering mission: "'The well-protected kingdoms through which you pass, the fortresses and towns, the strange and wonderful monuments, and each land's praiseworthy qualities and products, its food and drink, its latitude and longitude – record all of these and compose a marvellous work.'"[49] By obeying the injunction to record all, therefore, Evliya has obtained a licence to blaspheme; when recording foreign languages, for example, Evliya begins by listing numbers for doing business, followed by names for God, food, and drink, closely followed by obscenities and curses on the assumption that these words are what a visitor is most likely to hear. Evliya archly excuses himself for relating the "naughty expressions" of Balkan gypsies, for instance, because the "world traveller must have some inkling" of the actual spoken dialects "despite the impropriety of some expressions."[50] But there is a further injunction, an ethical and moral imperative in the saint's advice, not only to tell the truth but also to behave well and be a force for good: "'Do not abandon the path of truth. Be free of envy and hatred. Pay the due of bread and salt. Be a faithful friend but no friend to the wicked. Learn goodness from the good.'"[51] Fanaticism, however, is to be eschewed in keeping with a "vagabond Dervish-like nature," which Evliya characterizes for us further as being "ready to sacrifice my soul for my friends."[52]

Evliya's favourite characterization of himself is as a dervish, a follower of a Sufi order. He was most probably a member of the Gülşeni, a branch of the Halvetiyye,[53] the order traditionally closest to the Ottoman sultans.[54] He was very likely inducted into that order by his music teacher, Omer Gulşeni.[55] More precisely, Evliya describes himself as being, out of "the many kinds of dervishes in this world," "the kind who goes out among people, rides horses, and keeps servants."[56] He is a gentleman-dervish, a man of rank and property, not a poor man. Yet he consistently refers to himself throughout the ten volumes as "this humble one" or "this poor one" (*bu hakir, bu fakir*), asserting his dervish credentials.[57]

"Travel Knowledge"

If there is one principle of "travel knowledge" to be derived from the *Seyahatname*, it is to suspend judgment and inhabit imaginatively another's point of view.[58] This principle is most clearly articulated when in volume 8 Evliya is describing how in Gjirokaster, the Albanians, who are "devoted to Ali" (i.e., Shi'a Muslims), enjoy weddings and feast days by drinking alcohol and dancing in the streets: "Lovers go hand in hand with their pretty boys and embrace them and dance about in the manner of the Christians. This is quite shameful behaviour, characteristic of the infidels, but it is their custom, so we cannot censure it" (*bu dahi bir bed-sünnetdir kim âyîn-i ke[fe]redir, amma böyle göre gelmişler, bunı dahi 'ayblamazız*).[59] Dankoff observes how the very phrasing contains the refusal (*-ma-zız*) to attribute disgracefulness to acts that Evliya's audience would be likely to consider disgraceful (*ayıb* or *ayıp*): "*ayblamazız*":

> "We cannot censure it" is literally "We cannot say it is *ayıb*" – in other words, "*ayıb değil*!" ("No disgrace!"). No passage of the *Seyahatname* is more revealing of Evliya's attitude towards such customs.[60]

Here Evliya appears to fit Barkey's description of the Ottomans as heterogeneity-loving, prizing difference for its own sake. Gerald MacLean has argued that there is even a case to be made for Evliya as approaching what Jacques Derrida has theorized as an ethic of unconditional hospitality.[61] Glossing "it is their custom, so we cannot censure it," MacLean contrasts Evliya directly with Shakespeare, for whom hospitality is always so fraught as usually to be regretted: "For Evliya, differentiation within the imperial domains follows a logic of difference shaped by inclusion and conviviality rather than mere difference."[62]

For Evliya, Ottoman policies of toleration and protection provide a ground in which active affection can flourish, whether in the abode of Islam or in "*kafiristan.*" Friendship across difference is crystallized tantalizingly, if briefly, at the end of volume 7 when Evliya expresses to his Crimean Tatar host his heart-felt reluctance at leaving behind at Azov the envoy of Muscovy, with whom he has become friends. Feeling sad to lose the Muscovite as a companion, Evliya is snidely told by his Crimean host: "You have travelled so much in the land of the infidels that you have fallen in love with the infidels";[63] "*Kafiristanda geze geze kafirlere mahabbet etmişsin.*"[64] It is typical of Evliya to record the criticism he received for his friendship with a *kafir* instead of praising himself for open-mindedness. We are left to infer that friendship and love do not necessarily obey geopolitical or doctrinal differences.

Evliya's warm affection for the Muscovite envoy as a companion on the steppe resonates with an earlier passage in volume 7, when he compares and contrasts the Austrians and the Hungarians, theorizing what I call "a fellowship of the horse":[65]

> The Hungarians are Protestants while the Austrians are Catholics. Therefore these two infidel groups are opposites to one another, despite their both being Christians. And, as the saying goes, *Opposites do not join* … [C]ompared to the Hungarians the Austrians are like the Jews: they have no stomach for a fight and are not swordsmen and horsemen. Their infantry musketeers, to be sure, are real fire-shooters, but they have only a single rapier at their waist, and when they shoot they brace their muskets on a forked gun-rest – they

> can't shoot from the shoulder as the Ottoman soldiers do ... The Hungarians, on the other hand, though they have lost their power, still have fine tables, are hospitable to guests, and are capable cultivators of their fertile land. And they are true warriors. Like the Tatars, they ride wherever they go with a span of horses, with five or ten muskets, and with real swords at their waists. Indeed, they look just like our frontier soldiers, wearing the same dress as they, and riding the same [Arab] thoroughbred horses. They are clean in their ways and in their eating, and honour their guests. They do not torture their prisoners as the Austrians do. They practice swordplay like the Ottomans. In short, though both of them are unbelievers without faith, the Hungarians are more honourable and cleaner infidels.[66]

It seems that even when they are enemies, there may be fellow feeling among equestrian peoples. The fellowship of the horse underwrites codes of honour and hospitality not practised by others, transcending other differences among those whose power derives from the superiority bequeathed by equine mobility.[67]

This passage appears quite complex in its address to readers. On the one hand, there is Ottoman complacency and assumption of moral superiority, bolstered by a sideswipe at Jews for epitomizing an unwarlike people: the Hungarians are cleaner and more honourable than the Austrians *because they are more like us, with the same (equestrian) self-image.* That self-image is a concatenation: cavalrymen and swordsmen, hospitable hosts, riders of Arabian thoroughbred horses. On the other hand, it is insinuated, such smugness may be misplaced because the Hungarians are not us, and in fact *may be better than we are,* since even having lost their power to Austria, they maintain their honour, and their agriculture, tables, and stables, and do not torture prisoners. Evliya's style invites us to read between the lines, acknowledging Ottoman achievements but also insinuating a space for Ottoman self-critique. Either way, equestrianism is crucial both for Ottoman self-formation and for the assessment of others. Within the fellowship of the horse, honour and hospitality govern conduct in those expansive spaces of the steppe shared by the Ottomans and Tatars, Hungarians, and, I suggest, Muscovites or Russians, all people of the horse.

Not with Ships, but Horses

A horse is not a ship, the primary vehicle of early modern European exploration.[68] That the two could even be compared may strike readers as far-fetched, yet while in Cairo Evliya deemed donkeys to be "Egypt's caique and ferryboat," so ubiquitous were they for getting about.[69] Evliya's cavalryman's landlubber preferences were reinforced by an early misfortune at sea.[70] Yet horses for him always also exceed being just a convenient mode of transport.[71] They are at once companions, fellow expedition-makers, and allies in time of danger whether within or on the frontiers of the "well-protected domains."[72] Yet nowhere in the scholarship on Evliya to date has the importance of the horse been seriously considered. This essay is an attempt to fill this gap.[73]

On Ottoman Horses

The Ottomans were privileged to have immediate access to the best horses in the world, and they were equine multiculturalists.[74] Nowhere does Evliya refer to the "Turcoman horse" as foreign visitors did. Instead, he indicates the magnificence of the Nogai and Karaçubuk (Black Rod) breeds, both candidates for the Western Europeans' "Turcoman."[75] Evliya also uses the Tatar and Nogai word for a thoroughbred from the Eurasian or Central Asian steppe, *ağırmaq*, the same term as the Russian for a blood horse, *argamak*.[76] By far the most frequently mentioned breed, however, is the "Arab thoroughbred," or *küheylan*. The horses that Evliya describes at spring grass in the imperial pleasure park and resort lodge at Kağithane outside Istanbul are all *küheylans* in the general sense of Arab thoroughbreds, but in accordance with Bedouin usage, Evliya also employs *küheylan* to name a highly prized strain within that general category: "It is a beautiful meadow, where the Arabian horses [*küheylan*] called küheylan, jilfidan, tureyfi, ma'nek, musafaha, mahmudi and seylavi are fed on the finest grass, trefoil and oats."[77] *Küheylan* and *Seglawi* are two of the most celebrated Syrian and Central Arabian strains, also prized in Egypt; the Maneghi, the Cilfidans or Jilfans, and the Tureyfi or Treyfi strains are also esteemed.[78] The Mahmudis are likely to have been Kurdish Arabians since they appear in Evliya's account as gifts or booty from the regions known to Evliya as "Kurdistan."[79] That leaves us with Musafaha, which could well refer to a particular man who owned a substrain.[80] The very concept of "Arab thoroughbred" is for Evliya, then, a complex field, and a *küheylan*, an Arab thoroughbred, was *as Ottoman a horse* as one of a Turkic breed. Evliya also mentions riding a gelding of unspecified breeding on a campaign against rebels outside Iznik, and being given Tartar geldings (*alaşa*) to ride on the Kipchak steppe.[81] This evidence contradicts the popular belief in modern Turkey that the gelding of horses was not practised in Islam.

Care of the Horse, Care of the Self

Evliya states his love of the species with unusual frankness. In volume 8 he reports that because of this love, he has never been without the companionship of horses, having always owned between five and ten during fifty-one years of travel.[82] He cites the Qur'an regarding the divine gift of horses to Solomon:

> 31. Behold, there were brought before him, at eventide, coursers of the highest breeding, and swift of foot[.][83]

It is no surprise that Evliya, as a *hafiz*, should speak of his attachment to horses in religious terms. Horses are associated with the milk-white, Pegasus-like beast Buraq, upon whose back Muhammad journeyed, first to Jerusalem and then through the seven circles of heaven, during his *mi'raj* ("ascension") or *isra'* ("nocturnal journey").[84] Such a mystical construction of the horse suggests the possibility of "animal religion or animal religions," especially within animist philosophy and Sufism, and we shall find Evliya entertaining this possibility in Vienna.[85] However, horses are also humans' earthly companions, brotherly comrades, with whom a kinship of the road is formed: the horse as a second self, a companion species engaged in co-becoming.[86]

The centrality of this bond on the frontier is exemplified by Evliya's adventure with his horse Hamis in volume 6.[87] Evliya alludes again to the same Qur'anic verse when he claims that Hamis was "[o]ne of Solomon's *prancing steeds* (38:31)" and "noble as an Arab thoroughbred, dearer to me than my own brother," "my soul's companion, my zephyr-swift steed Hamis."[88] More than a brother, Hamis is Evliya's soul's companion (a soul brother);[89] he is also a nobly bred and swift steed. Accompanying the Ottoman army in Hungarian lands, and finding himself short of fodder for his horses, Evliya with Hamis joins a foraging party. Set upon by Hungarian troops near Komorn castle, his party are routed and Hamis is wounded by a bullet in the withers, but they manage to gallop away. Out of sight of the enemy, Evliya finds Hamis's wound gushing blood down his shoulder.[90] The practical and caring Evliya tears his handkerchief in two and stuffs the pieces into the wound to stop the flow. The dervish Evliya feels as if he himself is suffering the horse's pain, this horse that is dearer than a brother, observing, "My own heart seemed to be wounded because of his wound."[91]

The care of a horseman for his horse, and the resulting attachment-in-partnership, were matters of Ottoman pride. Evliya frequently mentions looking after his horses as a matter of the highest priority. Such care and attention could mean the difference between life and death. While in Bitlis in Kurdistan in 1656, pursuing damage control after a bloody conflict with the relatively autonomous Kurdish leader Abdal Khan and his sons, Evliya finds himself in a perilous situation. No Ottoman apologist, Evliya does not think that recent policy with regard to his hosts has been just, or is likely to be so: "[I]f you submit to the Ottomans, they will treat you well for a few months, but after that they won't look in your face."[92] Evliya's strategy is to ride out every day with his servants, not only to keep the horses fit, but also to prepare escape routes in the otherwise snowbound landscape. So when fratricide occurs in the Khan's family, and his own life is threatened, Evliya, two of his "slaveboys," and a local friend, Menteş Bölükbaşı, manage to escape:

> The snow was as high as a minaret. Fortunately, I had mounted every day and had opened paths, trampling down the snow drifts with five or six of my servants as a daily exercise. So the four of us pushed through; now at a jog-trot, now at a gallop, now at a run; often sinking in the snow, and looking back in the dark ... God be praised, our horses were in top condition, and went like lightning, for we had withheld their straw to make them lean, and we had mounted every day in Bitlis and trained them hard by pushing through the snow.[93]

Racing fitness demands a trainer's rigorous attention. The care of wounds too, as we have seen, is a matter of hands-on priority for the horseman. During the battle of the River Raab (St Gotthard) in 1664, when Evliya's horse is wounded, he goes immediately to request another from the grand vizier and then quickly repairs to his tent to dress the first horse's wound "with egg, salt, and alum."[94] Making the *haj* in 1672, when Evliya faces terrible weather that delays the Damascus caravan's departure for Mecca, he copes once again by giving priority to his horses' diet and exercise:

> I wrapped my three horses in kilims and felts, raced them over the ground and turned their rumps to the wind. Nor did I deprive their heads of provender bags filled with barley and straw. But the rain gave us no respite.[95]

Evliya also notes an equine gender difference in bearing such hardships as a desert crossing presents. Having been given several camels and "a grey mare" by the Governor of Damascus, who was in charge of the pilgrimage caravan, Evliya observes that the governor's "personal retinue and some of his troops use thoroughbred mares as their mounts," as did the Bedouin.[96] Evliya appears to have been travelling until then with stallions, as was customary for Ottoman Turks. He comments: "Stallions do not bear up very well."[97] He had taken particular care of his, as we have seen. Evliya opines rather archly that if "the authorities made an effort and kept good care of the road from Damascus to Medina, one could manage without camels and cover the stretch on horseback in comfort. *May God grant ease!*"[98] A horse's back is an Ottoman explorer's comfort zone.

Loving care and attention to horses' needs were richly repaid. Horses responded to kind leniency far more than to violent discipline. The Habsburg ambassador to the court of Süleyman the Magnificent (r. 1520–66), Ogier de Busbecq, had reported how different the Ottoman treatment of horses was from standard practice in Europe, and his views were widely known, remembered more than a hundred years later by John Evelyn:

> There is no Creature so gentle as a *Turkish* Horse, nor more respectful to his Master, or the Groom that dresses him. The reason is, because they treat their horses with great Lenity … [T]hey frequently sleek them down with their Hands, and never use any Cudgel to bang their Sides, but in case of great Necessity. That makes their Horses great Lovers of Mankind; and they are so far from kicking, wincing, or growing untractable by this gentle usage, that you shall hardly find a masterless Horse among them.[99]

I have written elsewhere of how such a theory of horsemanship models a theory of governance, and how in seventeenth- and early-eighteenth-century England horsemanship discourse mapped onto a discourse of "comparative imperialisms," in which the potential superiority of the Ottoman system was borne out by the superiority of the horses themselves when they were imported into Great Britain.[100] If kind leniency as opposed to brutality distinguished the Ottoman regime from the Habsburg one, then Ottoman horses were right to prefer the former, thereby bearing witness to Ottoman superiority. One of the most telling signs of Ottoman difference as it emerges from Evliya's sojourn in Vienna is that the rational preference of Ottoman horses for their own side becomes a diplomatic issue.

Exploration in Vienna

Vienna in volume 7 is the most extensively described Western European city in the *Seyahatname*.[101] Evliya is among the entourage of 299 people and 269 horses accompanying the envoy, Kara Mehmed Paşa, to ratify the 1665 peace treaty of Vasvar establishing friendly relations with the Habsburgs after the Ottoman defeat at the battle of the River Raab (St Gotthard).[102] Evliya is impressed by wondrous spectacles, "*garip seyirler*," including organ music at St Stephen's Cathedral, the care taken to preserve libraries,[103] elaborate clockwork figures on monumental buildings, painting, surgical operations, dentistry, and the forwardness and power of women, who "sit together with us Ottomans, drinking and chatting" (which is "no disgrace" ["*ayıp değildir*"]), and he makes friends in Vienna, reporting how he became "*gayet yakın dost*" (bosom friends) with the son of Marshall De Souche.[104] Evliya expresses some prejudices on this foreign and exotic terrain, but nowhere does his account do what we have come to expect from early modern European accounts – "reflect a European imperialist-colonialist ideology compelled to subordinate and alterize."[105] Yet before the visit is over, Evliya finds himself faced with irreconcilable differences that expose the limits of his boon companionship with infidels who are also imperial rivals.

His feeling of estrangement arises most acutely in two similarly structured episodes, which he names the "strangest spectacle" and the "Arab thoroughbred spectacle." That is to say, his cataloguing of Viennese marvels is interrupted by an Ottoman performance when a diplomatic gift horse refuses to be given to the Habsburgs. Perhaps the ambivalence, the attraction and revulsion, expressed in these two episodes could be best described by the early modern structure of feeling that Gerald MacLean has identified as "imperial envy."[106] MacLean's analysis focuses on the English among the Ottomans – the former feel wishful, covetous, and emulative – but for Evliya there emerges a comparable Ottoman structure of feeling, alongside the realization that the Habsburgs are likely to feel the same in the presence of imperial rivals: both difference and commonality are recognized.

For Evliya the "strangest spectacle" in Vienna is that of Muslim captives "pounding medicaments" at the "physicians' market," where there are "100 shops." This episode precedes and parallels the "thoroughbred spectacle" and so deserves quoting in full:

> In front of a number of the shops, on chairs, sit Muslim captives wearing white turbans, Bosnian kalpaks, Tekke and Hamid caps, and Tatar kalpaks, even with the appearance and dress of Tatars. All have their hands and feet chained, and some of the captives from the community of Muhammad are dark Arabs, some youths, and others white-bearded old men. With sad expression and bent necks, they sit on their chairs busily pounding

medicaments in huge bronze mortars – mace, cubeb, cinnamon, black pepper, cardamom, ginger, orris root, etc. Standing behind them are men with swords, as if to say, "Pound quickly!" But the older men pound slowly and feebly, looking right and left, their strength all spent.

Feeling pity for these older captives, I took out my purse and was about to give them a few *akçe*. But Boşnak Ali Zaim of Esztergom proved one of *those who prevent good works* (cf. 50: 25).

"Leave them alone for now," he said. "Give them alms when we come back through this quarter towards evening. Now the owners of these captives are standing next to them and will take from their hands whatever you give."

This seemed reasonable and I put the purse back in my pocket. After touring the markets and quarters and the ancient monuments that we had not yet seen, we returned towards evening to those captives. While we observed, the shops began to close. Several infidels came and unfastened the belts from the waists of the Muslim captives, then removed the turbans and kalpaks and caps from their heads and took off all their clothes. They inserted a watch key into each one's armpit and turned it. Immediately the hands and heads and eyes and eyebrows of all the Muslim captives stopped moving.

When they removed their headgear and clothing I noticed that they were bronze effigies of men, wound up like a clock and moving by means of clockwork mechanisms. I was lost in astonishment.

"Evliya Çelebi," joked my companion Ali Agha, "give these captives a few *akçe*, for God's sake!" It was truly a strange and wonderful spectacle.[107]

The story turns on Evliya's ignorance and on the locally knowledgeable Ali Agha's manipulation of it. Evliya first reacts as the naive but dutiful Muslim quick to dispense alms whenever there appears a need for charity. He ends astonished by Viennese technology. Yet more is intimated by this story; an experience is communicated rather than explained.[108] It first appears that captive representatives of the various Muslim peoples of the empire are in servitude in Vienna; then it is clear they are automatons. But that revelation means *both* that the Austrians possess the ability to produce such wonders, and that although they may have failed so far, they entertain precisely the fantasy of holding captive their Muslim rivals.

The "thoroughbred spectacle," more cryptic than the "strangest spectacle," resonates with the Muslim captives' episode in its structure, especially when Evliya's urge to act is curtailed by advice to wait and see: "'Hele görelim,'" says Kara Mehmed, cautioning him as the Bosnian *agha* had done. This enigmatic event suggests how resonantly animals, especially horses, could figure in geostrategic and political/diplomatic relationships. In this episode, two pedigreed Arab thoroughbreds are to be presented to the Habsburgs.[109] One of the horses seems to disappear from the text (did it go quietly?). The other horse, first referred to as "the famous küheylan named Tureyfi," after his celebrated Arabian strain (*Tureyfi adlı ünlü küheylan*), and thus echoing the presence of Arabs among the human captives, sees the black-hat-wearing infidel Austrian grooms, *siyah şapkalı kafirler*, to whom he is to be handed over – meaning that there are to be no properly dressed Muslim grooms in his future, *Müslüman kıyafetinde adam yok* – and promptly rebels. Rearing and striking out, he kills at least six stablemen, destroying two of their (unbelieving) heads with his forelegs before trampling members of the crowd in Palace Square, moving like lightning, *şimşek gibi*.

The violent action of the horse is conveyed in religio-political language, suggesting a violation of the horse's own religious and political boundaries. A sacrilege is being committed.[110] This is an Ottoman horse, Evliya emphasizes, sent by divine decree, *Osmanlı'dan ... bir at Allah'ın emriyle.* "This poor Arab thoroughbred horse," a humble being (like Evliya himself) (*bu fakir küheylan at*), has brought about an episode of mass injury now legendary: "There were so many kafirs injured it is still a legend in kafiristan" (*O kadar kafir yaralanmıştır ki hala kafiristanda destandır*). Commanded by the envoy, "'Hey, grab that horse'" (*Bre şu atı tutun*'), one of the Ottoman grooms tries to soothe the horse, whose unofficial, familiar name we learn is Ceyhun, calling "'Come my Ceyhun come'" ("'*Gel Ceyhunum gel*'"), the horse's name referring to the Central Asian river Jayhun (the Amu Darya or Oxus of antiquity, traditionally the border between Iran and Turan), the gentle tone exhibiting Ottoman leniency in action. Ceyhun responds by neighing with bloody tears (*kanlı yaşlar*) in his eyes and coming obediently.

Then comes the "wait and see" moment: the narration slides from the groom speaking to Evliya speaking ("I said"; *dedim*), and the horse's history is recounted to remind Kara Mehmed that he is a *gazi* horse, a war horse who has been ridden by the Ottoman sultan: "'*Sultanım bu at bir gazi attır ve bizzat Osmanoğlu padişahı binmiştir.*'" Fearing for the horse's life after this killing spree – what future treatment could be expected? (*Sonunda bu atı kafirler öldürürler*) – Evliya suggests it would be better to give a different horse: "'*Bu atı alıp yerine başka at verin' dedim.*'" This elicits from Kara Mehmed the now familiar caution to wait and see: "'*Hele görelim' diye aldırış etmedi.*" By waiting and seeing, Evliya witnesses more havoc and death with the second attempt to present the gift. The neighing (*kişneyip*) horse, breaking free of all restraints, killing seven more kafirs and wounding their seven horses, dashes from the Palace Square like a thunderbolt (*yıldırım gibi*) to erupt into the Çerkez Meydanı, the Circassian Square, the site of the martyrdom of a Çerkez cavalryman and his mount during the 1529 siege.[111] There, neighing bravely a few more times, Ceyhun gives up the ghost, delivering up his spirit (*ruhunu teslim etmiştir*) and expiring. The grooms bury this horse next to the fallen Circassian's horse – another martyr in a martyrs' square. Needless to say, this spectacle astonishes all the spectators, making a deep impression not only upon "*Bütün Islam askeri*," all the Muslim soldiery, but on all the people, "*Ve bütün halk.*" The story offers us a corporeal, animal experience for us to think about as we will.

The Ottoman delegation has itself become a foreign spectacle in Habsburg space. Coupled with the *faux* Muslim captives episode, the *küheylân* spectacle implies that diplomacy, gift exchange, and hospitality cannot totally displace the memory of previous warfare. Behaving as a horse well might – flight or fight being the species' operative responses – and acting up at being handed over to strangers who do not seem likely to treat him in the manner to which he is accustomed, Ceyhun has come as close to speaking a political truth as he could. It is as if the horse's actions re-enacted Sultan Süleyman's besieging of the city in 1529. Ceyhun has acted out what Evliya and the mission of 1665 cannot say: there remains unfinished business between the Ottomans and Habsburgs. Remember, Vienna, the horse's actions proclaim: once we Ottomans, including Çerkez cavalry and their brave horses, were nearly in possession of you. We died fighting here, our remains are buried here. War will indeed break out again, alas; the Ottomans will besiege Vienna again in 1683 while Evliya is putting the finishing touches to his description of the 1665 mission.[112] Historically speaking, the horse is by no means wrong in his neighing insistence on not burying the past, on refusing to go quietly into Habsburg service, as if all imperial and state rivalries and Muslim/Christian differences had been successfully overcome.[113]

By Way of Conclusion

In his differences from his Western European contemporaries, the Ottoman Evliya compels us to reflect anew upon both the modes and the ethics of exploration and encounter. Within and beyond the "well-protected domains," including such frontiers as Vienna, the Sudan, Kurdistan, Hungary, and the Kipchak steppe, the *Seyahatname* records the built structures and other achievements of Ottoman rule while also criticizing failures of good governance. Amassing encyclopaedic knowledge of humanity along the way, Evliya sought to uphold dervish ideals of heterodoxy and accommodation, not dictating or censuring but rather suspending judgment and befriending difference. These principles governed his knowledge gathering as well as his criticisms when Ottoman policies failed.[114] Ottoman traditions and practices were being actively contested during Evliya's lifetime, a period of self-questioning.[115] The Kadızadeli movement for reform, Karen Barkey suggests, advocated "scripturalism and orthdoxy" and "rigidity and harshness of rule" over and against Sufi "flexibility, complexity, and amalgamation of tradition and practice," the latter an apt description of Evliya's *modus operandi*, a mode of power/knowledge no longer valued by Ottoman officialdom as it had once been.[116] Evliya's playfulness, determination to see the funny side, and obedience to his own rules produces a stylistically distinctive, accomplished, and at times highly literary text; in the early modern European writing about exploration, these are far from common characteristics. Evliya's curiosity certainly extended to all aspects of the "indigenous populations and civilizations" he encountered but also beyond human society; he was a sensitive recorder of natural history, attentive to fellow creatures as well as fellow humans. For Evliya, horses were by no means simply vehicles of exploration; they were also intimate friends, more than brothers, companions in co-becoming, allegorical actors – even the conscience of empire. What Evliya the explorer expounds is a form of creaturely cosmopolitanism. To comprehend the "Ottoman age of exploration" requires us to attend to Ottoman horse power as well as sea power, and the concept of equestrian as well as maritime voyaging.

NOTES

1 Virginia Aksan, *Ottoman Wars, 1700–1870: An Empire Besieged* (Harlow: Pearson, 2007), 4.

2 Carter Vaughn Findley, *Turkey, Islam, Nationalism, and Modernity: A History, 1789–2007* (New Haven: Yale University Press, 2011), 211.

3 Karen Barkey, *Empire of Difference: The Ottomans in Comparative Perspective* (Cambridge: Cambridge University Press, 2008), 19, 20.

4 Ibid., 25.

5 Karen Barkey, "Rethinking Ottoman Management of Diversity: What Can We Learn for Modern Turkey?," in *Democracy, Islam, and Secularism in Turkey*, ed. Ahmet T. Kuru and Alfred Stepan (New York: Columbia University Press, 2012), 12–31, at 17.

6 Dominic Lieven, *Empire: The Russian Empire and Its Rivals* (2000; New Haven: Yale University Press, 2002), 13, 414.

7 Selim Deringil, *The Well-Protected Domains: Ideology and the Legitimation of Power in the Ottoman Empire 1876–1909* (1998; London: I.B. Tauris, 2011), 42.

8 Caroline Finkel, "'The Treacherous Cleverness of Hindsight': Myths of Ottoman Decay," in *Re-Orienting the Renaissance: Cultural Exchanges with the East*, ed. Gerald MacLean (Houndmills: Palgrave Macmillan, 2005), 148–74, at 168.

9 Bernard Lewis, *The Muslim Discovery of Europe* (1982; London: Phoenix, 1994), 55–7 and *passim*.

10 Nabil Matar, ed. and trans., "Introduction," *In the Lands of the Christians: Arabic Travel Writing in the Seventeenth Century* (New York: Routledge, 2003), xiii–xlviii, at xiv. See also Matar, *Europe through Arab Eyes, 1578–1727* (New York: Columbia University Press, 2009); and Gerald MacLean and Nabil Matar, *Britain and the Islamic World, 1558-1713* (Oxford: Oxford University Press, 2011).

11 Nabil Matar, "Arab Views of Europeans, 1578–1727: The Western Mediterranean," in *Re-Orienting the Renaissance*, ed. MacLean, 126–47, at 143.

12 Palmira Brummett, *Ottoman Seapower and Levantine Diplomacy in the Age of Discovery* (Albany: SUNY Press, 1994), 1–2.

13 Ibid., 2.

14 Giancarlo Casale, *The Ottoman Age of Exploration* (Oxford: Oxford University Press, 2010), 12. Brummett commends Casale's use of Portuguese as well as Ottoman sources and his "swashbuckling quality," but notes his tendency to downplay previous scholarship and his drawing of "exaggerated conclusions"; see Brummett, "Review of *The Ottoman Age of Exploration*," *Journal of the Economic and Social History of the Orient* 54 (2011): 417–20. For a meticulously exhaustive interrogation and (in some cases) refutation of Casale's claims, see Svat Soucek, "About the Ottoman Age of Exploration," *Archivum Ottomanicum* 27 (2010): 313–42.

15 Casale, *The Ottoman Age*, 10–11.

16 Adriana Craciun, "What Is an Explorer?," *Eighteenth-Century Studies* 45, no. 1 (Fall 2011): 29–51. Craciun describes the heterogeneity of practices, including those of the "traveler, adventurer, surveyor, factor, trapper, agent, interpreter," that preceded the nineteenth-century invention

of "the Explorer," recognizing how that term's Romantic authorial implications are "alien" to the early modern "corporate and military domains in which the business of exploration was typically carried out" (31). Evliya's circumstances as military actor and government agent should be understood as analogous to those of many of his Western European contemporaries.

17 Nuran Tezcan, "When did Evliyâ Çelebi Die?," in *Evliyâ Çelebi: Studies and Essays Commemorating the 400th Anniversary of his Birth,* ed. Nuran Tezcan, Semih Tezcan, and Robert Dankoff (Istanbul: Isbank Culture Production, 2012), 30–2.

18 Even Bernard Lewis acknowledges an exception to his incuriosity thesis in the case of "the great and ever-curious traveler Evliya Çelebi"; *The Muslim Discovery,* 81. For the seventeenth-century Ottoman intellectual context, see Cemal Kafadar, "Self and Others: The Diary of a Dervish in Seventeenth-Century Istanbul and First-Person Narratives in Ottoman Literature," *Studia Islamica,* 69 (1989): 121–50; and Rhoads Murphey, 'Forms of Differentiation and Expression of Individuality in Ottoman Society," *Turcica* 34 (2002): 135–69.

19 Robert Dankoff and Sooyong Kim, "Introduction," *An Ottoman Traveller: Selections from the Book of Travels of Evliya Çelebi,* trans. Dankoff and Kim (London: Eland, 2010), xi–xxix, at xi.

20 Robert Dankoff, *An Ottoman Mentality: The World of Evliya Çelebi* (Leiden and Boston: Brill, 2004).

21 Caroline Finkel, "Joseph von Hammer-Purgstall's English Translation of the First Books of Evliya Çelebi's Seyahatnâme (Book of Travels)," *Journal of the Royal Asiatic Society,* Third Series, 25, no. 1 (January 2015): 41–55, at 55.

22 Ibid., 41–2. The translation, of the first two volumes only, appeared in three parts (Book I, part i in 1832, Book I, part ii in 1846, and Book II in 1850). See also Pierre A. MacKay, "The Manuscripts of the *Seyahatname* of Evliya Çelebi, Part I: The Archetype," *Der Islam* 52 (1975): 278–98.

23 Dankoff, *An Ottoman Mentality,* 151.

24 On Evliya's "egocentricity" see Dankoff, "An Odyssey of Oddities: The Eccentricities of Evliya Çelebi," in *Eurasian Studies* 8 (2010) [Études en l'honneur de Jean-Louis Bacqué-Grammont]: 97–106, https://www.academia.edu/12820579/An_Odyssey_of_Oddities_The_Eccentricities_of_Evliya_%C3%87elebi.

25 Dankoff, *An Ottoman Mentality,* 126.

26 Ibid., 9. Laila Hashem Abdel-Rahman El-Sayed explores Evliya's "cosmopolitan emotions" in her PhD thesis, "Discourses on Emotions: Communities, Styles, and Selves in Early Modern Mediterranean Travel

Books: Three Case Studies," University of Kent/Freie Universität Berlin (2016).

27 Pinelopi Stathi, "A Greek Patriarchal Letter for Evliya Çelebi," *Archivum Ottomanicum* 23 (2005–6): 263–8.

28 Dankoff, *An Ottoman Mentality*, 106–14. See also Hakan T. Karateke, whose close analysis of Evliya's use of such terms as "bloodthirsty" (*hunhar*) reveals a critique of the abuse of power, in *Evliya Çelebi's Journey from Bursa to the Dardanelles and Edirne: From the Fifth Book of the Seyahatname* (Leiden: Brill, 2013), 7–10.

29 Evliya's "eccentricities do not necessarily contradict his typicalities" is Dankoff's judgment in *An Ottoman Mentality*, 115.

30 Dankoff and Kim, "Introduction,' *An Ottoman Traveller*, xi–xii and n2.

31 Ibid., xi.

32 Ibid., xi.

33 Ibid., xiii.

34 Ibid., xii–xiii.

35 See Nuran Tezcan, "Evliya Çelebi's 'White Man's' View of the People of Africa in the Seventeenth Century," in *Turkish Language, Literature, and History: Travellers' Tales, Sultans, and Scholars since the Eighth Century*, ed. Bill Hickman and Gary Leiser (London and New York: Routledge, 2016), 323–42.

36 Soucek, "About the Ottoman Age," 314.

37 Robert Dankoff, *An Evliya Çelebi Glossary: Unusual, Dialectal, and Foreign Words in the Seyahat-name*, Sources of Oriental Languages and Literatures 14 (Cambridge, MA: Harvard University, 1991), 8.

38 See Dr Yeliz Özay, "Analysis of *Evliyâ Çelebi's Book of Travels* in Terms of the Concept of *Acâib* Literature" [*EVLİYÂ ÇELEBİ SEYAHATNÂMESİ*'NİN *ACÂİB* EDEBİYATI AÇISINDAN DEĞERLENDİRİLMESİ], Gazi Üniversitesi Türk Halkbilimi Bölümü, Araştırma Görevlisi, Ankara/Türkiye, *Millî Folklor*, Yıl 26, Sayı 103 (2014): 123–33, http://millifolklor.com, accessed 22 January 2016. See also Houari Touati, *Islam and Travel in the Middle Ages*, trans. Lydia G. Cochrane (Chicago: University of Chicago Press, 2010).

39 Sooyong Kim suggests that Evliya's "thoroughness as a data collector sets him apart from the selectivity of earlier geographers," and that "when he does cross over into fiction, it is consistently with satirical intent"; "The *Seyahatnâme* in World Travel Writing," in *Evliyâ Çelebi: Studies and Essays*, ed. Tezcan, Tezcan, and Dankoff, 365–8, at 367.

40 Robert Dankoff, Nuran Tezcan, and Michael D. Sheridan, *Ottoman Explorations of the Nile: Evliya Çelebi's "Matchless Pearl These Reports of the Nile" map and his accounts of the Nile and the Horn of Africa in "The Book of Travels"* (London: Gingko, 2018).

41 Dankoff and Kim, *An Ottoman Traveller*, 389.

42 Ibid., 448.

43 Ibid., 450.

44 See Landry, "Horse–Human Companionship: Creaturely Cosmopolitanism across Eurasia," in *Cosmopolitan Animals*, ed. Kaori Nagai, Karen Jones, Donna Landry, Monica Mattfeld, Caroline Rooney, and Charlotte Sleigh (Houndmills: Palgrave Macmillan, 2015), 181–93. For more on the favourable treatment of animals in Ottoman society, see Benjamin Arbel, "The Attitude of Muslims to Animals: Renaissance Perceptions and Beyond," in *Animals and People in the Ottoman Empire*, ed. Suraiya Faroqhi (Istanbul: Eren, 2010), 57–74. For Islam and animals, see Sarra Tlili, *Animals in the Qur'an* (Cambridge: Cambridge University Press, 2012).

45 Dankoff and Kim, *An Ottoman Traveller*, 3. On the importance of dreams for the Ottomans, see Aslı Niyazioğlu, "Dreams, Ottoman Biography Writing, and the *Halveti-Sünbüli Şeyhs* of 16th-Century Istanbul," in *Many Ways of Speaking about the Self: Middle Eastern Ego-Documents in Arabic, Persian, and Turkish (14th–20th Century)*, ed. Ralf Elger and Yavuz Köse (Wisbaden: Harrassowitz Verlag, 2010), 171–84; and Caroline Finkel, *Osman's Dream: The Story of the Ottoman Empire 1300-1923* (London: John Murray, 2005), 2, 11–12.

46 Dankoff and Kim, *An Ottoman Traveller*, 3–4.

47 Ibid., 6.

48 Dankoff, *An Evliya Çelebi Glossary*, 5.

49 Dankoff and Kim, *An Ottoman Traveller*, 7.

50 Ibid., 277–8; this text has the distinction of being regarded as the earliest example of Balkan (Rumelian) Romani, 477.

51 Ibid., 7.

52 Evliya Efendi [Evliya Çelebi, Mehemmed Zilli ibn Derviş], *Narrative of Travels in Europe, Asia, and Africa, in the seventeenth century*, trans. The Ritter Joseph von Hammer, 2 vols. (London: Allen, 1834–46), vol. 1, pt ii, 246.

53 Dankoff, *An Ottoman Mentality*, 121–2.

54 Barkey, *Empire of Difference*, 184.

55 Dankoff, *An Ottoman Mentality*, 37–8n57, 122.

56 Dankoff and Kim, *An Ottoman Traveller*, 146.

57 Ibid., xxviii; Dankoff, *An Ottoman Mentality*, 151–2.

58 See Ivo Kamps and Jyotsna G. Singh, "Introduction," in *Travel Knowledge: European "Discoveries" in the Early Modern Period*, ed. Kamps and Singh (New York: Palgrave, 2001), 1–16.

59 Dankoff, *An Ottoman Mentality*, 72–3.

60 Dankoff, "Ayıb Değil! (No Disgrace!)," *Journal of Turkish Literature* 5 (2008): 77–90, at 82.

61 Gerald MacLean, "Hospitality in William Shakespeare and Evliya Çelebi," *Shakespeare Jahrbuch Band* 149 (2013): 117–35. See also Meyda Yeğenoğlu, *Islam, Migrancy, and Hospitality in Europe* (New York: Palgrave Macmillan, 2012).

62 MacLean, "Hospitality," 134–5.

63 Dankoff, *An Ottoman Mentality*, 65. Dankoff cautions against exaggerating or misreading Evliya's love of the foreign, suggesting: "[W]hile Evliya had a genuine appreciation of many aspects of European civilization, and even had some European friends, he did not 'fall in love' with them. Rather he treated the Europeans – as he did the Iranians – as a sounding board by which he could pass judgments on those he *was* in love with, namely the Ottomans"; "Did Evliyâ Çelebi 'Fall in Love' with the Europeans?," *Cahiers Balkaniques* 41: *Evliyâ Çelebi et l'Europe*, ed. Faruk Biligi (2013): 15–26; [en ligne], 41 (2013) [para. 23], mis en ligne le 19 mai 2015, http://journals.openedition.org/ceb/4002.

64 Dankoff, *An Ottoman Mentality*, 65. See also Evliya, *Evliya Çelebi Seyahatnamesi*, ed. Yücel Dağlı, Seyit Ali Kahraman, and Robert Dankoff (Istanbul: Yapı Kredi Yayınları, 1999–2007), vol. 7 (2005), 187b.2; and Evliya, *Günümüz Türkçesiyle Evliya Çelebi Seyahatnâmesi* [modern Turkish version], ed. Yücel Dağlı, Seyit Ali Kahraman, and Robert Dankoff, 10 vols., this vol. trans. Seyit Ali Kahraman (Istanbul: Yapı Kredi Yayınları, 2010), 7.2: 771.

65 See Landry, "Horse–Human Companionship."

66 Dankoff and Kim, *An Ottoman Traveller*, 230–1.

67 The horseman Bjarke Rink goes so far as to propose that equestrianism literally powered civilizational advancement, overcoming human limitations and conquering time, in *The Centaur Legacy: How Equine Speed and Human Intelligence Shaped the Course of History* (n.p.: The Long Riders' Guild, 2004). A more scholarly argument is David Anthony's thesis that Indo-European languages achieved dominance through being transported and disseminated by equestrian peoples of the steppe; *The Horse, the Wheel, and Language* (Princeton: Princeton University Press, 2007).

68 Lady Mary Wortley Montagu joked that among the Ottomans her side-saddle was "gaz'd at with as much wonder as the ship of Columbus was in America," writing to Anne Thistlethwayte, 1 April 1717, in Teresa Heffernan and Daniel O'Quinn, eds., *The Turkish Embassy Letters* (Peterborough: Broadview Editions, 2013), 128.

69 Dankoff and Kim, *An Ottoman Traveller*, 373.

70 When shipwrecked in the Black Sea in 1642, Evliya admits to having "some skill in swimming," and though from the depth of his heart he holds to the

noble Qur'an as his intercessor and recalls the great saints whose graves he has visited, he also thrashes "fearlessly and furiously, like a diver," until he lands upon a floating plank; Dankoff and Kim, *An Ottoman Traveller*, 50.

71 Tulay Artan investigates the symbolic resonances of seventeenth-century Ottoman horsemanship in "Ahmed I and 'Tuhfet'ül-mülûk ve's-selâtîn': A Period Manuscript on Horses, Horsemanship and Hunting," in Faroqhi, ed., *Animals*, 235–69.

72 Caroline Finkel describes Evliya as often fearful and in need of guides in Anatolia when travelling independently, as when making the *haj* in 1671, in "The Open Road: Thoughts on Evliya Çelebi as Wayfarer / Açık Yol: Bir Yolcu Olarak Evliya Çelebi Uzerine Düşünceler," *Journal of Turkish Studies / TUBA* 44 (2014): 1–22. For further "in the footsteps" (or hoofprints) approaches, see Finkel, 'With Evliya Çelebi from Alanya to Ermenek – An Initial Exploration of the Central Taurus Stages of His 1671 Pilgrimage Itinerary (October 2012)," *Journal of Turkish Studies / TUBA* 40 (December 2013): 97–117; and Caroline Finkel and Kate Clow with Donna Landry, *The Evliya Çelebi Way* (Istanbul: Upcountry [Turkey], 2011).

73 The Turkish republican writer Ahmed Hamdi Tanpınar describes the horse as playing a principal and "epic" role for the Ottomans, in "Evliyâ Çelebi and Empire," originally published in the newspaper *Cumhuriyet*, 27 June 1942, reproduced in Tezcan, Tezcan, and Dankoff, *Evliyâ Çelebi: Studies and Essays*, 394–6.

74 See Landry, *Noble Brutes: How Eastern Horses Transformed English Culture* (Baltimore: Johns Hopkins University Press, 2009), 5–9, 76–103, 172–4; Turkish translation, Landry, *Asil Hayvanlar: Ingiliz Kültürünü Değiştiren Doğulu Atlar*, trans. Sinan Akıllı (Istanbul: E Yayınları, 2015); further evidence is presented in "*Türk Atı, Türk Atlar, Nerede?* Turkish Horses Hidden from History Though Not from the Keen Eye of Lady Anne Blunt, 1884," delivered at the conference on "British and Turkish Literary and Cultural Interactions," Hacettepe University, Ankara, 13 May 2015, forthcoming in Burcin Erol, Deniz Bozer, and Sinan Akıllı, eds., *British and Turkish Literary and Cultural Interactions* (Newcastle: Cambridge Scholars Press).

75 Evliya in Von Hammer, *Narrative*, 1.i: 181; Dankoff and Kim, *An Ottoman Traveller*, 58.

76 Dankoff, *Evliya Glossary*, 12. For the *argamak*, see Ann M. Kleimola, "Cultural Convergence: The Equine Connection between Muscovy and Europe," in Karen Raber and Treva Tucker, eds., *The Culture of the Horse: Status, Discipline, and Identity in the Early Modern World* (Houndmills: Palgrave Macmillan, 2005), 45–62.

77 Evliya in Von Hammer, *Narrative*, vol. 1, pt ii, 85.

78 Lady Anne Blunt, "Pedigree of the Arabian Thoroughbred Stock," in *Bedouin Tribes of the Euphrates*, Ed., with a Preface and Some Account of the Arabs and Their Horses, By W.S.B., 2 vols. (London: John Murray, 1879; Reprint: London: Frank Cass, 1968), 1: facing page 276.

79 Dankoff, *An Ottoman Mentality*, 126.

80 Katrina Murray, executive secretary of the World Arabian Horse Organization (WAHO), further proposes that Mahmudi might refer to a Seglawi substrain belonging to Ibn Mahmoud or Ibn Amoud, both of the Shammar (private communication). Evliya's naming of strains, apart from the Mahmudi and Musafaha, is largely in agreement with Dr Hazaim Alwair's account of modern Syrian usage ["Syrian Strains"]; 2006 World Arabian Horse Organization (WAHO) Conference Proceedings, Damascus, Syria (Newbarn Farm: WAHO, 2007), 74–88.

81 Robert Dankoff, *The Intimate Life of an Ottoman Statesman: Melek Ahmed Pasha (1588–1662) As Portrayed in Evliya Çelebi's 'Book of Travels' ('Seyahatname')* (Albany: SUNY Press, 1991), 66; Dankoff and Kim, *An Ottoman Traveller*, 267.

82 Evliya in Dağlı, Kahraman, and Dankoff, eds., *Günümüz Türkçesiyle*, this vol. trans. Kahraman (2011): "Gerçekten de atlar yaratılmışların şereflisidir ki Cenāb-ı Hak küheylān atların hakkında *Kur'ān-ı Kerim'de 'Akşam üstü kendisine sāfin (üç ayağı üzerinde durup bir ayağını tırnağının üstüne diken) süratli koşan (saf kan Arap) atları gösterilmişti' [Kur'ān*, Şad, 31] buyurmuşlardır. Onun için bu hakir atları pek sevip 51 yıldarı beri 5–10 baş atsız olmamışımdır"; 8:1:27 [195a.8].

83 A. Yusuf Ali, *The Meaning of the Holy Qur'an* (Beltsville: Amana Press, 2000), Sura 38, Şad 31: 385.

84 See James W. Morris, "The Spiritual Ascension: Ibn 'Arabî and the *Mi'râj*," *Journal of the American Oriental Society* 107 (1987): 629–52; and 108 (1988): 63–77. See also Barnaby Rogerson, *The Prophet Muhammad: A Biography* (London: Little, Brown, 2003), 112–13, who remarks how without this particular story of Muhammad's night flight, as a religion, Islam would have evolved very differently (114).

85 Caroline Rooney, "Animal Religion and Cosmonautical Allegories," in Nagai, et al., eds., *Cosmopolitan Animals*, 58–71, at 59. Rooney's investigation of animist philosophy, *African Literature, Animism, and Politics* (London: Routledge, 2000), and of alternatives to secular Enlightenment, *Decolonising Gender: Literature and a Poetics of the Real* (London: Routledge, 2007), offers a broader theoretical framework for understanding Sufism beyond the Ottoman context.

86 On horses as "second selves," see Landry, *Noble Brutes*, 121, 132–5. On "co-becoming," see Landry, "Horse–Human Companionship," in Nagai et al., eds., *Cosmopolitan Animals*, 185–7; Vinciane Despret, "The Body We Care for: Figures of Anthropo-zoo-genesis," *Body and Society* 10, nos. 2–3 (2004): 111–34, at 121–5; Donna Haraway, *When Species Meet* (Minneapolis: University of Minnesota Press, 2008), 222–3.

87 For further analysis of this richly layered episode, see Landry, "Evliya Çelebi and Ottoman Enlightenment," in Oğuz Öcal, ed., *Evliya Çelebi'nin Sözlü Kaynakları* ([n.p.]: Turkish National Commission for UNESCO, 2012), 91–8, http://unesco.org.tr/dokumanlar/kitaplar/evliya_celebi_sozlu_kaynak.pdf.

88 Dankoff and Kim, *An Ottoman Traveller*, 184, 186.

89 Landry, "Horse–Human Companionship," in Nagai et al., eds., *Cosmopolitan Animals*, 185.

90 On the significance of such a wound and the "bloody shouldered Arabian," see Landry, *Noble Brutes*, 120–21.

91 Dankoff and Kim, *An Ottoman Traveller* 186.

92 Ibid., 159.

93 Ibid., 161–2.

94 Ibid., 229.

95 Ibid., 343.

96 Ibid., 342.

97 Ibid., 342.

98 Ibid., 346.

99 Ogier Ghiselin de Busbecq, *Travels into Turkey … Translated from the Original Latin of the Learned A.G. Busbequius* (London: J. Robinson and W. Payne, 1744), 131–2. In 1684 John Evelyn saw horses captured at the siege of Vienna: "[B]eautifull & proportion'd to admiration, spiritous & prowd," "with all this so gentle & tractable, as called to mind what I remember *Busbequius* speakes of them; to the reproch of our Groomes in *Europ* who bring them up so churlishly, as makes our horse most of them to retaine so many ill habits"; John Evelyn, *Kalendarium 1673–1689: The Diary of John Evelyn*, ed. E.S. deBeer, 6 vols. (Oxford: Clarendon Press, 1955), vol. 4: 398–9.

100 Landry, *Noble Brutes*, 127–36; Landry, "English Brutes, Eastern Enlightenment," in a special issue, "Animal, All Too Animal," ed. Lucinda Cole, *The Eighteenth Century: Theory and Interpretation* 52, no. 1 (Spring 2011): 11–30.

101 Dankoff and Kim, *An Ottoman Traveller*, 218.

102 A contemporary document attests to Evliya's presence in Vienna in 1665; K. Teply, "Evliyā Çelebi in Wien," *Der Islam* 52 (1975): 125–31; cited in

Lewis, *The Muslim Discovery*, 112, 317n34; Nuran Tezcan, "Documentary Traces of Evliyâ Çelebi," in *Evliyâ Çelebi: Studies and Essays*, ed. Tezcan, Tezcan, and Dankoff, 43–55.

103 In Vienna and at St Catherine's Monastery in Sinai, Evliya laments Muslim Ottoman failures to preserve libraries and other endowments, in contrast to Christian practice, which is exemplary; Dankoff and Kim, *An Ottoman Traveller*, 236–7, 366.

104 Ibid., 231; Dankoff, *An Ottoman Mentality*, 65.

105 Kim, "The *Seyahatnâme* in World Travel Writing," in *Evliyâ Çelebi: Studies and Essays*, ed. Tezcan, Tezcan, and Dankoff, 367.

106 "Where imperial discourses might be expected to produce empowered imperial subjects constituting themselves at the expense of colonized subalterns, the situation proves to be more complex in the case of English views of the Ottomans. Instead of any simple desire for domination, we will find instead a restructuring of desire, knowledge and power: imperial envy"; Gerald MacLean, *Looking East: English Writing and the Ottoman Empire before 1800* (Houndmills: Palgrave Macmillan, 2007), 20.

107 Dankoff and Kim, *An Ottoman Traveller*, 234.

108 Evliya conforms to Walter Benjamin's definition of the storyteller's art as keeping "a story free from explanation as one recounts it ... The most extraordinary things, marvellous things, are related with the greatest accuracy, but the psychological connections among the events are not forced on the reader. It is left up to him to interpret things the way he understands them, and thus the narrative achieves an amplitude that information lacks"; Walter Benjamin, "The Storyteller" [1936], in *Selected Writings of Walter Benjamin*, vol. 3: *1935–1938*, ed. and trans. Howard Eiland and Michael W. Jennings (Cambridge: Harvard University Press, 2002), 148.

109 My thanks to Sinan Akıllı for advice regarding the translation of this episode; Evliya, in Dağlı, Kahraman, and Dankoff, eds., *Günümüz Türkçesiyle*, vol. 7: pt i, 257–8 [66a–66b].

110 On the possibility of animals having a sense of the sacred, see Rooney, "Animal Religion."

111 Today in Vienna a statue of the Circassian cavalryman, the "Çerkez Dayı" (Circassian uncle), and his horse can still be seen on a palace wall; Claudia Römer, "Legends about Vienna in the *Seyahatnâme* and their Austrian Counterpart," in Tezcan, Tezcan, and Dankoff, eds., *Evliyâ Çelebi: Studies and Essays*, 290–5, at 293–4, fig. 2. According to Römer, the Ottomans' interpreter Franz von Mesgnien-Meninski (1620–1698) confirms Evliya's account in that "the Turks said that their gift horse wept" (294).

112 Dankoff, *An Ottoman Mentality*, 105.

113 After the peace mission, in 1667, Evliya relates his own plan for taking Vienna to the deputy grand vizier Mustafa Pasha; Dankoff, *An Ottoman Mentality*, 105.

114 Worldly justice by definition falls short of Sufi ideals, but Evliya continues to judge Ottoman actions according to those ideals. Cautioning against neo-Ottoman nostalgia, Caroline Rooney suggests that "the very spirit of Sufism may be seen to be at odds with imperialism"; she quotes Valerie J. Hoffman: "'One might argue that the political prominence of the Sufi Orders under the Ottoman empire represents a perversion of Sufism'"; Rooney, "Sufi Springs: Air on an Oud String" in "Postcolonial Springs," ed. Norbert Bugeja, *Counter Text* 1, no. 1 (April 2015): 38–58, citing Hoffman, *Sufism, Mystics, and Saints in Modern Egypt* (Columbia: University of South Carolina Press, 1995), 15.

115 On the "all-pervasive perception of rapid social change and dislocation" during Evliya's day, see Kafadar, "Self and Others," 125–7, 149–50.

116 Barkey, *Empire of Difference*, 191. Given Ottoman advances in "rational sciences" during the seventeenth century, Khaled El-Roayheb argues that the Kadızadelis' anti-intellectual influence may have been exaggerated, in "The Myth of 'The Triumph of Fanaticism' in the Seventeenth-Century Ottoman Empire," *Die Welt des Islams*, New Series, 48, vol. 2 (2008): 196–221.

chapter three

Indigenous Voyaging, Authorship, and Discovery

MICHAEL BRAVO

In the spring of 1810, two Moravian vessels set sail from Hopedale on the Labrador coast with the intention of spreading the Gospel to Inuit in the neighbouring region of Ungava. Separated by the rugged Torngat Mountains and boreal forest, Labrador and Ungava are to this day recognized as distinct Inuit regions, Nunatsiavut and Nunavik respectively. Connections between the two have for centuries been maintained by traditional trails, place names, and narratives. And so, too, there was a degree of separation marked by the presence of dangers and hostile spirits. Since the Labrador people are farther south than most Inuit groups, they are not people of the sea ice; their trails through snow tend to follow the coastline. Going inland becomes more difficult farther north, where the Torngat Range makes the going more forbidding. Travelling on the sea itself has always meant taking to boats – in others words, voyaging.

Heading north along the wild, rugged coast of Labrador (in present-day Nunatsiavut), the voyaging party wintered over at Okak, their northernmost mission settlement, marking the frontier of Inuit Christendom, and the staging post where they prepared for their remarkable journey the following year. In the spring of 1811 the small party set sail from Okak, heading north, rounding Cape Chudleigh on the northern tip of Labrador. Following the coastline westwards, they sailed until they reached the Kangiqsualujjuaq (Great Fjord), naming it the George River after the British monarch. The summer passing quickly, they weighed anchor and sailed onwards to the Koksoak River (meaning "Great River," Kuujjuaq in present-day Nunavik, Quebec). The Koksoak flows hundreds of miles from Quebec's interior northwards to the sea; its mouth was home to Inuit of the Ungava region. After spending the summer establishing contacts, surveying the riverbanks, assessing the local natural resources, and evaluating possible sites for a new mission station, they "considered the business committed to us to be accomplished" and sailed for home.[1] The journal detailing their voyage was published in London in 1814, complete with a chart carefully engraved and printed, containing many newly mapped indigenous place names (see Figure 3.1).[2]

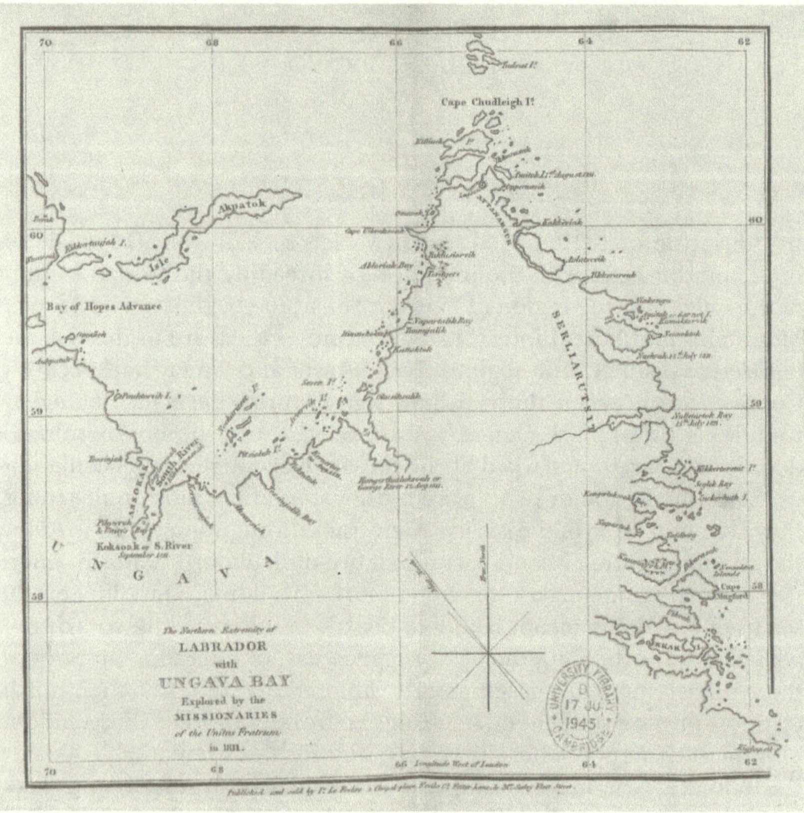

Figure 3.1 This remarkable fold-out map focuses close attention on the acquisition of knowledge of Inuit place names along the Labrador and Ungava coasts and testifies to the cartographic achievements of this collaborative evangelical expedition. The high standard of engraving affirms that the Moravian missions could, in the course of their coastal exploration, be authors of useful knowledge. "The Northern Extremity of Labrador with Ungava Bay explored by the missionaries of the Unitas Fratrum in 1811." Fold-out chart accompanying Kohlmeister and Kohl, *Journal of a Voyage from Okkak*, 1814. By permission of the Syndics of the Cambridge University Library.

This essay reflects on the experience of the Labrador Inuit on this northern journey. It argues that this ostensibly evangelical journey can reasonably be described as an example of "indigenous voyaging or exploration" and considers the implications of this framing. Carving out a historical space for indigenous voyaging is partly a matter of telling the story and teasing out the elements that give credit where it is due, as well as recognizing indigenous knowledge and expertise. Indigenous agency in long-distance travel is prone to being overlooked. In this case it was not because the missionaries sought to hide the contributions of their voyage partners – far from it. The complex skills and difficult work required on a long-distance journey are easy to overlook in the telling. Harder still is reading the nuances and deciphering the clues to the social and religious landscape of colonial frontiers like early-nineteenth-century Labrador. Genres of travel writing in the long eighteenth century such as missionary inspections, natural histories, colonial survey narratives, and accounts of geographical exploration and conquest tend to align the reader's understanding with the perspective and understanding of the author, and thus the recognition of authorship matters a great deal. These genres of travel writing tend to be porous. A close reading of the voyage narrative on which this essay is based – a narrative that defies easy classification – will to some extent merge those genres.

Simply labelling the voyage with national or ethnic categories such as "British," "German (Moravian)," or "Inuit" fails to capture the composition or allegiances of the party accurately. Moreover, colonial encounter was present in the social and religious fabric of the mission party itself, not merely in the anticipation of negotiating relations with the peoples of neighbouring indigenous lands. As we will see, in this evangelical expedition there was no hard and fast distinction between the figures of the explorer and the guide, or explorer and explored. This essay will provide a more complex and informative point of departure for a discussion of nineteenth-century Inuit travel traditions. It will also avoid the superficial temptation simply to contrast European and indigenous technologies of travel as a way of making visible indigenous expertise – this is itself a trope of imperial encounter. Rather, my concern is to examine the voyage as a window onto the different mobilities and the cultural ebbs and flows in this early period of region-building. The grand maritime passages (e.g., the Northwest Passage) would come to be experienced as an emotional narrative of imperial yearning; by contrast, the voyage to Ungava represents an important example of Inuit–settler long-distance travel. Journeys like these built on and reinforced an archipelagic region of connected trails and crossings.[3]

If the tomes devoted to the history of Victorian Arctic exploration have taught us a single important lesson about their successes and failures, it is that the personal, spiritual, and moral qualities of travel needed to resonate, if imperfectly, with their audiences. During the Napoleonic Wars, nationalist ideals shaped and filtered the reception of voyage narratives in Britain. Moral values were at least as important in giving purpose to Inuit travel, particularly where the church played such a prominent role.

Recognizing the spiritual content of the Moravians' journey to Ungava brings to the foreground a range of complementary cross-cultural relations. The fact that the expedition used Inuit-procured boats tells us something about who was directing the use of capital. Those boats were a two-masted forty-foot sailing ship with a tender, and an Inuit *umiaq* or "women's boat" – better thought of as a standard family-size boat – owned by the family of an Inuk man, Thukkekina. This took place against a background of technologies, materials, and skills that were shared between missionaries and Christian Inuit on the Labrador coast as early as Erhardt's 1752 exploration.[4] That these Inuit travellers were predominantly Christians, and that their journey would be assisted and mediated by an apparently non-Christian Inuit traveller from Ungava, invites a carefully considered response to the problem of what precisely made native travel "native." The missionaries, through their many years of evangelizing in Labrador, had the time and the moral mandate – which future Arctic explorers would only exceptionally have – to consider the value and use of local technologies in the context of local social values. The Moravians had the great advantage of coupling their voyaging methods to their shared religious values and a common purpose.

The Inuit–Moravian evangelical expedition to Ungava was predicated on a passage between two regions, albeit not a northwest passage. In navigational terms, the mission was seeking a safe coastal route from Labrador to Ungava. Its purpose was to connect the spiritual realms of the two regions and to prepare the ground for future religious instruction and conversion. Their evangelical passage was intended to open the gate that had hitherto blocked the passage of Christian belief and enlightened commerce between a Christian region and its pagan neighbour. The passage, encompassing the initiation of a new place into a Christian community, was analogous to a preparatory stage in baptism, the anticipation of a journey into a new phase of life, and was carried out with this sense of excitement and duty.

Indigenous region-building, of which this published voyage is an unusual example, was possible because the context of the long-distance travel that defined the journey was as much global as regional and local. As a number of historians have shown, the term "guide" masked the multiple cultural roles, context, and significance of knowledgeable people inhabiting colonial frontiers.[5] The term also implicitly signified the spatial boundaries where indigenous authority was deemed to begin and end. Communication and supply across long-distance imperial networks were often fragile and frequently reliant on and negotiated with local trading networks, knowledge, and social organization.[6] The Moravian network of missions spread across British and Danish colonies in distant parts of the globe epitomized this fragility and local dependence.

The circulation of correspondence between regional Moravian missions and their London headquarters through their published *Periodical Accounts* was crucial in shoring up the network and sustaining a collective identity, often in the face of great adversity.[7] Publishing their achievements, particularly where missionaries could demonstrate that they were helping build peaceful and stable relationships with indigenous peoples, also helped them secure and maintain patronage in Europe, where their status as a small Protestant church required the support of learned allies. In Britain, Sir Joseph Banks, president of the Royal Society (1778–1820) and a patron of many colonial projects involving scientific travel and collecting, was one such ally.[8] Thus this small-scale collaborative expedition along the coast of Labrador, by being brought to public light through publication, was part of a wider Moravian strategy throughout the long eighteenth century that entailed its missions collecting and publishing natural history.

The Moravian missionary society (the Brethren's Society for the Furtherance of the Gospel among the Heathen) had tools and conventions at its disposal for dressing the voyage to Ungava in a form familiar to readers of voyage and travel literature. *Journal of a Voyage from Okkak, on the Coast of Labrador, to Ungava Bay…* (1814) was a slim volume, fewer than one hundred pages, relatively concise but well-written, carefully edited, and accompanied by an engraved map of the Labrador and Ungava coast.[9] The title page of the published narrative described the journey explicitly as a "JOURNAL OF A VOYAGE" ("voyage" being in larger bold letters), suggesting a volume with a sense of purpose that was in some way substantial, or exceptional, that could sit on a bookshelf alongside other voyage narratives. The subtitle – "to explore the Coast, and visit the ESQUIMAUX in that unknown Region" – was explicit about exploration being at the core of the geographical purpose and holding the potential for new knowledge, commerce, or discovery.[10]

Recent historical and literary studies of the print culture of travel writing and exploration help us make sense of the *Journal of a Voyage from Okkak.* The attribution of authorship to the two European missionaries from Saxony, Benjamin Kohlmeister (1756–1844) and George Kmoch (1770–1857), reflected the fact that Kohlmeister's diary served as the basis for the narrative text and that Kmoch's record of toponyms was the basis for populating their chart of Labrador. As a co-authored narrative, the story and events made for an interesting account of missionary courage and encounter. Nevertheless, the packaging of the book as of Moravian authorship was not the whole story.[11] Through a critical postcolonial lens, the expedition can be recast, at least in part, as an Inuit journey in which the presence, roles, and religious convictions of the Inuit can be foregrounded to place a different emphasis on the significance of the voyage.

By contemporary standards, the expedition could claim to have brought home significant new knowledge. Admittedly, the waters along the coasts of Labrador and Ungava were near or adjacent to the heavily trafficked Hudson Strait, the principal shipping route into Hudson Bay, and the coast of Labrador had been surveyed by none other than James Cook when he was still a young naval lieutenant.[12] What the Moravian expedition did however accomplish was to record with care many previously unrecorded place names, some but not all of which were known to the people of Okak. The voyage narrative would become a rich source for subsequent cartographies of Labrador. Those toponyms would be incorporated, if selectively, by other cartographers and historians, including Arrowsmith (1814) and Anspach (1822).[13] Take for instance, Aaron Arrowsmith, leading chart maker and "Hydrographer to the Prince of Wales," whose coastline of Labrador on his *Chart of Labrador and Greenland, including the North West Passages of Hudson, Frobisher, and Davis* (Figure 3.2) was densely populated with the place names from the Moravian voyage. Thus Arrowsmith was able to explain to his chart readers that the "coasts of Labrador, Greenland, Baffins Bay, and the North of Hudson's Bay" were part of a "Karalit Nation" of tribes or peoples, each with its own dialect but linked by a shared history of contact, migration, and displacement. The distinctive histories of these Inuit sub-regions would continue to shape the Inuit Arctic into the late twentieth century.[14]

The Moravians' contributions to coastal mapping and natural history collecting, and their descriptions of indigenous encounter, added a degree of scientific seriousness to their missionary zeal and helped boost their reputation as reliable supporters of the British state, on which

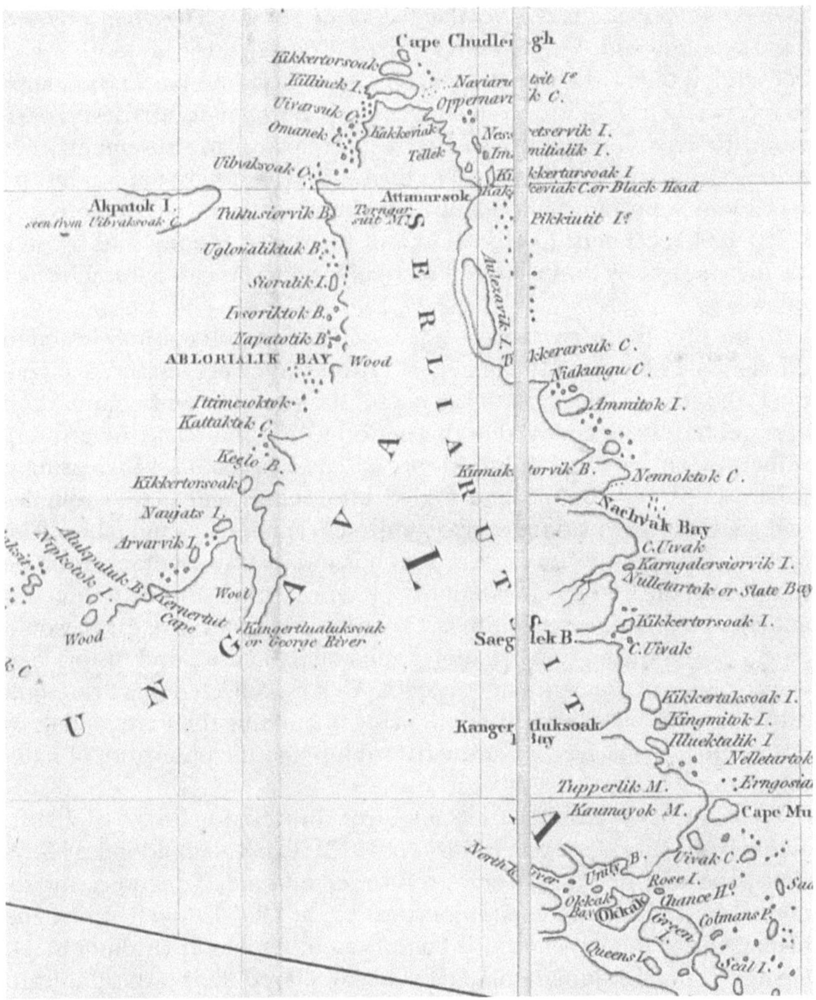

Figure 3.2 Aaron Arrowsmith, an authority in hydrography, added many place names from the chart of Kohlmeister and Kohl, engraving them on the plate of his 1809 chart of Labrador and Greenland. The reader can trace the voyage beginning with its departure from Okkak (lower-right), north along the coast to the tip of the peninsula, rounding Cape Chudleigh and Killinek Island (top), and then south to George River (mid-left), and onwards west to South River (far left), from where it returned following the reverse route. Section of the Chart of Labrador and Greenland, including the North West Passages of Hudson, Frobisher, and Davis, 1809 (detail). Maps 70915.(1). © The British Library Board.

they depended for access to the Labrador coast.[15] They had enjoyed good relations with Joseph Banks for many decades, for his mother had befriended them when he was still a child in London. Banks was happy to receive their help with collecting and observing natural history specimens; he also benefited from the meteorological measurements they made at their mission stations.[16] In the Caribbean, where natural history specimens were more abundant, the Moravians returned copious collections of specimens to Herrnhut and Leipzig in Saxony, and by publishing extensively they acquired recognition in Linnean natural history networks.[17]

By the time of the voyage to Ungava, scientific travel was imbricated in the standards by which the quality of European travel literature was routinely judged. As Nigel Leask has noted, the structure and organization of travel narratives changed in this period to accommodate the growing volume of natural history observations and measurements.[18] Increasingly, survey maps were bound and folded into quarto and octavo volumes and scientific observations were organized in appendices and tables. The Moravian expedition reminds us that missionary travel writing could be folded into the literary conventions of science, travel, and empire. It was anticipated that this expeditionary knowledge, in narrative form, would be circulated through international missionary and natural history networks.[19] Seen in that light, the voyage to Ungava reflected that Protestant missionary societies recognized the value of building their credentials by positioning themselves as worthy contributors to the enterprise of natural history.[20]

In the history of Labrador, Kippinguq or "Brother Jonathan" (d. 1813), and his wife Tukkekina or "Sybilla" (d. 1813), to use their adopted Moravian baptismal names, deserve to be remembered. They were instrumental in making the expedition possible at all.[21] Understanding the leadership of the expedition is complicated. Benjamin (Kohlmeister), George (Kmoch), Jonathan, and Sybilla all played their own significant roles, and their contributions as evangelicals, family members, and individuals are not simple to untangle. Kohlmeister did not intentionally hide this complexity, but neither did he draw attention to it. The conventions of authorship and journal writing were such that Kohlmeister was seen to be the designated leader of the expedition, with Kmoch his younger and stronger assistant, as well as co-author.

As an indigenous journey, the ensuing story of religious and economic exchange can be reframed as a particular moment or episode in an ongoing historical relationship between two neighbouring Inuit regions. Thus the expedition's track followed or ran alongside existing and precisely laid-down long-distance Inuit coastal routes that connected a shared ethnicity, beliefs, and commodity flows among Inuit groups who did not necessarily perceive themselves as a common people.[22] Kohlmeister had initially received his information about the Ungava Inuit from an Inuk named Arngaujak, who had been living on the east coast since 1801.[23] Inuit understandings of "life on the trail as home" draw attention to the connecting power of travel, and to forms of authority over land and territory that point away from what is often our usual understanding. In that context, the relationship between voyage narrative texts and maps is a good deal more complicated than meets the eye.[24]

The reception of the mission party was complex from the outset. Okak, the point of departure, was a community deeply divided between Christianity and shamanism. The settler impulse behind much colonial expansion was from the outset more fragmented and less dominant than often presupposed in writing about missionary travel. The voyage was arguably an assemblage of people, beliefs, and geographies with roots in the Inuit, Saxon, Moravian, and English worlds. In Europe the Moravians had a history of being persecuted for alleged religious dissent and heresies. Seen in those contexts, it is far from clear that this voyage, if understood as indigenous-led, can count as a postcolonial "third space." To the contrary, the evidence in the narrative suggests that there were already in Okak those who came out against the voyage ever leaving, seeing it as an outsiders' incursion into Inuit lands.

The voyage, which also served as a supply run to the northern mission stations, culminated in a new mission station being established farther up the Labrador coast at Hebron in 1831. Because of the fragility of its funding, logistics, and infrastructure as well as the unpredictable weather, the expedition stopped well short of building a station in Ungava. However, Hebron would not be the last stop on the line; further stations would later be established at Ramah (1871–1908) and Killinek (1904–1924). For the Inuit of Nunatsiavut, Hebron is remembered today as a site of deep tragedy because of the forced relocation of families from their homes when the Moravian church and state closed down the settlement in 1959. As Peter Evans has argued, this points to a tragic and very complex story of indigenous settlement, colonial domination, and resistance in Labrador's peripheries as a consequence of various temporal, cultural, and political dynamics.[25] Thus a critical reading of *Journal of a Voyage from Okkak* invites us to reflect on the differing experiences and responses to evangelical exploration among the expedition travellers and those they encountered. As Hans Rollmann has argued, the Moravians' commitment to spreading indigenized literacy and education across both genders and all ages left a remarkable legacy on the Labrador coast for more than a century.[26] However, this complex landscape of emotion, spirit, and belief also set the scene for more than a century of tension between a sense of place and belonging on the one hand, and shifting priorities of colonial rule at a distance from Herrnhut, St John's, and Ottawa, on the other.

Recovering the Voices of Indigenous Co-Travelling

The contrast in historical significance across the cultural divide between Europeans and Inuit, evangelicals and shamans, print culture and oral traditions, is of course familiar in studies in imperial history. The temptation remains to parse a cross-cross cultural expedition along these lines using a binary code of European and indigenous travel traditions. Doing so would throw into relief many remarkable features of indigenous societies. Inuit hunter-gatherer cosmology grounded in shamanism offers a very different understanding of a living landscape than the natural history traditions of Europe, and there is much to learn from these differences. However, as we shall see, the entanglement of "colonialism's [own] culture" across the divide was also present on this expedition in the Inuit evangelicals' own approaches to reading the non-human nature of animals and spirits.[27] This was a living landscape through which to navigate religious and commercial exchange, obligations and duties, threats and alliances. The spiritually charged coastal lands and seascapes of Nunatsiavut (Labrador) and Nunavik (Ungava) at times could make voyaging plainly dangerous and unpredictable, and thus navigation and orientation could also take on the character of moral as well as spatial necessities. Thus I argue that a critically informed reading of the expedition's diaries and print culture can lead us towards a deeper understanding of the complexity of the expedition's experience, rather than away from it as one might suppose from a text that also served a particular type of colonization. To the extent that the voyage from Okak to Ungava was an indigenous expedition in terms of both inspiration and execution, what might the expedition's journey through print culture have to teach us about the conditions of collaboration in what I term "cross-cultural co-travelling"?

A common and admittedly appealing aspect of encounter-based readings of co-travelling has been to focus on European debts to indigenous travel methods. Economic metaphors of appropriation, borrowing, and supplying figure prominently in such readings. Acquiring Inuit and First Nations travel methods and their associated material cultures had very practical economic value: consider the importance of canoes in the fur trade, sledges for polar exploration, and so on. Narratives of adopting indigenous travel methods have tended to turn on individual travellers who fashioned themselves in different ways to point to an authoritative access to the skills of other cultures. The moral of the story, where particular individuals have been concerned, is that by turning their backs on taken-for-granted European cultural superiority, they opened themselves up to be attentive observers and receptacles of local material cultures. The classic example from the mid-nineteenth-century North American Arctic was the Hudson Bay trader and explorer John Rae.[28] He adopted native materials and techniques of travel in the 1840s, while his contemporaries on British naval expeditions remained staunchly conservative in their reluctance to explore the potential of local ways. To be perceived by a Victorian audience as coming too close to a native culture in this period was to run the risk of moral censure. To abandon European conventions of dress, manners, and conduct suggested the possible loss of sound judgment. As Charles Dickens asked in *Household Words,* how could a European observer gone native be trusted to judge the truthfulness of native observations about the circumstances leading to the death of Franklin? Rumours of cannibalism reported by Rae were interpreted as an affront to the distance that guaranteed a sound perspective.[29] Both John Rae and Charles Francis Hall appreciated the practical advantages of Inuit travel techniques yet were careful to emphasize their utility while playing down their associated cultural meanings and beliefs.[30] What then of the risks taken by the Moravians and other missionaries who chose to live so fully in an indigenous society as to become intimate with its many rituals?

Kohlmeister had begun to contemplate such a voyage around 1800, at a time when the mission in Hopedale was beginning to see the fruits of its evangelical work. Ten years later he travelled to the Moravian congregations in Germany and England to win their support and to raise funds. Since well before the establishment of Moravian settlements on the north coast, traders from as far afield as Koksoak in Ungava Bay had been following the Labrador coast down to the Moravian colonies at Okak, Nain, Hopedale, and still farther south to Hamilton Inlet, where they could obtain a wider range of goods, including firearms and ammunition. The coastal journey from Ungava to Okak was between 600 and

650 miles. A trading voyage to bring firearms or luxury goods back to Ungava typically took two years to complete: a summer outward journey, wintering over in Labrador, and a return journey the following summer.[31]

These trade journeys are an important part of the story of the mission. A careful reading of Kohlmeister's journal shows that the Ungava Inuit were keen to increase their trade along the Labrador coast. Uttakiyok, a trader from Koksoak, appears to have been the key figure in this. During a trading voyage in 1800 he had met Kohlmeister, had given him extensive information about Ungava, and had expressly encouraged him to make a mission there. Kohlmeister, excited by news of the larger Inuit population in Ungava, resolved to do the groundwork for a mission colony.[32] Since the pilgrims could anticipate testing times ahead, it was essential for Kohlmeister's purpose that his Inuit companions on the voyage be strong and resolute in their Christian faith. The kind of seasonal lapses into shamanism that had undermined the mission stations for decades would be wholly unacceptable for an exploratory voyage; the missionaries required a total and year-round commitment to Christianity. This was especially important as the mission was to travel by ship during summer, the traditional season of dispersal to camps, where seasonal Christians might be most vulnerable to turning back to the ways of shamanism. What better time could there be to turn the idea of an exploratory mission into action than in the wake of an evangelical revival?

Kohlmeister, being the originator of the expedition, enrolled the help of Brother George Kmoch, who at age forty-one (fifteen years his junior) was very fit, energetic, and unmarried; he also possessed hunting skills that would be as important for the expedition as his spiritual support.[33] In seeking a partner from the Inuit community, Kohlmeister approached Jonathan, an elder, an experienced hunter and traveller, and a faithful, converted Christian, who is said to have been held in extremely high regard by other Inuit. Jonathan held a distinctive position in the Inuit Moravian world. Originally a native of Chateau Bay in southern Labrador, in 1784 he became the first Inuk to be converted to Christianity farther north at Hopedale. As a Moravian "national helper" he contributed to religious understanding in many ways, including by writing a spiritual letter to Christian Inuit in Greenland in 1799.[34] Nearly three decades on, Kohlmeister testified that Jonathan was "a man of superior understanding and skill, possessed of uncommon presence of mind in difficulties and dangers, and at Hopedale considered the principal person, or chief of his nation."[35] Thus Jonathan brought very considerable experience and intelligence to such a challenging undertaking.

Jonathan's *ateq* or Inuktitut name was Kippinguq. Sybilla's Inuktitut name was Tukkekina. Both deserve to be recorded and remembered. It seems probable that they would have continued to use their Inuktitut names, alongside their baptismal names, using one or the other depending on the circumstances.[36] The missionaries' respect for Jonathan's character was considerable, as frequently evinced in testimonies from Kohlmeister in his journal. A financial arrangement with Jonathan to show appreciation for his time and effort was consistent with the Moravian commitment to the synergy between trade and evangelism, a theme that would be repeated in the missionaries' dealings with other Inuit. His contributions would exceed those of his official role as the expedition's pilot. Kohlmeister's relationship to Jonathan was one of partnership, each shouldering more responsibility in different departments. Kohlmeister openly acknowledged Jonathan "as the captain of the expedition."[37] He would be responsible for navigating the ship, for organizing hunts for provisions, and for the party's safety.

The composition of the party was a significant indicator of the voyage's pace and style of travel. Most of the expedition members belonged to Jonathan's extended family. Envisioning the mission as a significant episode in the history of Inuit evangelism, Kohlmeister made a point of mentioning each member by name: Jonathan, Sybilla, and their son Okkiksuk; also Jonas, Agnes, and their five children, Sophia, Susanna, Jonathan, Thamar, and Sybilla; Paul and Mary; David and his mother Rachel.[38] Travelling as an extended family, the basic unit of Inuit sociality, also made sense as the way to evangelize: the more Inuit there were bound by kinship, the stronger their collective voice would be as they preached the word of God. The presence of women would create a channel of communication with other women not easily accessible to Inuit men. Moreover, hard experience in the early days of the missions had shown that a converted family was much more impressive to other Inuit than a few converted individuals, who could quite easily be alienated from their kin. More mouths to feed meant a greater need for food; at the same time, more hunters reduced the risk of going without any food. Women's skills – cooking, sewing, and speaking (women often conversed in groups and were therefore more articulate, whereas men often hunted alone, and spoke little) – though not reported by Kohlmeister, were central to Inuit mobility. One senses from Kohlmeister's writing that his rapport with Inuit men was a good deal more important to him than his rapport with the women. Kohlmeister's own wife and four children elected to stay at Hopedale. No explanation for this was given in the narrative, but one might speculate that his German wife had considerably less experience of travelling and perceived Hopedale to be the safer option for her children.

The goals of the expedition were both geographical and evangelical. The purpose was expressed modestly and clearly but with an official air: to gain "a more correct idea of the extent and dwelling-places of the Esquimaux nation."[39] A map showing Inuit place names as well as clusters of Christians among heathens was self-evidently both geographical and religious. The route to Ungava was a voyage, yes, but no great voyage of discovery. In fact, one could say that it was only one of hundreds of voyages to sail around the tip of Labrador into the Hudson Strait, the principal route into Hudson Bay. On those grounds, the claim implicit on the title page that this was a noteworthy voyage was potentially misleading. However, a collaborative evangelical journey shared some common features with nationalist, government-sponsored discovery expeditions. Both at times hugged the coastlines in comparatively small, shallow boats. Both mapped the land using scientific instruments, translating local places onto a global space, albeit with different levels of precision. Both solicited local knowledge to help them achieve their objectives. In other words, the technologies and methods of travel had a good deal in common. Yet the place names, and their linguistic and cultural histories, were Inuit in their remarkable specificity of place and particularity of historical meaning, whereas their appropriation was distinctly a cartographic tradition.

Historians have widely regarded the mastery of indigenous techniques as an index of a more profound understanding of landscapes traversed. Local technologies (e.g., dogs, kayaks) have struck a chord for those who respect the centrality of practical knowledge in scientific travel, besides appealing to a romantic sense of coming closer to the land. However, common technologies of travel do not imply that common meanings are attached to the landscape. Inuit evangelical travel is a case in point: the Moravian party, by virtue of co-travelling, adopted common technologies and methods of travel; yet the travellers to Ungava did not attribute a single, common meaning to the passage; rather, they perceived relationships between the regions quite differently. The point is not to identify the Labrador and Ungava coastline as a uniquely Inuit or British trade route; the proposition is true in both cases. The objects of imperial and local trade were thoroughly "entangled" in cross-cultural networks.[40] It was not as though the explorers and missionaries "inaugurated" the Arctic's "spatial history," as Paul Carter said of Cook and Australia.[41] The expedition to Ungava reveals a conjuncture of "spatial histories" – of missionaries, converted Labrador Inuit, and Ungava Inuit – the implication being that they came together, not that they merged. Why this was the case becomes clear when we look more closely at the travellers' perceptions of the journey.

By way of background, the most important spatial history of evangelical expansion in the Inuit world had been that from Greenland to Labrador, which was first attempted in the 1750s. Like the voyage to Ungava, it was formulated around a plan to use experienced missionaries fluent in the Greenlandic language and to make new inroads on the Labrador coast – an enterprise that however well thought out proved extremely difficult in practice.[42] The eighteenth-century Moravian colonies in Labrador caused only limited disruption among Inuit groups. Some of them clothed themselves in Christianity in the winter, then discarded the trappings of Christian religion in the summer. The missionaries initially mistook this simply as a sign of waywardness and lack of faith. Eventually however they began to understand that the seasonality of beliefs, like every other aspect of Inuit life, was dialectical, including their spatial mobility. Total conversion to a set of time-independent, uniform religious beliefs entailed a dramatically new understanding of spirit and landscape: either an eradication of the importance of seasonal life, or alternatively a fundamental reconceptualization of the dialectics of Inuit life. This did not necessarily mean abandoning all beliefs, but it did require a transcendental belief of monumental importance: that the Holy Spirit was the supreme spirit in summer and winter, on land and at sea, above and below the earth. Half of the battle of conversion was to make a successful translation of the seasonal dialectics of spirit into the transcendental dialectics of good or evil. In that way the missionaries might defeat the indigenous spirits and the shamans responsible for enforcing the crucial taboos that governed seasonal life. The missionaries could try to prohibit the taboos as evil, or suppress them and allow them to be followed as a matter of mere custom. Inevitably this also translated into a battle as to how one should travel, how the landscape should be named and respected, and whom one should rely upon in an hour of need.

What then were Kohlmeister's geographical aspirations? Since the expedition was to make brief evangelical calls at Inuit camps en route, their plan could enable them to solicit local geographical information, to record as many Inuit place names as possible, and to translate them on to a spatial grid. Inuit place names typically refer to very specific sites, particular points on the land, and much less often to circumscribed areas like peninsulas, bays, and inlets characteristic of the language of European navigation. The terminology, besides reflecting the specificity of linguistic suffixes or localizers in Inuktitut, also points to the specificity of landmarks as meaningful sites where particular events took place, people were remembered, or resources were to be found.[43] In this regard the missionaries were very disciplined. Unlike the officers of discovery voyages, the missionaries were to give only two new names in the course of the entire voyage, and these were for George River and Unity Bay, sites they deemed suitable for future mission settlements. They largely employed existing Inuit place names to identify important sites and landmarks. When they did formally take possession of land, it was marked by three-gun salutes and inscriptions on wooden tablets. For all that, the actual significance of such naval-inspired rituals was anything but obvious.[44]

Preparations for the expedition had begun in earnest the previous autumn at Okak, the northernmost of the Labrador missions, about two hundred miles from Hopedale, that is, almost halfway to the tip of Labrador. Jonathan repaired his boat, strengthening the timbers and dividing the interior cabin space into three sections, two for the Inuit and one for the missionaries, while Kohlmeister dedicated himself to the provisioning. Passing the winter at Okak offered the possibility of speaking with hunters who had more northern experience, but it also carried the disadvantages of being away from their traditional hunting grounds and family networks. Okak was still very much a religious frontier where new claims to spiritual authority were openly challenged. Although its Christian population was about the same size as Hopedale's (96 versus 102), there were many more non-Christians (110 versus 34).[45] There is some evidence that Inuit who had flirted with and abandoned Christianity in preference for a traditional hunting life, but who had also wanted the goods available from a trading post, found a more tolerant environment at Okak than at Hopedale. One such hunter, known to the missionaries as Solomon, had been unable to reconcile the missionaries' doctrinal expectations of total conversion with the most prized traditions of hunting and feasting. A glimpse of the true sadness that must have afflicted such individuals when confronted by the straightjacket of evangelical doctrine is indirectly conveyed by Kohlmeister in this passage:

> Solomon, who has left our community ... could not resist the temptation of going north to feast with the heathen Esquimaux, whenever they had caught a live, or found a dead whale. On such occasions, he was seduced to

> commit many irregularities and sins, but always returned to us with a show of great contrition and repentance. After many relapses, he was informed, that this would do no longer but that if he went again to these heathenish feasts, he would be excluded ... [He] perceived the justice of the sentence; but his love of that species of amusement overcame all his good resolutions. He not only went again, but took also another wife; a step which, of course, excluded him from our fellowship. Yet he is very desirous that his children receive a Christian education, and remain faithful to the precepts of the gospel.[46]

The celebratory feasts that followed a successful whale hunt involved eating large quantities of *maktaq*, the tasty fat beneath the skin. To the missionaries, Solomon's conduct was gluttonous, dissolute, and apparently adulterous, and his companions' behaviour was said to resemble drunkenness. The missionaries saw a strong correlation between the morality of Inuit and the place they inhabited, a contrast between life at the camps and at the missions, as evinced in Solomon's ambivalence towards his children's future in contrast to his own traditions.

The Hopedale party, while undoubtedly enjoying the hospitality of the Christian mission at Okak, could not take for granted the support of Inuit outside the congregation. Most people who ventured an opinion thought the voyage impractical and dangerous. This may have reflected the common view that journeys into the territories of neighbouring groups were, in general, cause for anxiety or even fear, in spite of the successful, if intermittent, trade between Ungava and Labrador. Almost certainly, they would also have had a different set of judgments about the risks of skirting the coastline by sea rather than by shore trail.

Finding oneself in a previously unvisited place was not in itself cause for alarm. Possessing the skills to find food and create shelter in one environment was a source of confidence when it came to applying the same skills in other similar environments. Getting lost could be a serious problem, but this could be solved in a number of ways, including the strategy of conserving energy and waiting to be found by family or friends. Thus historians need to think carefully before ascribing typically modern parameters of risk to Inuit experiences of their landscape; this is very easily misunderstood.

The much greater danger was the risk of isolation from families and family networks that had accumulated generations of specific knowledge about that land, and who had long experience of contact with the local spirits.[47] These spirits could restrict travellers' access to food and shelter if they were offended, angry, or simply malevolent. To tap into local knowledge about northern Labrador, the Moravians were able to persuade one Okak family (Thukkekina, his wife [not named], and their son, Mammak), to fortify their numbers. Kohlmeister also hoped to enlist Uttakiyok, the Ungava trader who had encouraged him from the outset. The previous winter, word had reached Okak that Uttakiyok was somewhere to the north and that he intended to return home to Ungava. Knowing the importance of the knowledge of Inuit travellers, Kohlmeister sent him the urgent message "that as we purposed paying his countrymen a visit, we wished him to wait for us, that he might conduct us through the straits of Killinek. But having heard nothing further concerning him, we remained in uncertainty respecting his intentions."[48]

While preparing to leave Okak, the Moravians' clash of faith with the evil of shamanism (as they perceived it) took on new proportions. Atsugarsuk, a shaman, was spreading intimidating stories around the community about the dangers awaiting the Moravian party. Powerful offshore currents near Killinek, the northern tip of the peninsula, would sweep them out to sea, or so he would have people believe. Whether the cause of this evil would be one of his helper spirits, or one of the Ungava Inuit's, was not revealed. Just in case they managed to pass the cape without harm, reports of "the hostile disposition of the Esquimaux in Ungava Bay" were likewise circulated. Kohlmeister heard that "if we even got there alive, we should never return."[49] Atsugarsuk and his party of dissenters certainly intended these threats to dissuade the Moravian party from taking Christ into northern Labrador and Ungava, or at least to demonstrate that their helper spirits were stronger than the Moravians' Holy Spirit. The Moravians on their part frankly admitted that they were frightened by Atsugarsuk's prophecies of doom, however clearly they grasped his motives. Crossing the boundary between the Labrador and Ungava Inuit now raised the prospect of the wrath of people and spirits on either side.

"Extremely Wild and Terrible": Power, Spirit, and Landscape

The party of seventeen Inuit and the two missionaries weighed anchor at Okak in the spring of 1811 and set sail along the Labrador coast north towards Cape Chudleigh and the nearby island of Killinek. Most nights, the Inuit went ashore with their bags and camped on the land; the two missionaries mainly slept in their berths on the ship. This tells us a lot about the Inuit attachment to the land and all that it offered in the way of comfort and the possibilities of harvesting food and looking for signs of other Inuit.[50]

The travelling party didn't wait to reach Ungava to begin their evangelizing; it was in their hearts, every moment of every day. Prayer services were held morning and evening. As they proceeded, they called in briefly at Inuit camps wherever they were sighted or anticipated. Great joy was felt upon meeting a small camp of Christians. At other camps, the Gospel was received, often with limited comprehension, but was reciprocated with generosity. Beyond the world of Christian camps, barter was the customary lubricant for exchange, and encounter the mode of narrative. The ships were especially well supplied with tobacco, a light but valued luxury, perfect for a gift greater than its explicit value as commodity or currency, which when needed served as an expression of thanks for hospitality or assistance with local knowledge.

As the party approached the Torngat Mountains (running along the northern Labrador coast), named after the spirits that resided there, "loud rejoicings on board" were occasioned by the sight on shore of Kumiganna of Saeglek, "who being bound to Killinek, had promised to accompany us thither."[51] When they attempted to land at Kakkeviak, a combination of wind, breakers, and (perhaps) ill-judged helmsmanship landed Jonathan's ship on the rocks, and the party only narrowly avoided shipwreck. Kumiganna, who came out in his kayak, directed them twenty miles up the coast to the safer haven at Oppernavik, with the news that their trusted friend Uttakiyok was awaiting them. It seemed that Kohlmeister's message the previous season had got through. Uttakiyok "had been upon watch in this place during the whole spring, was so anxiously intent upon meeting us, that he had erected signals on all the heights surrounding his tent."[52] The hunter, his two wives, and his younger brother enthusiastically welcomed the Moravian group with shouts and "firing of their pieces," as was their custom. The meeting with Uttakiyok was, as the evangelicals had hoped, a turning point in the voyage. His first-hand knowledge of the land was to prove invaluable to the expedition's safety and success. Uttakiyok, though not himself a Christian, joined the evangelicals in their worshipping.

Kmoch wasted no time in learning the local geography. Sitting with Uttakiyok in his tent, "looking down the coast as far as Kakkeviak, [Kmoch] got him to name all the bays, ports, and islands."[53] The chart showing "the Northern Extremity of Labrador with Ungava Bay" was a testimony to Uttakiyok, who then named each place as they passed by in their ships. Kohlmeister, having learned to use a quadrant to take an elevation and calculate a simple latitude, took down the position of each site they visited.[54]

Just beyond Oppernavik lay the dangerous strait, Ikkarasak, situated between the northern tip of the Labrador Peninsula and a number of off-shore islands. As they entered this strait, shifting winds were driving the ice, making it dangerously unpredictable. Jonathan and Utakiyok knew the ice could tear away their anchors and rip holes in the ship's hull. For two weeks they met this threat with persistence, prayer, and navigational tactics. Then, circumventing the powerful whirlpools about which they had been warned, they rounded the peninsula and set a south by south-west course along the largely uninhabited Ungava coast for one hundred miles. As the ship passed Abloriak Bay, Uttakiyok remarked on a particularly evil group of mountains along the coast, also called the Torngats.[55]

Holding a raven's claw in front of his chest for protection and fastening an inflated seal's intestine on a pole to the gunwale, Uttakiyok pointed to a cavern "in shape like the gable end of an house, situated at the top of a precipice, in a black mountain, of a very horrid and dark appearance." Kohlmeister concurred that "the scenery was, indeed, extremely wild and terrible, and the before-mentioned prospect of the rocks and islands at low water gave to the whole country a most singularly gloomy character."[56] The reality of the terror, he comforted himself, lay in the powerful tides.[57]

At Kangertlualuksoak Bay, Uttakiyok showed them a suitable place for a settlement with access to plenty of food. The arrival of the expedition generated much excitement, and Uttakiyok predicted that a mission, once established, would soon be visited by many Inuit. Kohlmeister conducted a brief ceremony in which he declared British sovereignty over the large river draining into the bay, naming it the George River after the British king. Still some seventy miles from Koksoak, their final destination, with the winter freeze-up not far off, Jonathan and Jonas advised Kohlmeister and Kmoch to begin the return journey to Labrador rather than risk being iced in for the winter. These Ungava Inuit struck Kohlmeister as materially poor, even though Koksoak seemed a rich environment with strong potential for trade.

After preaching against the Torngak, the "evil spirit ... [of] eternal darkness and misery."[58] Kohlmeister again reported that the local people had expressed a willingness to convert and had given promises that more families would follow if the missionaries were willing to set up a mission. Kohlmeister concluded his visit by taking possession of Unity Bay, much as they had done at the mouth of the Koksoak (George River). Thus one can see that a willingness to convert was being negotiated through a promise to construct a mission settlement where trade might grow and flourish.

Guiding and Gatekeeping

Throughout the voyage narrative, the reader cannot escape the conclusion that gatekeepers played a very active role at many key moments and in many places: Hopedale, London, Okak, Upernavik, Killinek, the Torngat Mountains, Kangertlualuksoak Bay, and Koksoak. This raises the question as to what sort of gateway or passage the Moravian expedition passed through in travelling from Labrador to the Ungava coast. This is complicated by the fact that the members of the same evangelical expedition, these co-travellers, while sharing a common purpose and means of transport, adopted different roles as well as different views of the voyage's significance. Now I want to explore to what extent the co-travellers' religious or spiritual beliefs shaped their perceptions of the passage between Labrador and Ungava. It will be no surprise to discover that a missionary and a shaman perceived the environment in very different terms. However, the presence of Christian and non-Christian Inuit from different regions adds some subtleties to the range of ways they conceptualized the environment. Neighbouring groups with distinctive histories have not always valued places according to the same stories and therefore have not necessarily shared a common understanding of geographical features.

Among the expedition's participants, Christians were in the minority. Let us begin with Uttakiyok, for he possessed the most intimate knowledge and experience of the trails between Labrador and Ungava; he felt at home "on the trail."[59] He very effectively escorted the expedition past several serious hazards en route to Ungava. Described with admiration by Kohlmeister as a "steady, faithful guide," he was actually far more important to them than that. Before considering who was doing the guiding, the term itself requires some qualification.

The term "guide" has drawn considerable critical attention in recent historiography of exploration.[60] Taken at face value, it implies the role of an assistant, whose own interests are subordinated to and often effaced by those of an expedition's leader. It has become increasingly clear, though, that guides are far more complex figures, often playing multiple roles ranging from host to leader, negotiator, navigator, translator, ethnographer, and – in the case of Brother Jonathan – evangelist. Thus the role of the Labrador Inuit in this account speaks to a long-eighteenth-century narrative tradition of constructing non-European communities through "guides" or "go-betweens" as diverse as the Polynesian chieftain, Tupaia, and the Greenlandic artist-traveller Sacheuse (see Craciun and Terrall in the Introduction).[61] As Paul Carter argued in *The Road to Botany Bay*, the act of naming in voyaging is simultaneously an act of imposing erasure on the landscape, recasting it in the image of its imperial surveyors, ultimately at the expense of the rights of traditional peoples to lands they have inhabited for millennia. In some of the most celebrated eighteenth-century encounters, such as that of Captain Cook and the Polynesian chief Tupaia, whatever their shared experiences and however much they respected each other the dynamic remained asymmetric as a consequence of the now familiar mechanisms of imperial travel and collecting.

Uttakiyok resists easy integration into the literature on guides and go-betweens because one cannot assign Inuit, man or woman, a clear place in a social hierarchy of leadership and command. Neither individualists nor collectivists in a sense familiar to Western societies, Inuit are traditionally very cautious about assuming or demonstrating status among their kin, not that reputations are not accrued. Uttakiyok is a case in point: in the narrative we are discussing, he assists without subordinating himself, possesses knowledge without owning it, and belongs to the Ungava people without ambassadorial pretensions of representing them. He does not enter the voyage narrative through encounter; rather, he has been an interested party going back ten years to the time the idea of the expedition was first mooted. The concept of the "co-traveller," as I have defined it, is more appropriate here, for the multiple meanings of passage surpassed in richness and variety the authority invested in a single leader by the sponsoring institution, in this case the Moravian church. Uttakiyok's importance for the expedition can be traced to his knowledge of the Ungava region and its people, this privileged access having been acquired through many years' experience of life on the trail. His plausible status as a broker was supported by the apparent demand among Ungava Inuit for goods from southern Labrador and was presumably further heightened by the disposition of the spirits, and unimpeded by any animosity from Labrador Inuit. Thus he offered a kind of access to Ungava that the Moravians could not themselves take for granted. To what extent he felt obliged to reciprocate previously enjoyed hospitality, precisely how he thought that a trading post in Ungava would be advantageous to himself and his people, or whether he hoped to earn a tidy commission, must remain matters of speculation.

From the Moravians' perspective, they were gaining access through Uttakiyok to some part of the extended family networks in Ungava. His willingness to make essential introductions and to explain the visitors' purposes doubtless contributed to their safety and warm reception in Ungava. That such privileged access across ethnic boundaries could not be taken for granted was demonstrated to Kmoch upon his arrival at Koksoak. His hosts sent out a search party shortly after he went hunting alone, not because they suspected he might get lost, but because they feared that other Inuit, not knowing him, might mistake him for a Cree hunter and thus take him to be an unlicensed outsider and dispense rough treatment.[62] The shaman Atsugarsuk in Okak, who had earlier warned the party that Ungava Inuit could be extremely dangerous, had not been fabricating his threats, though he may have exaggerated and twisted them to his own ends.

According to Kohlmeister, when the expedition was sailing past the Torngats, Uttakiyok nervously described the terrifying cavern as "the dwelling place of Torngak, the evil spirit." Interpreting his use of the term "Torngak" is semantically complicated. J. Garth Taylor has argued that the term had a range of possible suffixes with subtly different meanings with significant regional variations between Ungava and Labrador.[63] The name of the range "Torngets" (pl.) would refer to the shamans' many helper-spirits. If Kohlmeister was correct in his understanding, Uttakiyok was referring to the Ungava notion of Torngak, meaning the great spirit in control of the minor spirits, which obey his commands.[64] As Lucien Turner, the most reliable ethnologist of Ungava Inuit in the late nineteenth century, explains,

> each person is supposed to be attended by a special guardian who is malignant in character, ever ready to seize upon the least occasion to work harm upon the individual whom it accompanies ... Besides this class of spirits, there are spirits of the sea, the land, the sky ... the winds, the clouds, and everything in nature. Every cove of the seashore, every point, island, and prominent rock has its guardian spirit. All are of the malignant type and to be propitiated only by acceptable offerings.[65]

Hence there is some doubt as to whether Uttakiyok was referring to Tungak as a proper name for the master spirit, or to *torngak* as a common name, a malevolent but not all-powerful spirit among many.

The significance of Torngak for the Labrador Inuit was markedly different than for the Ungava Inuit, and hence there is an added difficulty in relying on Kohlmeister to identify the spirit of the cavern on the Ungava coast. Maps of Labrador showed the Torngat range of mountains along the northern coast, which Kohlmeister appears to have called Attanarsuk. Inuit do not distinguish linguistically between common and proper nouns. Naming the mountains Torngat may have been the way that Labrador Inuit referred to the spirit-helpers (*tuurngait* = pl. of *tuurngaq*) residing in the range of mountains bearing that name. When Atsugarsuk threatened the missionaries with the currents off Cape Chudleigh, he was likely deferring to the power of a malignant *tuurngaq*, one of the helper spirits that could exercise control over the winds, the ice, or the currents, and that may have resided in the Torngat mountains. There is no evidence, however, that Labrador Inuit had any equivalent to the Ungava notion of Tungak, a master spirit.[66]

The missionaries' view of Torngak was more clearly documented, thanks to their diaries, and less ambiguous, thanks to some distorting generalizations. The Moravians used the term *torngak* both as a common noun and a proper noun during the eighteenth century.[67] As the Moravians increased their presence along the Labrador coast in the 1770s, their use of the term increasingly came to denote the Christian idea of the devil. The Moravians needed a vernacular equivalent to the devil with which they could vilify shamanism, and chose torngak for that purpose.[68] When Kohlmeister reported Uttakiyok's use of Torngak, he represented Uttakiyok as superstitious, remarking that had time permitted, it would be amusing to visit the cavern. He also remarked that the place was actually dangerous "in reality" because of the difficult navigation conditions. This implies that Kohlmeister did not take very seriously that this site was the devil's residence. One also has to acknowledge the possibility that Uttakiyok was referring to a different spirit, but that Kohlmeister referred to it, regardless, as the devil, torngak, to deny the complexity of Inuit spirits and to drive home the evil of shamanism to his readers in simple terms.

What do the variations in the uses of the label torngak tell us about the gateway between Labrador and Ungava? Inuit perceptions reveal three contrasting perspectives about the relative power of the spirits, the meaning of the gateway, and the expedition's passage through it. Uttakiyok pointed to the cavern of Tungak as a barrier between life and death, not immediately dangerous but potentially so vexatious as to threaten to take the travellers to their death. Regarding the currents and ice-strewn waters at Ikkarasak, Kmoch drew on Inuit sources for what reads as a mechanical explanation: "the Eskimos told us about the vortex, that it pulls the strongest ice floes down to the bottom and they reappear, smashed into small pieces, on the surface again."[69] Kohlmeister says nothing that leads one to suppose that Uttakiyok regarded these hazards as being under the power of a torngak, rather than just dangerous in their own right. Whatever Uttakiyok thought about Ikkarasak, or the torngak at the cavern, his perception of the obstacles separating Ungava from Labrador was highly localized and place-specific.

Atsugarsuk, an Okak shaman who figured in the narrative as resisting the spread of Christianity, seems to have been intent on disrupting the missionaries' ambitions. The mission's reception, he predicted, would be obstructed in the vicinity of Ikkarasak and again at the Ungava camps. The currents, aided by the winds, would endanger their lives, like a gate or barrier that would deflect their momentum off course, out to sea. Insofar as he was deferring to a spirit to back up his threat, he sought to close the gate to Ungava and to prevent the spread of Christianity. It may also be that his helper-spirit was less powerful than the helper-spirits of Uttakiyok, who brought their spiritual forces to support Jonathan and Kohlmeister and their respective collection of helper-spirits.

Jonathan, who came from the same region as Atsugarsuk, but who lacked local knowledge and experience of northern waters, understood that the passage might be blocked by a malevolent spirit, or by a shamanistic force that he could recognize as an enemy, as shown by his fear. As a convert, however, he had the Holy Spirit and the support of the missionaries for guidance. Jonathan, visiting Okak from a different part of the same region as Atsugarsuk, had every reason to perceive their disagreement over the wisdom of the journey as a contest. A shaman's power to attach hostile intent to the currents, so as to divide Ungava from Labrador, was clearly able to hold sway over Jonathan's perception of the passage. As a convert, Jonathan was able to resist Atsugarsuk, at least enough to undertake the journey, but not sufficiently to entirely dismiss or discredit his predictions as to what lay ahead.[70]

In a world governed by shamanism, spirits can exist independently, without bodies. Some spirits are thought to have been people or animals, who having died now live without their bodies. It makes sense to speak of a "geography of spirits." Inuit have long recognized that spirits have special powers to act causally on the environment (e.g., to stir up a gale somewhere, to prevent access to seals in a particular area) and that they reside in particular locations, which may be subterranean, celestial, on the land, or in the sea. To call on a spirit, a shaman conducts a ritual whereby he leaves his body and makes a flight to visit the spirit, during which visit he may be able to question the spirit or hold a conversation. For Inuit, the places where spirits reside are specific, real places, like the cavern that prompted Uttakiyok to hold the raven's claw as the ship sailed past. A good hunter must therefore anticipate obstacles, consider the causes, and use skill and knowledge to circumscribe them.

The meaning of the passage to Ungava for the missionaries also had to do with access, but with very substantial differences. If the passage to Ungava was a contest or a power struggle between good and evil, as the Moravian missionaries truly believed, they required a combination of spiritual fortitude (as much as the shaman needed a helper-spirit) and well-honed skills to safely navigate the hazards. Where the missionaries' perspective *differed* was in their understanding of spirit and where and how it could be brought to bear upon their travels along the coast. Moravian doctrine rejects the premise that distinct spirits reside at specific geographical locations on the earth's surface. Transcendental good or evil can in principle manifest itself anywhere and at any time. The principal battleground in Protestant theologies takes the form of a struggle for the human soul. Hence the Moravian missionaries rejected as idolatry the shamans' claim to privileged access to a helper-spirit, identifying it as a projection of an evil heart onto a neutral object or landscape. The Holy Spirit, by contrast, is known through its immanence in the human soul.

The missionaries' main challenge when seeking converts was to convince Inuit that God and the devil were all-powerful, not divisible into hierarchies of minor powers; that their power was expressed within the person, not as an exclusively external force; and that God's presence was universal, not confined to specific geographical locations. The Moravian missionaries' interpretation of torngak as a universal and all-powerful evil was an attempt to square the circle by teaching that a transcendental devil could be the cause of particular actions or conditions and by denying that particular actions must have correspondingly distinct spiritual causes.

For the missionaries, the passage to Ungava was therefore a question of faith to be settled in the heart. Attributing causal efficacy to the currents and ice around Cape Chudleigh was acceptable to the missionaries provided they were couched as an explanation based on mechanical and not spiritual forces. The Christians acknowledged the dangers of powerful currents as natural hazards but were reluctant to believe that a malevolent spirit would exercise specific control over local currents. So they made the passage a microcosm of a Christian life, and required regular prayer marked by services at the beginning and end of each day to fortify their hearts and resolve.

The missionaries could of course recognize the dangers of strong currents, quite independently of speculation about metaphysical causes. Since a journey or passage was a Christian euphemism for life, practical skills were the point at which a universal spirit immanent in the body could meet the practical dangers of adverse travel conditions. Embodied skill could in other words bridge cultures, particularly for the Moravians, who placed unusual value on the practice of artisanal skill as a means of demonstrating a faithful life in preference to a more lettered approach to teaching theological exegesis. Hence Kmoch's love of the rugged life on the land was typical of an approach to mission work appreciated by Moravians more widely.

Throughout his journal, Kohlmeister showed great respect for Inuit skills and for their mechanical arts, describing Jonathan as "a steady, intelligent Christian Esquimaux" and recognizing him as "one of the most skilful commanders on the whole coast of Labrador."[71] Moreover, skill was a category that could be compared and assigned a rank or index. For instance, Jonathan's cousin, Paul, was judged to be "in activity and skill ... next to Jonathan."[72] Moreover a skilful, disciplined body was grounds for respecting unbaptized Inuit and for being optimistic about their prospects of conversion. If a shaman's contortions were a sign of an evil spiritual activity, this also allowed that the virtuous bodily actions of other hunters corresponded to benign mental dispositions. Kohlmeister described Uttakiyok as a "steady, faithful guide" and as having "superior sense, and skill in all the Esquimaux arts." Such high praise was undoubtedly well-deserved for the person who rescued them from near disaster on more than one occasion.

Uttakiyok was undoubtedly a skilful guide for the evangelical party, but we might pause to ask: To or through *what* was he guiding them? I use "what" to suggest that the object of guiding is the making of a passage, not geography, not information, and above all, not the map. There is a sense in which every traveller is a guide for whom orientation is a continual process in relation to the world around him. Consider two different senses of the term "guide" in relation to orientation. To "be guided by" a person, a spirit, or an impulse can point to a source of inspiration that may or may not be visible or material, in contrast to a guide as a tablet, animate or inanimate, inscribed with local knowledge. On an evangelical voyage, both meanings of the term are crucial. To follow the call of God, or a helper-spirit, is to be drawn by another, or to allow its will to be inscribed on oneself. To follow a human guide is to delegate some of one's orientation to another. The relationship between these meanings of "guide" is as important as the meanings individually. The German missionaries allowed themselves to be guided by their faith and simultaneously by their "faithful guide." If the missionaries were being guided in both senses of the term in the same direction, it made perfect sense for them to follow confidently. If, by contrast, the guides opposed each other, the missionary risked being torn apart in the proverbial manner of having each limb bound to a different horse, with the horses then sent running in opposing directions. Had Kohlmeister or Jonathan relied equally on the shamanistic and Christian spirits, this sort of disastrous conclusion might well have been the result. We know of course that they fared rather better. Their guidance was selective, and the phenomena of the Labrador–Ungava regions entered the "traveller's narrative only in so far as they align[ed] themselves with the direction of his desire."[73] To understand how potentially conflicting kinds of guidance are aligned with desire is to understand how to navigate through spatial histories.

Since a map is a product of an expedition, Carter advises us to examine the origin of the map in the journal, the record of the expedition, rather than in the landscape itself. In the journal lie the literary codes and conventions, the clues to the alignment of the coastline and the traveller's desire. When he writes that Cook "inaugurates a new spatial history for Australia," he means that by carving a new maritime track that circumscribes the coast, Cook is creating a new way of conceptualizing Australia. And though Cook's voice in his journal is ironic, even self-mocking, so that he seems reticent to impose his presence on the landscape, Carter is adamant that the surveyor's journal is a dominant discourse that in time will overlay the aboriginal presence like a blanket smothering the land beneath it.

The Moravian expedition travelled the very same Labrador coast on which Cook had cut his teeth and learned his trade as a youthful surveyor.[74] Kohlmeister would have used a chart of the coast based on Cook's survey or possibly an earlier Moravian map informed by Inuit knowledge of place names and trails. Nevertheless the Moravian expedition, which repeatedly made for shore, continually immersed itself in indigenous meanings of travel, with the intent of making as much contact as possible with Inuit groups en route. Kohlmeister never tried to hide the fact that his track followed an Inuit trade route and was led by an Inuit hunter, whereas many contemporary travel writers preferred to exaggerate the novelty of their travels in order to promote themselves.

If we follow Carter's materialist metaphor, in saying that the ship's track inscribed itself in Kohlmeister's journal and on his chart, then the raging surf, the malevolent spirits, the raven's claw, Uttakiyok's identification of landmarks, and Jonathan's handling of the helm were all aligned with that track. Above all else, the Moravian chart is a record of this alignment with Kohlmeister's (specifically) evangelical desire.

At least three interlocking spatial histories are relevant to the mission: the traces of Ungava Inuit, Labrador Inuit, and the missionaries. In fact, there are four, if one includes the imperial traces of the surveyors. The meaning of the passage was demonstrably different for Uttakiyok, Jonathan, and Kohlmeister. Their readings of the landscape, knowledge of the intricacies of the coast, and relationship to the world of spirits, and the significance they attached to the voyage, have already been contrasted. Just as the object of the guide is the passage, so, too, the object of travel writing, as Carter astutely comments, is "to constitute space as a track": "the life of this space resides in succession, in its demonstration that the parts link up, looking forwards and backwards along the orientation of the journey."[75] The spatial histories of Ungava and Labrador were constantly being aligned by the co-travellers with their desires, individual and shared. It is instructive to note that one of the greatest impressions recorded in Kohlmeister's narrative was recounted by Kmoch after he had sat alongside Uttakiyok on the promontory, naming and recording the features of the coast. That moment, perhaps better than any other, demonstrates the relationship between the Ungava spatial history and Kohlmeister's map. Contrary to appearances, engraving Inuit place names on the map did not restore Inuit meaning to the landscape. At most, it signalled surfaces or gateways to Inuit worlds of meaning. Kohlmeister's slightly amused observation of the cavern home of the malevolent spirit is cut short when he gently mocks Uttakiyok's "superstitious customs" and names it, tongue-in-cheek, the "Dragon's Dwelling."

Kohlmeister remarked that "there was no time to examine the place," effectively closing the door on the possibility of exploring relationships of interiority between spirits and features of the land. Indeed, his narrative and map scarcely dwell upon movements along one of the three key axes for Inuit spatial orientation, the inland/out-to-sea axis.[76] Beyond landing the party to evangelize, a little inland hunting, and forays at their destination in Ungava, the displacement was dictated by the coast, winds, and sea currents. Where coastal displacement gives continuity to the journal and the map, inland movement gives the journal only unwelcome diversion and repetition. The arrival of the ship at Kangertlualuksoak, and then Koksoak, signals an arrest of littoral displacement. The evangelical gaze turns inland, along the rivers, in search of resources and sites suitable for a future mission.

After the Expedition

Upon his return to Hopedale, Kohlmeister edited his notes and sent them to London, where Christian Latrobe (1758–1836), secretary to the (Moravian) Society for the Furtherance of the Gospel, arranged for publication. Kohlmeister's *Journal of a Voyage from Okkak* was intended to show the Labrador mission in a favourable light, to reflect well on Moravian colonial expansion as a whole, and to appeal to the widespread supporters of overseas missionary work.

Preparations for Moravian expansion into Ungava got under way quickly. The Labrador Moravians had the full support of the Synod at home to finance another expedition and to build a mission at Koksoak. Kohlmeister and Uttakiyok had arranged with the Ungava Inuit to expect them in the summer of 1813. This time it would be easier to rendezvous with Uttakiyok. He had agreed to await the ships at the meeting place beyond the islands, having "taken care to preserve the boards and other signals ... that we might not seek the former places in vain."[77] In the meantime Kohlmeister had travelled up to Nain, and then on to Okak, to make further arrangements.

Jonathan and Sybilla, anxious to advance their cause in Ungava, followed Kohlmeister up to Nain. Events however took a dramatic turn for the worse when these two Inuit elders fell ill and died soon after. How these two Inuit evangelicals were remembered, and to whom in subsequent generations their *ateq* (Inuit names) would be passed on, would be interesting to know. That their lives were cut short must have been a source of immense sadness for all those who had journeyed with them. The Brethren in their piety were warm but succinct: "Thus this excellent man ended his life here below. He was a faithful, willing servant of the Mission, and always rejoiced, when he could render any kind office to the Missionaries, for which he had frequent opportunity. His loss will be severely felt."[78]

Over at Koksoak in Ungava, preparations for the co-travellers' return were undertaken with excitement and diligence. The council of the village elders had considered the planning and conservation required if Koksoak were to become a regional entrepôt: "they would cut no timber for the repairs of their kayaks and boats in the Koksoak, that the woods might not be injured, when we should come and build a settlement."[79] They opted instead to travel farther to "the great river Aksaviok, where large timber trees are found."

Word had spead widely in the Koksoak hinterland so that twenty-one large boats, each carrying twenty to thirty people, packed full of trading goods, arrived in the summer of 1813 at the mouth of the Koksoak River, followed by another thirteen boats the following spring. Inuit from Igluarsuk, near the entrance to Hudson Bay to the west, came down, "exceedingly astonished when they saw wood for the first time." News that the Cree people had also "expressed their joy at the arrival of Europeans" reached the missionaries by way of Atsugarsuk and Aveinek, who had been sent by the Ungava Inuit in the spring of 1814 to hasten the missionaries' return. This was welcome news, strengthening the missionaries' hopes that the expedition would bear fruit, and providing them them with more details of the location of the Ungava Inuit, of whom they supposed the Labrador population to be a smaller extension.

The ambitious missionaries on the Labrador coast faced hard times. A harsh winter in 1813 had left their colonies short of food and oil. The situation at home in war-torn Europe was no better. The Moravian Church had been deprived of much of its income as armies brought fear and havoc to individual settlements in their paths. Kohlmeister readily acknowledged that "on account of the consequences of the war, it is not possible just now to begin a new establishment in the Ungava country." The other critical factor was the question of permission as "the Ungava country seems to lie within the boundaries of the district granted by charter to the Hudson Bay Company ... that we may be treated not as intruders, but as friends."[80]

Missionaries Kohlmeister and Stürmann undertook a further journey to explore a possible station in Saglek, Nullerkartok, or Nachvak.[81] But just as the war in Europe came to a close, and a follow-up expedition to Ungava looked more promising, misfortune struck the missions, albeit temporarily, from a new direction, less predictable than the human folly of warfare. The winter of 1815 in Labrador was severe, leading to a shortage of provisions. From the missionaries' perspective, excessive exposure to the cold injured the soul as well as the body, so that they "seemed in a manner stupefied, and scarce able to attend to the concerns of their souls with becoming seriousness."[82] The Moravians, themselves famous for never panicking or succumbing to fear of death, were also subdued when their supply ship, the *Jemima*, failed to reach Hopedale in the summer of 1816 due to the severe ice conditions. The absence of four missionaries aboard the *Jemima* (which had had to winter in England), and the fear that the ship had been lost, obliged Kohlmeister to abandon his hope of taking three other missionaries in 1817 to live in Ungava, build a traditional sod house, and live there for a full year.[83] The brethren in Okak with evident disappointment conceded "we are sorry that, by circumstances, our ardent wish to bring the Gospel to the Ungava country, cannot be fulfilled for the present."[84]

Kohlmeister's concern about the possessiveness of the Hudson's Bay Company proved well-founded. The directors, alerted to the economic intelligence concerning the strategic importance and wealth of the Ungava coast contained in Kohlmeister's narrative, refused the Moravians permission to settle in Ungava.[85] The HBC instead sent four of its own expeditions to Ungava from its posts on James Bay over the next sixteen years to expand its trade and to pre-empt the Moravians. They established a permanent trading post at Koksoak (Fort Chimo) in 1830, the first of a number on Ungava Bay, whose purpose was to buy goods from Inuit and Naskapi Innu, to sell in distant markets.[86]

The missionaries, forced to scale back their ambitions, eventually settled on a station just sixty miles to the north of Okak at Hebron, which they established in 1830. The Inuit were at the time living on a nearby island. This new spiritual territory, according to the missionaries, "had but lately been a den of murderers, dedicated, as it were, by the *angakoks* [shamans] to the service of the devil." The construction of the mission required, in addition to the missionaries' efforts, an enormous amount of Inuit labour. The materials for the Hebron mission were delivered by ship; local hands managed to bring "44,900 bricks ashore in three days." The rest of the materials were fetched by ten dog teams and *kamotiks* (sledges), with supplies of wood coming up from Hopedale. "One hundred and thirty-seven journeys" over a distance of 120 miles – or 16,440 miles – gives some indication of the work involved.[87]

Sledge travel between Okak and Hebron also shows a different kind of evangelical travel, more mundane and repetitive than Kohlmeister's and Jonathan's unique voyage but of no less consequence. The increased traffic necessary to sustain a new mission is evidence of the growing commercial activity around mission settlements in the north of Labrador in this period. Inuit were instrumental in supporting this new traffic. They created a demand for trade, they provided overland transportation between the settlements, and they brought new prospective converts. The expansion of Christian numbers on the Labrador coast proceeded apace. Religious instruction in the colonial environment led to significant social change.

The Print Culture of the Moravian Labrador Coast

Journal of a Voyage from Okkak, though exceptional as a voyage narrative, was in fact part of an extended network of print culture reaching missions around the globe orchestrated by the indefatigable C. Ignatius Latrobe at the mission headquarters in London. Thus the voyage narrative was not out of place alongside other respectable Moravian mission literature edited, sometimes authored, and published by Latrobe: serialized news in the *Periodical Accounts*, mission visitation reports, and natural history accounts and meteorological registers.

In decentring the key protagonists of the voyage to Ungava, it is instructive also to be alert to the geography of literacy and print culture on the Labrador coast, which relied upon the metropolitan guiding hand of Latrobe but also took on a life of its own. The circulation of Bibles was of course central to the work of the missions. The New Testament remained the key: "they read it daily in their houses and tents, with the greatest earnestness, delight, and edification. We have, indeed, ever since the arrival of this most precious gift, observed a great change."[88] The missionaries collaborated with the British Foreign and Bible Society in revising the translations of the Gospels from Greenlandic into the Labrador dialect. Complete copies of the New Testament were presented to Labrador Christians in 1820 as a gift from the British and Foreign Bible Society. To acknowledge their appreciation for this spiritual literacy, Moravian Inuit "of their own accord, began to collect seal's blubber, by way of making a small contribution towards the expenses of that Society. Some brought whole seals, or half a seal, or pieces, as they could afford it. Others brought pieces of blubber in the name of their children, requesting that their poor gifts might be accepted."[89] Boiled down, this produced no less than thirty gallons of oil.[90]

The acquisition of literacy was thus made a part of everyday life, as it had been in Greenland and elsewhere throughout the Moravian network. School was held through the winter months between November and April. Pupils were counted, classes were started punctually at the sound of the church bell at the same time every day, and biblical literacy was tested. Where literacy prospered, religious devotion seemed to follow. The Okak school, for example, was attended by both children and adults, whose interest was apparently motivated by a desire "not so much to learn to read and write, as to hear what may be said in them of our Saviour." Reading, writing, and mathematical skills were a means to measure the mission's progress, and also a way of demonstrating that their missions were producing results. One examination proved that some students "could read a whole page without hesitation, and were tolerably expert in the rudiments of mathematics."[91] According to Kohlmeister, "children of five and even four years of age are able to read."[92]

Just as literacy was a barometer of evangelical success, a new school was a sign of Christian travel breaking new ground in an institutional form. For example, the missionaries opened a school at Hebron around 1832, shortly after the new mission was established. The following year, missionary Freytag was able to announce with visible pride that "Eskimo children manifest a decided predisposition for learning." The problems faced in schools were glossed over in the missionary reports, though in places they do allude to some difficulties. For instance, the school at Hebron, attended by twenty-eight children, was an unheated building with an indoor temperature that during winter hovered between the –15° and –20° Fahrenheit. Learning was a blend of the heroic and the long-suffering. One winter was "so severe that the books not unfrequently fall out of the children's hands in consequence of their being benumbed."[93]

The significance of evangelicalism for Inuit is also evident from its place within Inuit travel, beyond the confines of the institution of the mission. According to the perhaps overoptimistic Moravian official historiography, the Inuit "value the Scriptures above every other gift, and always carry the books with them, as their choicest treasure, whenever they go any distance."[94] On long-distance winter hunting trips, Inuit could pass the long nights in their igloos by reading the Scriptures. As children were generally quicker learners than adults and elders, they were usually asked to do the reading. As one missionary explained, "the children or young people read aloud, while the rest are quietly mending their tackle, or sitting down and doing other work." Hymn-singing was another pastime, which included "short and easy anthems, in three or four parts."[95] This offers a glimpse into the reach of learning beyond schools and church, evidence as to how print culture became part of the seasonal mobility of Inuit life on the land.

The establishment of regular correspondence between Inuit at different settlements reveals that literacy included a widespread capacity to write as well as to read. The widespread absorption of biblical literacy into Inuit life extended to the adoption of the conventions of written letters and an intermittent postal service. Literacy was reshaping communication between extended families living at different colonies. Kohlmeister remarked (c. 1824) that he "has sometimes had nearly fifty short letters committed to his care by the Esquimaux" when travelling between communities.[96] Fifty letters from a community with between one and two hundred converts is very substantial evidence of the role of Christianity in transforming Inuit social relations in this period. The letters were said to contain "information respecting the families and friends of the writers, and, [included but were not limited to] ... edifying remarks and meditations on religious subjects, which may have peculiarly been impressed on their minds and hearts."[97]

Although evangelical travel followed the coastal contours of the Inuit world, the missionaries' engagement with Inuit culture should not be dismissed as superficial. Literacy on the Labrador coast was an engine of evangelical expansion and not simply a means of witnessing and propagating a record of it. The Bible having been indigenized in Inuit culture, the practice of spreading the Gospel to other Inuit kinship networks was becoming indigenized as well. This was the context in which it makes sense to speak of the voyage from Okak to Ungava as an indigenous voyage. The remarkable evidence of widespread Inuit literacy in Labrador in the 1820s suggests how deeply the written word had penetrated the lives of Inuit. As the activity of reading spread from schools in the settlement, to correspondence between settlements, and into the igloos and tents of families hunting on the land, far-reaching changes regarding perceptions of Inuit Christians, their unconverted kin, their helper-spirits, their shamanistic customs and taboos, and their distant neighbours in other regions were well under way.

ACKNOWLEDGMENTS

I would like to express my gratitude to Professor Dorinda Outram for inspiration in studying this voyage and visiting Herrnhut together, Professor Hans Rollmann for extensive scholarly guidance, information, and advice about the Moravian Church in Labrador, Dr Peter Peucker for advice when consulting the Archives in Herrnhut, and John MacDonald for sharing his research on the history of George River, as well as to Peter Evans, Peter Hansen, Nigel Leask, John MacDonald, Andy Martin, and the editors of this volume.

NOTES

1 Benjamin Kohlmeister and George Kmoch, *Journal of a Voyage from Okkak, on the Coast of Labrador, to Ungava Bay, Westward of Cape Chudleigh: undertaken to Explore the Coast, and Visit the Esquimaux in that Unknown Region* (London: Society for the Furtherance of the Gospel among the Heathen, 1814).

2 The Koksoak appears on topographical maps today as Kuujuaq River, Kuujuaq meaning "large or great river" in Inuktitut.

3 *The Pan-Inuit Trails Atlas* (www.paninuittrails.org) is one such representation of the regional character of Inuit trails criss-crossing the North American Arctic. Note however that the atlas is incomplete and does not yet show the world of Inuit trails in what is present-day Labrador or Québec.

4 Hans Rollmann, personal communication, e-mail message to author, 30 July 2017.

5 Felix Driver and Lowri Jones, *Hidden Histories of Exploration: Researching the RGS-IBG Collections* (Egham: Royal Holloway, University of London, in association with the Royal Geographical Society with Insitute of British Geographers, 2009); Michael Bravo, *The Accuracy of Ethnoscience: A Study of Inuit Cartography and Cross-Cultural Commensurability*, Manchester Papers in Social Anthropology no. 2 (Manchester: Department of Social Anthropology, 1996).

6 Simon Schaffer, ed., *The Brokered World: Go-betweens and Global Intelligence, 1770–1820.* (Sagamore Beach: Science History Publications, 2009); Peter Hansen, "Debate: Tenzing's Two Wrist-Watches: The Conquest of Everest and the Imperial Culture in Britain 1921–1953," *Past and Present* 157 (1997): 159–77.

7 Hans Rollmann, "Moravian Education in Labrador: A Legacy of Literacy," in *Conference Proceedings – 2008 Symposium: Post-Confederation Education Reform: From Rhetoric to Reality*, ed. Gerald Galway and David Dibbon (St John's: Memorial University Newfoundland, 2008), 227–36; Gisela Mettele, *Weltbürgertum oder Gottesreich: Die Herrnhuter Brüdergemeine als globale Gemeinschaft* 1727–1857 (Göttingen: Vandenhoeck & Ruprecht, 2009).

8 Michael Bravo, "Mission Gardens: Natural History and Global Expansion, 1720–1820," in *Colonial Botany: Science, Commerce, and Politics*, ed. Londa Schiebinger and Claudia Swan (Philadelphia: University of Pennsylvania Press, 2005), 49–65; John Mason, *The Moravian Church and the Missionary Awakening in England, 1760–1800* (London: Royal Historical Society, 2001).

9 Kohlmeister and Kmoch, *Voyage from Okkak*.

10 The German manuscript of Kohlmeister and Kmoch's travel account is in the Moravian archives in Herrnhut. "Bericht von der im Jahr 1811 ausgeführten Recognoscirungs-Reise, der nördlichsten Gegend von Labrador u[nd] der Hudsons-Straße in der Ungava-Gegend, durch die Brüder Benjamin Kohlmeister und Georg Kmoch," K.a.10.6.c, Unity Archives, Herrnhut.

11 Kohlmeister's biographical information is from James Hiller's entry in the *Dictionary of Canadian Biography*, vol. 7, 473–4; Kmoch's biographical information is from *Memori of Br. George Kmoch, Missionary in Labrador...* (London: W. Mallalieu, 1858). On authorship in Arctic voyaging, see Adriana Craciun, *Writing Arctic Disaster: Authorship and Exploration*, (Cambridge: Cambridge University Press, 2016); Innes M. Keighren, Charles W.J. Withers, and Bill Bell, *Travels into Print: Exploration, Writing, and Publishing with John Murray, 1773–1859* (Chicago: University of Chicago Press, 2015).

12 W. Glover, ed., *Charting Northern Waters: Essays for the Centenary of the Canadian Hydrographic Service* (Montreal: Canadian Nautical Research Society and McGill–Queen's University Press, 2004).

13 Aaron Arrowsmith, *Chart of the Northern Seas between Europe and America from Latitude 50° to 72° North, including the Baltic and North Cape on the Eastern Side; and on the American Coast, parts of Newfoundland, Labrador and Greenland* (London: Arrowsmith, 1808, updated to 1814); Lewis Anspach, *Geschichte und Beschreibung von Newfoundland und der Kuste Labrador* (Weimar: Verlag des G.H.S. priv. Landes-Industrie-Comptoirs, 1822), trans. from English ed. 1819.

14 Arrowsmith, *Northern Seas* [chart].

15 Mason, *The Moravian Church.*

16 Gaston Demarée and Astrid Ogilvie, "The Moravian Missionaries at the Labrador Coast and Their Centuries-Long Contributions to Meteorological Observations," *Climatic Change* 91 (2008): 423–50; Jacques Cayouette, *À la Découverte du Nord: Deux Siècles et Demi d'exploration de la Flore Nordique du Québec et du Labrador* (Québec: Editions Multimondes, 2014).

17 Christian Oldendorp, *History of the Mission of the Evangelical Brethren on the Caribbean Islands of St. Thomas, St. Croix, and St. John* (Ann Arbor: Karoma Publishers, 1987).

18 Nigel Leask, *Curiosity and the Aesthetics of Travel Writing, 1770–1840: From an Antique Land* (Oxford: Oxford University Press, 2002).

19 Sujit Sivasundaram, *Nature and the Godly Empire: Science and Evangelical Mission in the Pacific, 1795–1850* (Cambridge: Cambridge University Press, 2005).

20 Nicholas Jardine, James A. Secord, and Emma C. Spary, eds., *The Cultures of Natural History* (Cambridge: Cambridge University Press, 1996).

21 For biographical information on Jonathan and Sybilla, see Hans Rollmann, "Hopedale: Inuit Gateway to the South and Moravian Settlement," *Newfoundland and Labrador Studies* 28 (2013): 1719–26; Rollmann, "A Memorable Voyage to Ungava Bay: Marking the 200th Anniversary of a Moravian Mission," *The Telegram* (St John's), 8 January 2011.

22 *Pan-Inuit Trails Atlas* at www.paninuittrails.org.

23 Hans Rollmann, personal communication, e-mail message to author, 30 July 2017.

24 Claudio Aporta, "The Trail as Home: Inuit and their Pan-Arctic Network of Routes," *Human Ecology* 37 (2009): 131–46; Michael Bravo and Claudio Aporta, "Cartographic Gestures," in *Atlas: Geography, Architecture, and Change in an Interdependent World*, ed. Renata Tyszcuk, Joe Smith, Nigel Clark, and Melissa Butcher (London: Black Dog Press), 142–5.

25 Peter Evans, "Transformations of Inuit Resistance and Identity in Northern Labrador, 1771–1959" (PhD diss., University of Cambridge, 2013).

26 Rollmann, "Moravian Education"; Rollman, "Christian Gottlob Barth and the Moravian Inuktitut Book Culture of Labrador," paper presented at Newfoundland and Labrador Book History Symposium, Memorial University of Newfoundland, St John's, 7–8 May, 2016.

27 Nicholas Thomas, *Entangled Objects: Exchange, Material Culture, and Colonialism in the Pacific* (Cambridge, MA: Harvard University Press, 1993). His invocation to be alert to comparisons of the cultures of colonialism, rather than that of the colonizer or the colonized, is very apropos here.

28 Kenneth McGoogan, *Fatal Passage: The Untold Story of John Rae, the Arctic Adventurer Who Discovered the Fate of Franklin* (Toronto: Harper Flamingo, 2001).

29 Kenneth McGoogan, *Lady Franklin's Revenge: a True Story of Ambition, Obsession, and the Remaking of Arctic History* (Toronto: HarperCollins, 2005).

30 By the end of the century, the use of dogs and sleds for winter overland travel was more common but still not the rule. In Britain the validation of Inuit travel methods came in the first half of the twentieth century in the guise of logistics, a sub-category of polar research where the merits of travel techniques could be analysed, explained, and judged as practical knowledge, vital to the institutional organization of polar research. In France, travel technologies acquired central importance in the comparative study of the human sciences under the rubric of techniques.

31 For a regional history of Ungava that provides context for the *Voyage from Okkak*, see John MacDonald, *Historical Overview of Human Occupation of the*

Monts-Pyramides Park Project Study Area, Nunavik, report presented to the Kativik Regional Government (2010) (internally published report).

32 Kohlmeister and Kmoch, *Voyage from Okkak*, 3, 40.

33 Ibid., 6.

34 Hans Rollmann, "'So that in this part you should not lag behind other missionary congregations': The Introduction of National Helpers in the Moravian Mission among the Labrador Inuit," forthcoming in *Journal of Moravian History* 17 (2017).

35 Kohlmeister and Kmoch, *Voyage from Okkak*, 5.

36 Rollmann, "Hopedale: Inuit Gateway," 167. Rollmann, a distinguished historian of Labrador, identifies Br. Jonathan as Kippinguq. Whether he alternated between names remains a matter of speculation, but it has been a custom among most baptized Inuit in the twentieth century.

37 Kohlmeister and Kmoch, *Voyage from Okkak*, 8.

38 Ibid., 8–9.

39 Ibid., 4.

40 Thomas, *Entangled Objects*.

41 Paul Carter, *The Road to Botany Bay: An Essay in Spatial History* (London: Faber and Faber, 1987), 33.

42 For further analysis of the Moravian's Labrador coast exploration journeys of 1752, 1764, 1765, and 1770, see Hans Rollmann, ed., *Moravian Beginnings in Labrador: Papers from a Symposium Held in Makkovik and Hopedale*, an occasional publication of *Newfoundland and Labrador Studies*, no. 2 (St John's: Faculty of Arts Publications, 2009).

43 John MacDonald, *The Arctic Sky: Inuit Astronomy, Star Lore, and Legend* (Toronto: Royal Ontario Museum and Nunavut Research Institute, 1998), 162.

44 Patricia Seed, *Ceremonies of Possession in Europe's Conquest of the New World, 1492–1640* (Cambridge: Cambridge University Press, 1995).

45 This is based on statistics for 1810 and refers to the winter and not the summer population. The category "Christians" included people baptized, awaiting baptism, or baptized and excluded for some offence. Taken from James Hiller, "The Foundation and the Early Years of the Moravian Mission in Labrador, 1752–1805" (MA thesis, Memorial University of Newfoundland, 1967), appendix 4, table 6: Congregations and Wintering Populations, 1771–1810. Hiller's statistics are taken from the *Memorabilia*, year-end summaries of events, spoken in church as addresses and recorded in mission diaries published at the end of each year.

46 Kohlmeister and Kmoch, *Voyage from Okkak*, 10–11.

47 Jean L. Briggs, *Never in Anger: Portrait of an Eskimo Family* (Cambridge, MA.: Harvard University Press, 1970).

48 Kohlmeister and Kmoch, *Voyage from Okkak,* 40.

49 Ibid., 8.

50 George Kmoch, "Lebenslauf des am 21. December 1857 in Ockbrook selig entschlafenen verwitweten Bruders Georg Kmoch," *Nachrichten aus der Brüdergemeine* 1858: 639–74 at 658.

51 Kohlmeister and Kmoch, *Voyage from Okkak,* 38.

52 Ibid., 39–40.

53 Ibid., 41.

54 Obtaining longitude at this stage of the voyage was less critical because the coast of Labrador runs more or less on a north–south axis. Hence locating place names on a coastline previously surveyed by Capt. James Cook required only determining the latitude.

55 Uttakiyok's nomenclature, judging from Kohlmeister's description, appears to refer to a specific set of mountains in the coastal area visible on the Ungava coast where they sailed past. The missionaries' appellation "Torngat mountains" appears to have referred to the entire range of mountains, of which different parts were visible from the Labrador and Ungava coasts. This is a good example of the contrasting specificity of nomenclature by Inuit and missionaries.

56 Kohlmeister and Kmoch, *Voyage from Okkak,* 50.

57 The Rev. J.W. Davey, *The Fall of Torngak: or, the Moravian Mission on the Coast of Labrador* (London: S.W. Partridge and Co., 1905). In writing his history of the Moravian missions in Labrador, Davey selected Kohlmeister's description of their passage past the cavern for the book's opening vignette. It aimed to depict, explained Davey, "the domain of this evil influence in the heart and life of the poor haunted Eskimo, and to mark its gradual surrender to the resistless power of the Gospel of the Grace of God." Davey, *The Fall of Torngak,* 5–6.

58 Kohlmeister and Kmoch, *Voyage from Okkak,* 72.

59 Claudio Aporta, "The Trail as Home: Inuit and their Pan-Arctic Network of Routes," *Human Ecology* 37 (2009): 131–46.

60 See, for example, Driver and Jones, *Hidden Histories,* 2009; Kapil Raj, *Relocating Modern Science: Circulation and the Construction of Knowledge in South Asia and Europe, 1650–1900* (Basingstoke: Palgrave Macmillan, 2007).

61 On go-betweens, see Simon Schaffer, Lissa Roberts, Kapil Raj, and James Delbourgo, eds., *The Brokered World: Go-Betweens and Global Intelligence, 1770–1820* (Uppsala: Science History Publications, 2009); Joan Druett, *Tupaia: The Remarkable Story of Captain Cook's Polynesian Navigator* (Auckland: Random House, 2011).

62 Kohlmeister and Kmoch, *Voyage from Okkak,* 72.

63 Garth J. Taylor, "Deconstructing Deities: Tuurngatsuak and Tuurngaatsuk in Labrador Inuit Religion," *Études/Inuit/Studies* 21 (1997): 141–58.
64 Lucien M. Turner and John Murdoch, *Ethnology of the Ungava District of Hudson Bay Territory*. (Washington, D.C.: Smithsonian Institution, 1894), 194.
65 Ibid., 193–4.
66 Taylor, "Deconstructing Deities," 141–58.
67 Christian Drachardt, manuscript copy of Drachardt's private diary, 10 May 1771–9 August 1773, 1771-73 in Herrnhut, Germany, Archiv der Brüder-Unität; cited by Taylor, "Deconstructing Deities," 145.
68 Taylor, "Deconstructing Deities," 149.
69 *George Kmoch,* Lebenslauf des am 21. December 1857, in *Ockbrook Selig Entschlafenen Verwitweten Bruders Georg Kmoch, Nachrichten aus der Brüdergemeine* (1858), 639–74. The quotation taken from this original German edition was redacted in the briefer account published in the *Periodical Accounts* 22 (1858): 379–84, 433–40, made available online by Hans Rollmann at http://www.mun.ca/rels/morav/texts/kmoch.html.
70 Kohlmeister and Kmoch, *Voyage from Okkak,* 8.
71 Ibid., 5, 8.
72 Ibid., 9.
73 Ibid., 77.
74 Nicholas Thomas, *Cook: the Extraordinary Voyages of Captain James Cook* (New York: Walker and Co, 2003).
75 Kohlmeister and Kmoch, *Voyage from Okkak,* 76.
76 The three spatial axes of Inuit orientation revealed though linguistic analysis are governed by (1) the prevailing wind, normally a north or northwesterly axis; (2) the coastal axis, up and down the coast; and (3) the inland/out-to-sea axis that runs orthogonally to the coastline. This is considerably further complicated by terms that position sights and objects relative to the subject. For further reading, see Michael D. Fortescue, "Eskimo Orientation Systems," *Meddelelser om Grønland,* "Man and Society" issue, 11 (1988); and Fortescue, *Orientation Systems of the North Pacific Rim* (Copenhagen: Museum Tusculanum Press, 2011).
77 "Extract of a Letter from Br. Benjamin Kohlmeister to the Secretary of the Society, written August 5, 1815, at Okak," *Periodical Accounts* 6 (1814): 343.
78 Anon., *Periodical Accounts Relating to the Missions of the Church of the United Brethren Established Among the Heathen* 5 (1812): 263.
79 Ibid., 343.
80 Ibid., 402.
81 "Kurze Anmerkungen von einer Besuchs-Reise auf einiger der von Okkak noerdlich liegenden Wohnplaetze der Eskimos mit Capt. Fraser

in Begleitung der Brr. Kohlmeister u[nd] Stürmann vom 4. bis 18. Aug. 1814" [Brief Remarks about a Visitation Journey of Some Dwelling Places of the Inuit North of Okak, with Capt. Fraser, in the Company of Brethren Kohlmeister and Stürmann from 4–18 August 1814], R15.K.a.No.26, 137–40, Unity Archives, Herrnhut.

82 John Holmes, *Historical Sketches of the Missions of the United Brethren for Propagating the Gospel among the Heathen, from their Commencement to the Present Time* (Dublin, 1818), 107.

83 Ibid., 110.

84 Anon., *Periodical Accounts* 6 (1814): 396.

85 Davey, *The Fall of Torngak*, 230.

86 Bernard Saladin d'Anglure, "Inuit of Quebec," in *Handbook of North American Indians*, vol. 5 (Arctic), ed. David Damas (Washington, D.C.: Smithsonian Institution, 1984), 476–507, at 499.

87 Davey, *The Fall of Torngak*, 221–3.

88 Anon., *Periodical Accounts* 5 (1812): 262.

89 Anon., *Missions in Labrador from their Commencement to the Present Time* (Dublin: Religious Tract & Book Society for Ireland, 1832), 232.

90 Davey, *The Fall of Torngak*, 216.

91 Anon., *Missions in Labrador*, 230.

92 Ibid., 250.

93 Davey, *The Fall of Torngak*, 225.

94 Anon., *Missions in Labrador*, 231.

95 Ibid., 252. Music, provided it was "confined to the service of religion," was deemed conducive to leading a godly life. Mrs Kohlmeister, during a visit to Nain, reported that the missionaries had formed a grand orchestra; "missionary Koerner played the violincello, missionary Henn the clarionet, and two young Eskimoes the violin" (228). Violins and French horns were played as accompaniments to singing.

96 Anon., *Missions in Labrador*, 252.

97 Ibid., 252.

chapter four

The World in a Nicknackatory: Encounters and Exchanges in Hans Sloane's Collection

MILES OGBORN AND VICTORIA PICKERING

Among the many volumes of letters sent to Sir Hans Sloane, the renowned physician and collector, and now held among his manuscripts at the British Library, there is one that contains an object that did not make it into his extensive collection. It is the outline of a smiling face burnt onto a thin sliver of wood, probably with a piece of metal heated in a flame (Figure 4.1). The letter that came with it on 25 April 1713 was sent from someone calling himself "Tim Cockleshell." It read:

> Most Curious S^{r},
> Having, in my Travels thro' ye West Indies, met with this Catoptrical Adustion I thought it might not be altogether unworthy a place in your famous Nicknackatory. 'Twas given me by a Bramine who affirm'd it to be an Original of one of the Antient Kings of Mexico. I desire, S^{r}, you wou'd please to shew it to your Fellow Naturals, especially to the learned & ingenious Dr Woodwd, upon whose approbation I intend to be at the Charge of having a Print taken from it. I am S^{r},
>
> *Your most humble admirer and Servt.*

Signing off, he informed Sloane that "[y]ou may direct to me at the sign of the Cham of Tartary's Slipper in York Buildings, next door to the Yorkshire Cushion, over against the Cinnamon Broom-stick."[1]

We don't know from whom it came. The sender is clearly having fun with Sloane's own past history of collecting in the Caribbean, with his collection and what he might be convinced to take into it, and, as many others had done and would do, with Sloane as a symbol of what collecting itself meant as a problematic practice.[2] "Tim Cockleshell" offers a natural philosophical curiosity from a far-off land – one that mixes the "Indies,"

Figure 4.1 Tim Cockleshell's Catoptrical Adustion. Sloane MS 4043, f. 145. © The British Library Board.

east and west, by combining Brahmins and Aztecs – and a distant time. It is an obscurely but precisely named object, a burnt reflection, that might be circulated among learned and ingenious men, but that would show quite how easily such men would believe something so obviously made up. A joke on them.[3] Yet the question is open as to whether this was a joke that Sloane was in on, or, indeed, whether he found it funny or not.[4] The year 1713 was a high point in the controversy over the authenticity of the shield that John Woodward – a fellow member of the Royal Society and Royal College of Physicians, and erstwhile rival and enemy of Sloane's – had taken to be Roman, but which was found to be a sixteenth-century piece of French classicism. A joke on him. Yet it was also the year that Sloane resigned as secretary of the Royal Society, forced out by Isaac

Newton and Woodward, who had often criticized Sloane for his eclectic and miscellaneous approach to natural philosophy.[5] A joke on Sloane. His collection – later described as "an ornament to the nation," and providing the foundation for the British Museum – is here a "Nicknackatory": a toy shop, a horde of trinkets of no discernible value, and about as useful as a cinnamon broomstick.[6] Whether Sloane laughed (maybe knowingly) or not, we do know that he kept the letter and the object, at least among his correspondence if not in his collection.

Our aim here is to take this joke seriously and to explore how the world was encountered in the seventeenth and early eighteenth centuries through Sloane's collection, as a "Nicknackatory." We will do this by considering the implications of Sloane's collecting practices – and their global modes of exchange – for his collection, and then by interpreting how the encounters with the world that this vast and eclectic collection afforded were shaped by its management of scale, its spatial organization and modes of presentation, and its translation into being a founding collection for the British Museum after Sloane's death in 1753. Through this we argue that Sloane's collection, rather than acting as a single "centre of calculation," offered instead a multitude of locally ordered, partial, temporary, and changing ways of engaging with, and trying to know, the early modern world.

Hans Sloane: A Collector and His Collection

Across his long lifetime Hans Sloane (Figure 4.2) amassed a huge and varied collection. There were more than three hundred volumes of dried plants in his herbarium, around fifty thousand books and manuscripts, more than one hundred albums of drawings, and over thirty-two thousand coins, as well as fossils, shells, corals, and animal parts (horns, bones, and preserved specimens). While we will consider the contents of this collection in more detail later, it is important first to focus on the process, or rather processes, by which it was gathered, and on Sloane as a collector, for what that can tell us about his collection as a mode of encounter with the early modern world.

Sloane was an active collector of natural history "in the field," at least in his early years. Although this only makes up a very small part of his final collection – nine herbarium volumes out of the more than three hundred – it was a significant part of his activity, as well as an important starting point for his collecting and his collection. So while there is one volume of dried plant specimens that is identified by Sloane as "gathered in the fields and gardens about London about the year 1682 for my own and Mr [William] Courten's collections," there are only a few others that

Figure 4.2 *Sir Hans Sloane*, by Stephen Slaughter, 1736.
© National Portrait Gallery, London.

contain similar material.[7] More significant, however, are the eight volumes of plant specimens collected by Sloane in Jamaica in the late 1680s.

Sloane travelled to Jamaica in 1687 as physician to the new governor, the Duke of Albemarle. He later stated that he did so since he was already a fellow of the Royal Society and the Royal College of Physicians, and he wanted "to cast in my Mite towards the Advancement of Natural Knowledge, and the Faculty of Physic, and by that means endeavour to deserve a Place amongst so many Great and Worthy Persons: [so] This Voyage seem'd likewise to promise to be useful to me, as a Physician; many of the antient and best Physicians having travell'd to the Places whence their Drugs were brought, to inform themselves concerning them."[8] While in Jamaica he travelled the island, or at least those parts of it he felt he could safely visit, collecting specimens, of which he brought back around eight hundred. Some of the plants he had drawn for him in Jamaica by the Reverend Garret Moore, who also depicted fishes, birds, and insects for Sloane. Sloane noted that in order to get the best possible representations of the natural world, he "carried him [Moore] with me into several places of the Country, that he might take them on the place."[9]

This was, inevitably, an encounter with people as well as with places, plants, and animals, as Sloane and Moore explored Jamaican nature. As one of the practitioners of "colonial" natural history, Sloane was interested in the uses of nature, at home and abroad.[10] He wanted one purpose of his work to be "to teach the Inhabitants of the Parts where these Plants grow, their several Uses, which I have endeavour'd to do, by the best Informations I could get from Books, and the Inhabitants, either *Europeans, Indians* or *Blacks.*"[11] So, alongside using his library, he had talked to the island's inhabitants about their plants and what they did with them. His explorations and encounters aimed to produce a coherent collection of Jamaican plants that would be of practical use, and make his reputation in natural history.

Albemarle having died, Sloane returned to London in 1689 with the duke's body preserved in a cask, and hundreds of other specimens. There he had the dried plant material drawn by Everardus Kickius, in ways that reproduced the characteristics of the particular specimens, and he published, in Latin in 1695, a concise catalogue of Jamaican plants. This worked through his specimens and his library of botanical works on the Americas to set out the details of the island's plant life and what was known of it. This was a somewhat dry, unillustrated text for botanical specialists.[12] It was followed, however, in 1707 – nearly twenty years after Sloane's return from the island – by the publication of the first volume of his *Natural History of Jamaica.* Besides engraved images of his botanical specimens taken from the drawings by Kickius, it included engravings of insects, birds, fish, and quadrupeds, as well as some other artefacts. It gave brief, descriptive accounts, from observation and from previous authors, of all these plants and animals. It staged an encounter with Jamaican nature for its predominantly European readers.[13]

Yet this book also signals a difference in the mode of encounter with the world from Sloane's Jamaican collecting. The full title of the work gives a clearer sense of the broad frame within which Sloane's more particular collection of specimens was located. He called it *A Voyage to the Islands Madera, Barbadoes, Nieves, St Christophers, and Jamaica; with the Natural History of the Herbs and Trees, Four-Footed Beasts, Fishes, Birds, Insects, Reptiles, &c. Of the last of those islands. To which is prefix'd, An Introduction, Wherein is an Account of the Inhabitants, Air, Waters, Diseases, Trade, &c. of the Place; with some Relations concerning the Neighbouring Continent, and Islands of America. Illustrated with the Figures of the Things described, which have not been heretofore engraved. In large Copper-Plates as big as the Life.* It included a description of the island's topography, climate, and rivers; a brief account of its history; an account of Sloane's voyage to and from the island; and a whole series of medical case histories that Sloane had attended to; as well as reflections on diet and an account of life on the islands, including the punishment of the enslaved.

There was, in what was included in this first volume in 1707, a broad sense of what might be gathered together to understand Jamaica, and other such places, even if the relationships between those things were not readily specified. The book itself is, therefore, something of a collection of parts that make an unsteady whole.[14] Its version of natural history is certainly a very capacious one. Moreover, by the time it was published, Sloane had long been back in London and was very actively engaging in forms of collecting that greatly expanded his collection in both extent and scope. Jamaica certainly played a part in this via the connections he had made there. Most notably, in May 1695 he had married Elizabeth Rose, the widow of Fulke Rose of Jamaica, by which, as Thomas Birch noted, "[h]e made a very considerable Addition to his Fortune," not least by incorporating into his investment portfolio the one-third share she held in her former husband's sugar plantations.[15] It was this fortune that Sloane used to build his collection in and from London through other forms of collecting and other ways of exploring and encountering the world.

As James Delbourgo has shown, Sloane turned himself from a collector of Jamaican plant specimens into perhaps the eighteenth century's

East India Company employees permanently based at settlements along the coast – including the surgeons Samuel Browne and Edward Bulkley, and the clergyman George Lewis, at Fort St George, Madras – engaged with local knowledge and gathered substantial botanical collections now found among the Vegetable Substances. Likewise, East India Company ship surgeons such as James Cuninghame and Alexander Brown viewed company voyages as ideal opportunities to collect all sorts of botanical items, including "[d]iffering gums resins or substances brought from the Nicubar Island."[19] Often, however, Sloane's access to this material was through the London apothecary James Petiver, and Petiver's own global correspondence network, rather than via direct contact with these collectors himself. Sloane also took advantage of people working beyond the English company. One specimen in the collection is described as "[t]he fruit of a small triangular coco-nut esteemed in the East Indies a great antidote" and is one of twenty-four items sent "From Dr. Kempfer."[20] The German physician Engelbert Kaempfer was based at a Dutch East India Company trading post in Japan in 1692. Kaempfer's collecting gave access to places beyond the scope of English company trade. His contributions to the Vegetable Substances are also a reminder of how Sloane added substantially to his collection through wholesale purchase. After Kaempfer died in 1716, Sloane bought his entire collection.

As a result of Sloane's curiosity and sense of wonder, and the range of his contributors, the Vegetable Substances contains a great variety of sorts of specimens. Sloane's catalogue describes objects such as "[a] snake stick being a branch of an oak tree so involuted as to imitate the coiling of a snake the ends of which are shapd to resemble the head & tail"; "A knot of an Oak from Yorkshire wherein the fibrills are turn'd very curiously into circular and other forms. The whole resembling in some manner the Head of a Dogg"; and "shoes made of ... bark & straps of seals skins."[21] This variety is also true for his collection as a whole, which he greatly expanded in size and scope during the early eighteenth century by buying the collections of other collectors, Kaempfer included. The first such major purchase was William Courten's collection in 1702. Courten had been a close friend, and Sloane's purchase served to keep the collection together and to provide funds to clear debts Courten had inherited from his father. Courten's collection contained antiquities, coins, plants, and paintings, so acquiring it was an important moment in substantially broadening the remit of Sloane's own collection. It invites reflection on the point at which having things becomes having "a collection," a form of possession that means acquiring more things, as well as decisions about what they should be. It also raises the question of the implications for the mode of encounter with the world when what John Evelyn, in 1691, called a "universal Collection of the natural productions of Jamaica" became a collection "of every conceivable kind of object."[22]

In short, this is the problem of the "Nicknackatory." The wonder of Sloane's collection was the huge variety of things it contained from all over world (or at least those parts of the world where the extended tentacles of European imperial and commercial ventures reached), as a consequence of which his collection was always challenged by questions of its coherence, its utility for making knowledge, and its meaning. Such a "universal" collection could encounter the world – it might even aspire to contain the world – but this did not necessarily render it knowable. This is the tension in early modern modes of exchange and encounter that we want to explore in what follows. Considering the organization of Sloane's "Nicknackatory" itself, those who encountered the world through it, and its translation into the founding collection of the British Museum, points to how different attempts to manage these problems of diversity, variety, and (in)coherence offered encounters with the world through the collection that were always partial, obscured, only locally ordered and temporary. We start with how Sloane brought some local order to one part of his global collection.

Making a Collection

It is not unfamiliar to think about the making of a collection as a series of processes that create and stabilize the entities that make it up, and the gathering, ordering, and managing of information about them. For a natural history collection this involves making and preserving specimens, just as Sloane did in Jamaica. It can also involve translating them into other forms, such as the images he had drawn by Moore and Kickius. It also means making objects comparable and commensurable through certain forms of classification or ordering, so that what is produced does become a collection and not just a bunch of stuff or a heap of matter. In doing so, one of the things that must be attended to is scale. Once again, this can be well illustrated through Sloane's Vegetable Substances collection.

Sloane's own three-volume handwritten catalogue for this collection lists 12,523 items, and there are more than eight thousand surviving objects. As we have seen, the collection is made up of seeds (about half the collection), roots, leaves, bark, gums, and balms, but also the curious

Figure 4.3 A selection of samples from Sloane's Vegetable Substances collection, now held in the Natural History Museum. © The Trustees of the Natural History Museum, London.

objects noted above. However, the most striking thing about the collection is how it is made or made up into a collection. Each "item" – which may in itself be multiples of the same thing – is in its own box. These have glass tops and bottoms and wooden sides and are sealed with decorative, often marbled, papers glued down to seal the edges. So there are lots and lots of boxes (Figure 4.3). They are of a range of different sizes and shapes but are at broadly the same scale: perhaps the scale of the hand.

Various sorts of managing and ordering accompany the bringing of the collection to a single scale. Most pragmatically, the boxes simply keep separate things that would be easily lost or confused: scoopfuls, or pinches, of tiny seeds or small dried fruits – often hard to differentiate one from the other – or twigs, roots, and bark. All are at risk from insects and other pests, or from damp. These vegetable substances may share a scale and object-ness with coins and medals, or gemstones, but they have a different, more fragile materiality. The boxes fix them. Doing so brings the specimen to knowledge in particular ways. It makes them accessible to the eye, but much less so to the hand, nose, or tongue, or, indeed, to experimentation.[23] Like all forms of ordering, it opens up that which is ordered to some ways of knowing, but necessarily closes others down.

This is also true of the scale that is produced for the Vegetable Substances collection as a whole. It is a good example of the geographers' contention that scale is not something that simply exists – most of the debate being about the scales of the local, national, and global; rather, it has to be "socially constructed."[24] Here we see how scale is constructed through material practice: the practice of boxing vegetable substances. Specimens must be brought to that scale to be part of the collection. Nature is cut to fit. It also means disconnecting parts of plants and separating them from their ecologies of animals, other plants, and growing conditions. What does it mean, then, to encounter and explore the world's nature at this scale, box by box, rather than in a botanical garden, for example? The scale and materiality of the Vegetable Substances seems to suggest a focus on comparability and the visual – on placing boxes out on the tabletop or holding them up to the light, which is a three-dimensional equivalent of botanical illustration for the parts of plants that can be preserved dried.[25] There is no evidence that the boxes were made to convey specimens to others, unlike illustration and publication. Indeed, their use is difficult to assess, for no definable contributions to knowledge were made through the collection as a whole, as opposed to indications of specific work with particular plants undertaken by Sloane and his correspondents.

Sloane's catalogue provides another technology for seeing this vast collection of boxes: a paper technology.[26] Each box is identified by a number that keys it back into the catalogue, another attempt to guarantee certainty against the dangers of confusion and multiplicity. But while opening up for each item a space that can be filled with information, the catalogue often undercuts this by being unable to fulfil its promise. Entries can be so short as to be virtually meaningless – "a seed"; or highly speculative and full of question marks – "Long cocoon divided?" or "Spongia species? Insects nest?"[27] The material object has been fixed in its box, but what it is, where it is from, and what it might be used for is still in question. The collection offers the promise of identification – knowing what everything is and where it came from – but it was not, for Sloane, a step towards systematization or classification, as such collections would be for Linnaeus and his followers. Behind the uniformity and universality suggested by the scale of the boxes, and the promise of identification given by the catalogue, the encounter with the world and its nature through the Vegetable Substances collection is one that is fundamentally shaped by the differentiated forms of encounter that brought its elements to Sloane. There are pockets of order – sub-collections with their own protocols of naming and information, such as the fifty-three entries labelled "Chinese druggs" that were contributed by James Petiver with descriptions that included Chinese names and therapeutic properties – and lines of connection between boxed specimens and other parts of the collection, such as the herbaria. But these exist within an unassimilated plethora of diversity and variety. This can also be seen when we consider the Vegetable Substances as part of the organization and display of Sloane's collection as a whole.

Presenting a Collection

It was certainly the case that visitors to Sloane's collection – and we have a number of descriptions of it, both in Bloomsbury and in Chelsea – noticed the ways in which he stored, organized, and presented it as well as the objects themselves. Per Kalm, a Finnish naturalist who worked with Linnaeus in Sweden, and who visited Sloane's collection at Chelsea, was quite taken with its boxes and described, in particular,

> [a] large collection of insects from all parts of the world, all of which were now preserved in four-sided boxes, with clear glass glued on both over and under, so that one could see them quite well, but these boxes or cases were also so well stuck together and so tight that no worms or other injurious insects could get at them, and spoil them. The sides were of wood. In some both lid and bottom, were of a very clear glass, but in most only the lid. At the joints the glass was stuck or glued fast with paper. Where the bottom was of glass, the insect was gummed on to the middle of the bottom.[28]

He also noted that the same type of boxes were used for "all kinds of seed."[29]

Kalm also described the rooms in which the collection was housed, as well as various other modes of display for Sloane's specimens, such as the glass-fronted cabinets for displaying corals and the artfully constructed wooden box that held in its various stacked layers 1,300 gemstones. As a botanist, Kalm needed to have an eye for such issues of preservation and presentation. However, what mainly comes across in his account of Sloane's collection is its extent – in both variety of categories of material and the numbers of things contained within them (indeed, before moving it to Chelsea Sloane had bought the house next door in Bloomsbury so that he could display his collection) – and its focus on particular interesting or curious objects.

Thus, a French visitor in 1729 provided a lengthy numbered list, of which this is a part, including, at "12," what was probably the Vegetable Substances collection:

> 2. A collection of medals; there are as many ancient as modern; 23,000.
> 3. Skeletons of leaves of various trees, produced by insects.
> 4. Various birds, amongst others humming birds and "oiseaux du mogol."
> 5. Skins of all sorts of animals.
> ...
> 12. A cupboard where there are 7,000 different fruits.

But he also noted, in particular, the whale skeleton that Sloane had in the courtyard and "the plant called lagetto of which the stem, the leaves and the bark provide four different kinds of fibre."[30] This plant, lace-bark (*Lagetta lagetto*), was particularly associated with Sloane, who probably brought the first scientific specimens to Britain from Jamaica.[31] It features in the portrait painted of him by Stephen Slaughter in 1736 (Figure 4.2), and in the *Natural History of Jamaica* it was discussed in terms of both its natural historical properties and its uses. Kalm, for his part, also listed the categories of objects: gemstones, shells, corals, insects, seeds, volumes of bound plants, and "an endless number of other items," while noting particular objects that were shaped by nature or human hands or both: "Egyptian pebbles shaped like a man's face"; "A polished agate which displayed in a most naturalistic manner an eclipse of the sun"; "An apparatus made of elephant bone with which the women of the East Indies scratch their backs"; and "An Indian god to be carried in the pocket." Some of the items he noted were evidently of interest to him, or to others who might read his account. Other items were also noted by fellow visitors: the lace-bark; edible birds' nests; the paintings by Maria Sybilla Merian; and "[a] *Cochlea* which laid eggs of the shape and size of swallows' eggs and white in colour, in which were found little *Cochleae*, which then grew into big ones."[32] While he was there he was under strict instructions to inspect a particular snake for Linnaeus, and had to spend much time counting its abdominal plates and scales "while the others went round and looked at everything."

There are two points to make here. First, about Sloane's spatial organization of the collection; and second, about his presentation (or performance) of it for visitors. Regarding the first, we can get no clear overall picture of the collection's exact organization, and there are no images of it on which to draw. However, the rather brief descriptions given by visitors do broadly accord with Marjorie Caygill's interpretation of the pencilled numbers in the margins of some of Sloane's catalogues as indicating locations in rooms or cabinets, although she only looked in detail at the *Miscellanies* and *Antiquities* catalogues.[33] This was a matter of ordering like with like across the collections. For example, "181" seems to have coded various forms of *materia medica* but also included straps made from manatee hide used for whipping the enslaved. Indeed, of the more than 1,200 Vegetable Substances specimens given the code 181, many are not specifically designated in the catalogue as also having therapeutic properties, even though they might do.[34] There is also "245," which includes virtually all of the musical instruments, but also a considerable number of items associated with smoking; and "252," which contains weapons. However, as Caygill concludes, "while there are clusters, most of the large cabinets or spaces would have housed a wide range of objects."[35] Thus, for example, as Kalm notes, there was

> [a]nother room, with the clothes of native people in various kinds of leather and other materials. In this room were also
>
> A stuffed camel
>
> A striped donkey from the Cape of Good Hope: *Equus lineis transversis versiculor.* Linn
>
> West Indian boats made of bark.[36]

Was there a form of ordering here concerned with covering materials and their uses, or were things more haphazard than that? Clearly, the organization of the collection did not disclose a single system. Its encounter with the world was, at best, one of local pockets of order within a more indeterminate set of juxtapositions and what must at times have just been an overwhelming – but perhaps "wonderful" – sense of the extent and variety of what had been brought together as a microcosm of God's creation.[37]

Second, this organization of things into boxes, drawers, cabinets, and rooms was then actively mobilized in the performance of displaying the collection to its visitors. Sloane was a key part of this. Despite the press of other business, and later despite his old age, he was often on hand to show people around. In 1710 the German scholar Zacharias Conrad von Uffenbach noted Sloane's "vast politeness" and "that he did us a very great honour by sparing us the time between half past two and seven o'clock" to show the collection, even though he could have been earning a guinea an hour in his doctor's practice instead. When the Prince and Princess of Wales visited in 1748, Sloane was in his nineties, but he was still there to receive them and talk to them despite "being antient and infirm."[38]

Such visitors were taken through the collection and shown its highlights. Some objects – the legatto, edible birds' nests, particular manuscripts or images – were picked out for them; others they chose themselves. It was certainly an interactive experience: handling agates, turning the pages of books and manuscripts, holding the cochlea up to the light to see the smaller ones within, even tasting the bird's nest.[39] Through such performances the meanings of objects in Sloane's collection could be, by whatever interpretative hand or eye, turned to particular ends. For example, Kalm, the naturalist, gave an account of the collection that focused on the gems insofar as they showed evidence of material transformations by or of nature; but he hardly mentioned the extensive collection of coins and medals. In contrast, the account of the royal visit that same year published in *Gentleman's Magazine* orchestrated a truly global and extensively historical encounter with questions of ethnographic difference, value, and kingly virtue and vice:

> When their Royal Highnesses had view'd one room, and went into another, the scene was shifted, for, when they returned, the same tables were covered for a second course with all sorts of *jewels*, polish'd and set after the modern fashion; or with *gems* carv'd or engraved; the stately and instructive remains of antiquity; for the third course the tables were spread with *gold* and *silver ores*, with the most precious and remarkable ornaments used in the *habits* of men, from *Siberia* to the Cape of *Good Hope*, from *Japan* to *Peru*; and with both ancient and modern *coins* and *medals* in gold and silver, the lasting monuments of historical facts …

The account took the trouble to focus on a few of these:

> … of a *Prusias*, King of *Bithynia*, who betray'd his allies; of an *Alexander*, who, mad with ambition, over-run and invaded his neighbours; of a *Caesar*, who inslaved his country to satisfy his own pride; of a *Titus*, the delight of mankind … [O]thers shewing the effects of popular rage, when overmuch

> oppressed by their superiors, as in the case of the *De Witts* in *Holland*; the happy deliverance of *Britain*, by the arrival of King *William*; the glorious exploits of a Duke of *Marlborough*, and the happy arrival of the present illustrious *royal family* amongst us.

These objects "raised the mind to praise the great creator of all things" and "ye great beauty of all parts of the creation." But in addition, there were clearly lessons – although who was delivering them was unclear – to be drawn from Sloane's collection about the value of nature and the nature of power.[40]

Visitors, then, actively worked – and were worked on and with – to make meaning in Sloane's collection. They could experience wonderment at its extent and variety, be intrigued by particular things, and find (or be guided towards) meaningful paths through its objects and categories that provided very different forms of knowledge: from the number of scales on a snake's belly to the legitimation of the Hanoverian succession. Yet the particular shape of each of these paths, their diversity, and the uncontainable variety of the collection as a whole, meant that the purpose of Sloane's collection *as a collection* was always in question. The Prince of Wales might have "expressed the great esteem and value he had for him [Sloane] personally, and how much the learned world was obliged to him for his having collected such a vast library of curious books, and such immense treasures of the valuable and instructive productions of nature and art." He might also assert that this meant "esteeming it an ornament to the nation" that should be "established for publick use to the latest posterity."[41] But for others, its rationale was less clear. It remained a "Nicknackatory," with Sloane "the foremost Toyman of his Time," and this raised a question: what could a collection of everything actually mean?[42] What was the value of encountering and exploring the world if doing so involved all possible objects? What sort of meaning and value could be derived from such a collection if anything and everything could be in it? This became part of the discussion as Sloane's collection underwent a post-mortem transformation as it was remade into the British Museum.

Transforming a Collection

Sloane, who had absorbed many other people's collections into his own, was well aware of what might happen to it after his death: that it might be broken up, dissolved into parts that would be much less than the whole.

His will, in its various versions from the late 1730s onwards, attempted to secure his collection for the future by narrating its purpose and the mechanisms for its continuation. As to its purpose, he wrote, combining the spiritual and the temporal, that

> [w]hereas from my youth I have been a great observer and admirer of the wonderful power, wisdom and contrivance of the Almighty God, appearing in the works of his Creation; and have gathered together many things in my own travels or voyages, or had them from others ... Now desiring very much that these things tending many ways to the manifestation of the glory of God, the confusion of atheism and its consequences, the use and improvement of physic, and other arts and sciences, and benefit of mankind, may remain together and not be separated, and that chiefly in and about the city of London, where I have acquired most of my estates, and where they may by the great confluence of people be of most use.[43]

The mechanism was to entrust it to the care of a body of, eventually sixty, trustees – an interlinked group of men of money and learning, with significant political clout – who were charged with offering it at the bargain price of £20,000 to George II. And if the British king did not want it, it was to be offered to the academies of science at Saint Petersburg, Paris, Berlin, and Madrid, in that order. There were, as might be expected from what has already been said, different judgments of its worth. The *London Magazine* called it "the most valuable private collection (perhaps publick one) that has ever appeared on earth." Whereas Horace Walpole, one of the trustees, privately wrote to Sir Horace Mann that he had his doubts:

> You will scarce guess how I employ my time; chiefly at present in the guardianship of embryos and cockle-shells. Sir Hans Sloane is dead and has made me one of the trustees to his museum, which is to be offered for twenty thousand pounds to the King ... He valued it at fourscore thousand; and so would anybody who loves hippopotamuses, sharks with one ear, and spiders as big as geese! It is a rent charge to keep the foetuses in spirit! You may believe that those who think money the most valuable of all curiosities, will not be purchasers.

Indeed, the king did turn the opportunity down, saying, as Walpole put it, that "he [George II] did not believe there are twenty thousand pounds in the Treasury."[44]

Fortunately for Sloane's legacy, his trustees were not defeated. They raised the matter in parliament, arguing successfully there that the founding of a museum with Sloane's collection at its heart could be funded by a lottery. The House of Commons recorded its view that the collection be "kept intire, and maintained for the use and Benefit of the Publick," and the act to establish the British Museum passed on 7 June 1753. The museum was to be a universal collection, as Sloane's had been, combining productions both natural and artificial, and books and manuscripts as well as objects, all designated for the "use and Benefit of the Publick." As Marjorie Caygill notes, Sloane's will served as the catalyst for the first of a new sort of collection: one that was owned publicly and was *of* and *for* the nation, instead of being the private collection of an individual or monarch.[45]

There were, of course, significant continuities with what had gone before: there was no simple shift from private to public. Sloane's collection had always been open to the learned, albeit that openness was shaped by the collector's sense of who he wanted to show it to; and as Anne Goldgar has deftly shown, the British Museum as it actually operated was marked by a restricted sense – or series of restricted senses – of the public for whom it was intended and how they would benefit from even the limited access provided.[46] So it is important to recognize that the British Museum was not simply an act of will by Hans Sloane, or an act of Hans Sloane's will. His death provided the opportunity not just to turn one man's private collection into something public, or *for* the public, but to effect a more telling transformation in the bringing together of Sloane's collection with other collections to make something new.

To understand what happened we need to return to the houses of parliament and the crucial debate of 19 March 1753.[47] There, the long-standing speaker, Arthur Onslow, gave up the chair to another Whig grandee, Philip Yorke, Lord Hardwicke, and made the case, along with Henry Pelham (the First Lord of the Treasury) that not only should the cost of purchase and management be met by a lottery, but that there were other great collections that should be part of this too. Pelham reminded the house of the Cottonian library, a great collection of works, especially its 958 volumes of manuscripts, amassed by the Cotton family and given to the nation in 1700. This had been rather neglected and had nearly been destroyed by fire in 1731. Onslow was one of the trustees of the collection, which included the Lindesfarne Gospels and two copies of the Magna Carta. Handily, it also came with a bequest of £7,000. Pelham also suggested the purchase of the Harleian manuscripts from the Duchess of Portland. This was the collection of the first and second earls of Oxford, containing eight thousand volumes and more than fourteen thousand rolls and other documents. It was, therefore, not simply a matter of Sloane's collection becoming the British Museum; rather, the British Museum was assembled by bringing together into one collection – albeit across different spaces in Montagu House – Sloane's collection, the Cottonian library, and the Harleian collection of manuscripts.

It seems that these collections were at first kept separate. Then in 1758 they were divided into three broad categories: printed books, manuscripts, and "Natural & Artificial Productions," so that the Sloane collection was slowly transformed in its organization and display. James Empson, who had worked with Sloane for many years and who supervised the collection's move from Chelsea back to Bloomsbury, noted that it could no longer be displayed as it had been by Sloane himself:

> How much soever a private Person may be at Liberty arbitrarily to dispose and place his Curiosities; we are sensible that the British Museum being a public Institution subject to the Visits of the Judicious and Intelligent, as well as Curious, Notice will be taken, whether or no the Collection has been arranged in a methodical Manner.[48]

Again, it is unclear what this meant in the rooms of Montagu House, but the distinction between the "Curious" and the "Judicious and Intelligent" is one that Anne Goldgar has seen as a structuring principle of the new museum's different spaces. It provided a distinction between the Reading Room as a preserve of the Republic of Letters and the galleries that afforded more public access to the curious, although that was still closely circumscribed. She has argued that for many of the trustees "the Reading Room was the core of the Museum, and the research that took place there was the main point of the institution." Here, Sloane's collection of books and manuscripts was subordinated to the Cottonian and Harleian collections with their Whiggish political project to preserve English political liberties (notably those copies of the Magna Carta). Goldgar argues that in the eyes of its creators, it was the institutionalization of a political perspective that made the museum public, or for public benefit, not access for the curious to displays of "Natural & Artificial Productions."[49]

Now that it was housed – if not displayed – alongside a combined collection of manuscripts that, as their catalogue boasted, "happily secured to this Country the most compleat and extensive Fund of national

Antiquities, that any Kingdom can boast of," the meaning of Sloane's collection was altered.[50] In this new context, Sloane's items meant something different than they had in Chelsea or in his Bloomsbury townhouse. Even while Sloane's collection had always been able to tell a story of English liberties, this had only been one among many stories. The eclectic and open-ended mode of engagement and encounter with the world that Sloane's "Nicknackatory" had afforded was pushed from the centre of the museum's account of Britain's relationship with the world as a new national narrative (or Whig) history was being crafted. Sloane's objects, and his means of arranging them, were also devalued, as well as subjected to a new methodical organization, as curiosity slid down the social scale.

Conclusion

One influential way to understand the modes of global encounter and exchange afforded by collections – particularly natural history collections – is through Bruno Latour's notion of "centres of calculation."[51] Here, repeated "cycles of accumulation" bring back "home" the "events, places and people" encountered by "inventing means that (a) render them *mobile* so that they can be brought back; (b) keep them *stable* so that they can be moved back and forth without additional distortion, corruption or decay, and (c) are *combinable* so that whatever stuff they are made of, they can be cumulated, aggregated, or shuffled like a pack of cards." When this practical work has been done, Latour argues, places "that were at first as weak as any other place will become centres dominating at a distance many other places." This, he argues, is "simply a question of scale," since those centres of calculation mean that scientists "in their Natural History Museums, without travelling more than a few hundred metres and opening more than a few dozen drawers, travel through all the continents, climates and periods." As a result they "*see new* things … [T]hat's all there is in this mysterious beginning of a science."[52]

It is tempting to interpret Sloane's collection in this way, but that would be to deny that its characterization as a "Nicknackatory" did get at something important about the ways in which it was formed from and, in turn, formed particular sorts and varieties of encounters and exchanges with the world beyond London. As a "universal collection" it had earlier Renaissance precedents as well as pointing towards Enlightenment forms of universalism.[53] Yet the great range of relationships with all sorts of people that brought materials together into the Vegetable Substances collection could not, despite the boxed uniformity of the collection and the promise of the catalogue's information system, simply be productive of new forms of knowledge as a centre of calculation. Moreover, even if that inability in relation to this corner of the collection was just a matter of practical incapacity, what was brought together in the collection as a whole was gathered and displayed under quite different regimes of knowledge and value, as much produced by the visitors as by Sloane: wonder as well as systematic comparison; theology alongside utility; political lessons as much as natural philosophical ones. And when Sloane died, and the collection formed part of the British Museum, its meanings were relativized again within a new institution established for new purposes. The collection's organization was, therefore, always a matter of local forms of order, interesting juxtapositions, and an effect of abundance and particularized curiosity. Visitors to this cabinet of curiosities – from naturalists to royalty – could certainly "*see new* things," but they were each led to do so in very different ways, and in ways that differed from the forms of vision characteristic of "centres of calculation." These were also ways that were not necessarily the beginning, mysterious or not, of a new science, as critics like John Woodward had complained.

It is, therefore, important to avoid a teleological view of Hans Sloane's collection. Thinking of it as a "Nicknackatory" situates it more firmly within early modern London and the particular relationships with the world that Britain was making during that period.[54] It recognizes that the virtue and value of collecting (and of natural history) was in question. It recognizes that the multiple, partial, differently powerful, and differently productive relationships that were being forged – through commerce, enslavement, settlement, warfare, and diplomacy – with people and places across the globe did not necessarily add up, and neither did the knowledge they produced.

ACKNOWLEDGMENTS

We would like to thank James Delbourgo and Charlie Jarvis for their comments on this essay. Victoria Pickering's research was funded by the *Reconnecting Sloane* project (AHRC grant number AH/J00989X/1) and we thank, for ongoing discussion of its subject, the project members: Elizabeth Eger, Anne Goldgar, Arnold Hunt, Alice Marples, Felicity Roberts, Kim Sloan, and Charlie Jarvis once more. Miles Ogborn would like to thank Adriana Craciun and Mary Terrall for their invitation to give a keynote address on "Collections in Flux" which enabled him to work through some of these ideas.

greatest individual collector of every conceivable sort of object. He did so not by travelling further but by staying put and becoming "a collector of collectors."[16] Delbourgo then shows in great detail how Sloane's vast collection was amassed. It involved commercial transactions – especially buying the collections of others such as William Courten in 1702, Leonard Plukenet in 1714, and James Petiver in 1718 – as well as personal favours and gifts. It also involved much more mediated chains and systems of exchange, with Sloane acquiring things from distant places after they had passed through many hands.

If we look at just one part of Sloane's collection we can see some of the complexities of this process. The Vegetable Substances, for instance, which sits alongside the Sloane Herbarium in the Natural History Museum in London, originally contained more than twelve thousand botanical samples ranging from balms and oils to skeletonized leaves, as well as many fruits and seeds of various shapes and sizes. From Sloane's own catalogue of the collection we know that more than three hundred people contributed to the Vegetable Substances from around the world. These people varied in their professions, status, and relationships with Sloane, and while some items came directly to him, others passed along complex chains, giving Sloane access to many different sorts of natural history.

Much material came from the New World. Characterized as they were by settlement, agricultural colonization, and slavery, the Americas offered Sloane a diverse set of collectors and correspondents, from independent merchants and planters to surgeons, women, and permanent residents. Many of them were keen to find a place in the transatlantic republic of letters and used a variety of sources of specimens and knowledge – including indigenous and enslaved people – to do so.[17] Sloane at times engaged with and thereby influenced their natural history collecting, as was the case with the naturalist Mark Catesby, whose travels to the Carolinas in the 1720s he helped sponsor. At other times, he developed more mutually beneficial relationships – for example, with the physician Henry Barham in Jamaica, and the Pennsylvania-based Quaker John Bartram – that involved exchanging different sorts of natural knowledge.[18] Sloane did not simply accept botanical specimens from these people; rather, he engaged in years of correspondence with them, thus adding to his own medical knowledge and establishing lasting friendships.

To access natural history specimens from the "East," Sloane used a different sort of network. These vegetable substances almost always came via agents connected to established European trading companies. English

NOTES

1 Tim Cockleshell to Sir Hans Sloane, London, 25 April 1713, Sloane Manuscripts 4043 ff. 144–5, British Library, London.

2 Barbara M. Benedict, "Collecting Trouble: Sir Hans Sloane's Literary Reputation in Eighteenth-Century Britain," *Eighteenth-Century Life* 36 (2012): 111–42; James Delbourgo, "'Exceeding the Age in Every Thing': Placing Sloane's Objects," *Spontaneous Generations* 3 (2009): 41–54, who quotes a satire on Sloane from 1700 that notes that for any "pebble or a cockle-shell" from the Indies or China "he would soon write a comment upon it, and perpetuate its memory upon a copper plate" (42). For the most thorough treatment, see Delbourgo, *Collecting the World: The Life and Curiosity of Hans Sloane* (London: Allen Lane, 2017).

3 This may have been a collective joke, since the letter was directed to Sloane "at the Grecian Coffeehouse in Devereaux Court" (f. 143r), a favourite spot for Royal Society fellows; see Jonathan Harris, "The Grecian Coffee House and Political Debate in London, 1688–1714," *London Journal* 25 (2000): 1–13; and Larry Stewart, "Other Centres of Calculation, or, Where the Royal Society Didn't Count: Commerce, Coffee Houses, and Natural Philosophy in Early Modern London," *British Journal for the History of Science* 32 (1999): 133–53.

4 He was, for example, "stung" by the attack on him in William King's *The Transactioneer* (1700); see Delbourgo, *Collecting the World,* 168.

5 Joseph M. Levine, *Dr. Woodward's Shield: History, Science, and Satire in Augustan England* (Berkeley: University of California Press, 1977), although by then Woodward was on Sloane's side against Isaac Newton.

6 See [Francis Grose], *A Classical Dictionary of the Vulgar Tongue* (London, 1785), 114. This letter's usage postdates Thomas Brown, *Letters from the Dead to the Living* (London, 1702), 29, in another humorous letter for a coffeehouse audience, but predates that by Sir Charles Hanbury Williams quoted in Benedict, "Collecting Trouble," 126.

7 Quoted in Charlie Jarvis, Mark Spencer, and Robert Huxley, "Sloane's Plant Specimens at the Natural History Museum," in *From Books to Bezoars: Sir Hans Sloane and His Collections,* ed. Alison Walker, Arthur MacGregor, and Michael Hunter (London: British Library, 2012), 138.

8 Hans Sloane, *A Voyage to the Islands Madera, Barbados, Nieves, S. Christophers and Jamaica,* vol. 1 (London, 1707), Sig. A1^{r}.

9 Ibid., Sig. A2^{r}.

10 Londa Schiebinger and Claudia Swan, eds., *Colonial Botany: Science, Commerce, and Politics in the Early Modern World* (Philadelphia: University of Pennsylvania Press, 2007).

11 Sloane, *A Voyage to the Islands*, vol. 1, Sig B2[r].
12 Hans Sloane, *Catalogus Plantarum Quæ in Insula Jamaica* (London, 1696). On Kickius, see Jarvis, Spencer, and Huxley, "Sloane's Plant Specimens."
13 Although see James Robertson, "Knowledgeable Readers: Jamaican Critiques of Sloane's Botany," in *From Books to Bezoars*, ed. Walker, MacGregor, and Hunter, 80–9; and James Delbourgo, "Sir Hans Sloane's Milk Chocolate and the Whole History of the Cacao," *Social Text* 29 (2011): 71–101.
14 Kay Dian Kriz, "Curiosities, Commodities, and Transplanted Bodies in Hans Sloane's 'Natural History of Jamaica,'" *William and Mary Quarterly* 57 (2000): 35–78; Christopher P. Ianinni, *Fatal Revolutions: Natural History, West Indian Slavery, and the Routes of American Literature* (Chapel Hill: University of North Carolina Press, 2012).
15 Thomas Birch, "Memoirs Relating to the Life of Sir Hans Sloane," Additional Manuscripts 4241 f. 5v, British Library, London. Much of Sloane's wealth came from his medical practice.
16 Delbourgo, *Collecting the World*, 202.
17 Susan Scott Parrish, *American Curiosity: Cultures of Natural History in the Colonial British Atlantic World* (Chapel Hill: University of North Carolina Press, 2006).
18 Catesby contributed 215 specimens to the Vegetable Substances collection, Barham and Bartram contributed 155 and 35 respectively.
19 Vegetable Substances Catalogue, Natural History Museum, London (hereafter VS), 586.
20 VS 8184.
21 VS 11802, 12435, and 69.
22 Arthur MacGregor, "The Life, Character and Career of Sir Hans Sloane," in *Sir Hans Sloane: Collector, Scientist, Antiquary*, ed. MacGregor (London: British Museum, 1994), 11–44 (Evelyn quote at 22).
23 Although we do know that Sloane boxed some of what he received and experimented – or had others experiment – with the rest, see Victoria R.M. Pickering, "Putting Nature in a Box: Hans Sloane's Vegetable Substances Collection" (PhD diss., Queen Mary University of London, 2017).
24 Sallie Marston, "The Social Construction of Scale," *Progress in Human Geography* 24 (2000): 219–42.
25 Daniela Bleichmar, *Visible Empire: Botanical Expeditions and Visual Culture in the Hispanic Enlightenment* (Chicago: University of Chicago Press, 2012).
26 Isabelle Charmantier and Staffan Müller-Wille, "Worlds of Paper: An Introduction," *Early Science and Medicine* 19 (2014): 379–97.
27 VS 451 and 218.

28 Per Kalm, *Kalm's Account of his Visit to England on his Way to America in 1748*, trans. Joseph Lucas (London: Macmillan, 1892), 100–1.
29 William R. Mead, *Pehr Kalm – His London Diary, 1748* (London: [the author], 2013), 53.
30 Sauveur Morand, reproduced in MacGregor, "The Life, Character, and Career of Sir Hans Sloane," 31.
31 Emily Brennan, Lori-Ann Harris, and Mark Nesbitt, "Jamaican Lace-Bark: Its History and Uncertain Future," *Textile History* 44 (2013): 235–53.
32 Mead, *Pehr Kalm*, 50–2, 54–5.
33 Marjorie Caygill, "Sloane's Catalogues and the Arrangement of His Collections," in *From Books to Bezoars*, ed. Walker, MacGregor and Hunter, 120–36.
34 On the "manati strap," see James Delbourgo, "Slavery in the Cabinet of Curiosities: Hans Sloane's Atlantic World" (2007), British Museum website, http://www.britishmuseum.org/PDF/Delbourgo%20essay.pdf, accessed 25 May 2017.
35 Caygill, "Sloane's Catalogues," 127.
36 Mead, *Pehr Kalm*, 55.
37 James Delbourgo, "Collecting Hans Sloane," in *From Books to Bezoars*, ed. Walker, MacGregor, and Hunter, 9–23.
38 Von Uffenbach, reproduced in MacGregor, "The Life, Character, and Career of Sir Hans Sloane," 30; "An Account of the Prince and Princess of Wales visiting Sir Hans Sloane," *Gentleman's Magazine* 18 (1748): 301.
39 Von Uffenbach notes its "taste, appearance and feeling"; see MacGregor, "The Life, Character, and Career of Sir Hans Sloane," 30.
40 "An Account," *Gentleman's Magazine*, 301.
41 Ibid., 301–2.
42 Quoted in Benedict, "Collecting Trouble," 128.
43 Quoted in Marjorie Caygill, "Sloane's Will and Establishment of the British Museum," in *Sir Hans Sloane*, ed. MacGregor, 46–7.
44 Quotations in Caygill, "Sloane's Will," 47–8.
45 Quoted in ibid., 50.
46 Anne Goldgar, "The British Museum and the Virtual Representation of Culture in the Eighteenth Century," *Albion* 32 (2000): 195–231.
47 See Caygill, "Sloane's Will."
48 Quoted in ibid., 55.
49 Goldgar, "The British Museum," 205.
50 Quoted in ibid., 220.
51 Bruno Latour, *Science in Action: How to Follow Scientists and Engineers through Society* (Cambridge, MA: Harvard University Press, 1988); David P. Miller

and Peter H. Reill, eds., *Visions of Empire: Voyages, Botany, and Representations of Nature* (Cambridge: Cambridge University Press, 1996).

52 Latour, *Science in Action*, 223, 225.

53 Delbourgo, *Collecting the World.* Lizzie Eger has also pointed out to us the resonances between Sloane's collection and the idea of "strange varieties" or "Order in Variety" (from Alexander Pope's *Windsor Forest*) in eighteenth-century poetry.

54 Miles Ogborn, *Global Lives: Britain and the World, 1550–1800* (Cambridge: Cambridge University Press, 2008).

chapter five

A Slaving Surgeon's Collection: The Pursuit of Natural History through the British Slave Trade to Spanish America

KATHLEEN S. MURPHY

On the morning of 30 March 1716, a recent traveller to Buenos Aires visited James Petiver's apothecary shop on Aldersgate Street in London bearing a dead armadillo (Figure 5.1). The visitor, Dr John Burnet, had recently returned to England after spending more than a year as a slave ship surgeon in the service of the South Sea Company. His posting aboard the *Wiltshire* brought him to West Africa's Gold Coast, where Captain Digory Herle, with Burnet's assistance, purchased 298 captive Africans. After spending a few months on the West African coast, the *Wiltshire* sailed to the Rio de la Plata region, where the 247 individuals who survived the passage were disembarked in Buenos Aires and sold to Spanish American colonists. During the voyage, the ship surgeon gathered a small collection of natural curiosities. While the rest of his collection consisted of preserved specimens, Burnet managed to keep the armadillo alive during the return voyage. But a few days after arriving in England, the animal died. The physician brought it to Petiver in the hope that the avid collector could arrange for it to be properly preserved.[1]

Knowing the rarity of such animals in British collections, Petiver had more ambitious plans for the specimen. He sent the armadillo to Dr James Douglas, a fellow member of the Royal Society who was known for his anatomical work. Petiver observed to Douglas that it was likely the first armadillo to reach England's shores alive and concluded by declaring, "I doubt not but you may make some Discoveries in its Viscera for which reason I have sent it to you, but must desire you will deface it as little as possible because it must be returned to the Gentleman."[2] A week later, Douglas presented the Royal Society with the first of two descriptions of the animal. Despite Petiver's predictions, they did not include

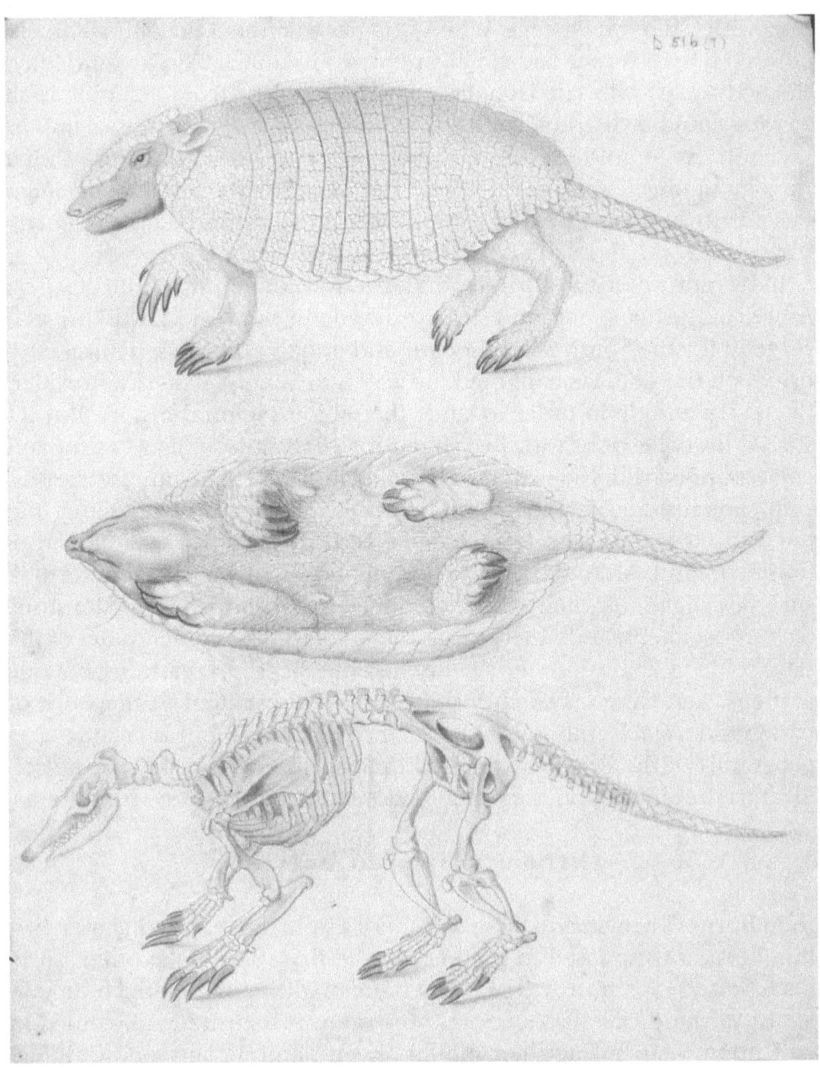

Figure 5.1 James Douglas, "The Description and Natural History of the Animal Called Armadillo or ye Hog in armour from South America by J.D." (1716). MS Hunter D516, f. 7. Special Collections, University of Glasgow.

discoveries about its viscera. When Douglas examined the animal he discovered that its owner had already removed its internal organs and filled the body cavity with salt. Douglas's paper, therefore, had to confine itself to what could be learned from the animal's external appearance and its skeleton. As he told the Royal Society, he "endeavoured to make what remains of the creature as usefull as I can." Even an incomplete specimen was worthy of study, given how rarely British naturalists had the opportunity to study the flora and fauna of Spanish America.[3]

In an era when most foreigners were forbidden entry into Spanish America, Burnet spent more than a decade in the region, working as a surgeon for the South Sea Company and quietly collecting natural curiosities on the side. He exploited the access to Spanish America provided by the slave trade in order to study the region's natural history. Burnet shared his collections with British natural historians such as Petiver and corresponded with them about his observations. Burnet, other surgeons, ship captains, and factors of the South Sea Company were among the few Britons with access to investigate Spanish America's natural wonders first-hand. Although only a handful of company servants undertook such investigations, their efforts uniquely shaped British natural history. Seeds, specimens, and observations they gathered along the routes of the slave trade to Spanish America enriched the British herbariums, botanic gardens, and cabinets of curiosities that were essential to the work of early modern naturalists. Their reliance upon the infrastructure and geography of the British slave trade to Spanish America shaped the collections they made and the natural knowledge that resulted from them.

Britons in Spanish America

John Burnet's activities in Spanish America were the reason that men like him were not supposed to be there in the first place. Like other European powers, Spain strove to restrict trade to within its imperial boundaries. Spanish officials also knew that the value of their trade depended in part upon maintaining their monopoly on natural commodities indigenous to their empire. They understood that given half a chance, their imperial rivals would smuggle the natural sources of Spanish American dyes and medicines into their own territories. Consequently, the Spanish crown strictly forbade the entry of foreigners into Spanish America and closely guarded natural knowledge about the region.

The stakes for doing so were high. Spanish America was home to some of the most valuable natural commodities known to early modern Europe.

These included cinchona, the antifebrile indigenous to the Andes that contains the natural source of quinine, and cochineal, a brilliant red dye that was more valuable by weight than silver. For more than two hundred years, Spain's policies of secrecy and exclusion of foreigners largely worked, leaving naturalists in other parts of Europe often ignorant about the flora and fauna of Spanish America. As late as 1734, European naturalists still debated the basic classification of cochineal; was it an animal, a vegetable, or a mineral? British naturalists were confident that an environment home to such natural treasures must surely contain others. The only reason they had not yet been discovered, they chauvinistically assumed, was simply that so far only the Spanish had looked.[4]

British naturalists had long been eager to learn more about the region's natural wonders. The second volume of the Royal Society of London's *Philosophical Transactions* (1667) included a series of questions the society's fellows hoped travellers could answer about distant regions, including Spanish America. These inquiries sought, in particular, to determine whether the more fantastical claims made in travel literature would stand up to eyewitness inspection. In a classic articulation of the Baconian ideals upon which the society was founded, the article's introduction explained that "'tis altogether necessary, to have confirmations of the truth of these things from several hands, before they be relyed on." The article asked, for example, whether in Panama "[t]oads are presently produced, by throwing a kind of Moorish Water found there, upon the Floors of their Houses," as the Dutch author Jan Huyghen van Linschoten had reported. The society's interest in Spanish America also led the editor of *Philosophical Transactions* to include reviews of travel narratives about the region among the journal's many descriptions of natural wonders, novel experiments, and other advances in natural knowledge. Merchants, imperial officials, and naturalists shared the conviction that Britain could only benefit if her subjects gained admittance to Spanish America.[5]

The exclusion of foreigners and foreign traders from Spanish America was never absolute, and the slave trade represented a key exception. Like colonists throughout the Atlantic World, Spanish colonials desired slaves to work in their fields, mines, and homes. Unique among European imperial powers, however, before 1800 Spain generally abstained from direct participation in the slave trade due to the Treaty of Tortesillas (1494).[6] In order to supply its colonies with slaves without participating directly in the slave trade, the Spanish crown negotiated a series of long-term contracts for foreign traders to deliver a set number of slaves to its colonies each year. The *Asiento de Negros,* or asiento, offered its holder a monopoly on the legal trade in slaves to Spanish America.[7]

Although British merchants engaged in an extensive illicit slave trade to Spanish America for more than a century, their ability to sell slaves legally in the region was confined to a few decades in the early eighteenth century. In 1713 the British received the *asiento* for the first (and only) time as part of the peace negotiations that ended the War of the Spanish Succession. Under this agreement, the British South Sea Company was required to supply 4,800 prime slaves each year for thirty years to Spanish America. To do so, the company was granted permission to establish trading factories to house unsold slaves in a handful of Spanish American towns, including Buenos Aires, Cartagena, Havana, Portobelo, and Vera Cruz. Each factory employed British factors (agents) to oversee the sale of slaves and a factory surgeon who was responsible for their health.[8]

Like those who had held the *asiento* before them, the British hoped it might create an opening to Spanish American markets through which more than just slaves would flow. The possibility that the *asiento* would serve as the cover for a broader contraband trade was a source of tension between Spanish officials and the South Sea Company from the beginning of the contract. The Spanish crown worried that the South Sea Company would smuggle manufactured goods and provisions such as flour, as well as bribe Spanish officials to countenance the illicit trade. For British investors, this possibility was part of the trade's appeal. Merchants saw potential profits not necessarily in the slave trade itself but in the access to Spanish American markets and bullion that such a trade would make possible. Historians of the *asiento* have argued that the terms of the British contract were perfectly contrived to enable contraband trading by both the company and individuals employed in its service. The activities of a few South Sea Company men such as Burnet demonstrate that flour and manufactured goods were not the only things being smuggled onboard the company's vessels. A few also used their unusual access to Spanish territories to surreptitiously collect specimens, to record natural knowledge, and to gather seeds of desired natural commodities.[9]

A Slaving Surgeon's Collection

Burnet was among the first group of Britons to engage in the legal slave trade to Spanish America. After completing his medical degree at the University of Edinburgh, the physician entered the South Sea Company's service in 1715.[10] Burnet's first posting was as the *Wiltshire*'s ship surgeon.

After the slave ship returned to London, the physician presented most of the items he had collected to the South Sea Company's Court of Directors. The following year, the company appointed the physician as factory surgeon in Portobelo on the Isthmus of Panama. Along with the rest of the factory's employees, Burnet evacuated to Jamaica in 1718, at the beginning of the War of the Quadruple Alliance (1718–21). After peace was restored in 1721, Burnet returned to Spanish America as the South Sea Company's factory surgeon in Cartagena (in modern Columbia), where he remained until 1729. Burnet's collecting practices demonstrate the possibilities open to South Sea Company employees who were determined to use their access to Spanish America to survey the natural resources and natural curiosities of the region.[11]

Over the course of nearly fifteen years, Burnet gathered a wide-ranging collection of specimens from Spanish America, West Africa, and the Caribbean. Rather than amass his own cabinet of curiosities, Burnet gave the *naturalia* he collected to his British correspondents. Hans Sloane, James Petiver, and James Douglas, all medical men and members of the Royal Society of London, were the primary beneficiaries of the physician's efforts. Burnet's habit of referring collectively to the specimens he gathered makes it impossible to fully determine the extent of his collections. Yet his correspondence, along with manuscript catalogues to Sloane's museum, reveals the diversity of the objects he gathered.

The sixty-two specimens that can be identified included medicaments, dyes, culinary plants, shells, astronomical observations, and man-made curiosities.[12] Seventeen of the objects, or almost 30 per cent, were plants or minerals reported to have medicinal virtues, as one might expect one medical man to send to another. For example, Burnet gathered specimens of *terra macomachi*, a cure for ringworms, from Cartagena, *raiz rouge*, used to stop fluxes, from Buenos Aires, and counter-poisons from Jamaica.[13] But Burnet certainly did not confine himself to medicaments. His collection contained more than twenty animals and insects, including butterflies, a wingless cockroach, a marine caterpillar, a variety of fish, a pair of sloths, and, of course, an armadillo. The Portobellan scorpion that Burnet sent to Sloane enabled the metropolitan naturalist to compare the Jamaican insect with its Portobellan counterpart. In his natural history of Jamaica, Sloane concluded that the two were different species based on the specimens he had received from Burnet.[14]

Burnet also gathered four samples of minerals, including a large amethyst and what he believed was a type of gold. Such specimens manifested British interest in the mineral riches of Spanish America. Similarly, the four specimens of plants renowned as dyes that Burnet collected reflected British interest in dyes indigenous to a region already famed for cochineal. And unlike the mineral wealth of Spanish territories, dyes and other types of "green gold" might easily be transported out of Spanish America and introduced into cultivation in British colonies.[15]

Like dyes, medicaments were a frequent focus of Burnet's efforts to discover green gold in Spanish America. Shortly after arriving in Cartagena, Burnet sent Sloane samples of four medicaments popular among local residents. "I should be glad to know if any of these things be Esteemed in England," he wrote, "& whither a quantity of the Earths or Balsam would sell." The South Sea Company physician frequently complained about the inadequacy of his salary and his limited opportunities to increase his income through private practice. He hoped that the minerals and balsams he sent to Sloane would solve his financial troubles if, like other medicines imported from Spanish territories, they commanded high prices in Britain. Based on the surviving correspondence, it seems that Burnet never received a response from Sloane about whether the medicaments he sent might sell.[16]

The dyes and drugs Burnet investigated would also have been of interest to the South Sea Company, given the high prices Spanish commodities commanded in British markets. Furthermore, since Spanish buyers could pay for *asiento* slaves in cochineal, cinchona, indigo, or other natural commodities, the company's profits might depend on its employees' command of natural knowledge. The directors of the South Sea Company frequently worried that their factors might unknowingly exchange slaves for inferior or even counterfeit natural commodities. They frequently berated factors who misjudged the quality of dyes and drugs exported to Britain. In 1717, concern over such issues led the directors to send John Hoskins, an expert on dyes, to Vera Cruz. They explained that he would "assist our Factory at Vera Cruz in viewing & Examining Cochineal Indico, and other Dying War[e]s & Drugs." The company's directors hoped that under Hoskins's tutelage the factors at Vera Cruz could learn to distinguish good-quality dyes and drugs from impostures. Hoskins brought with him samples of Spanish American commodities, along with strict instructions that any drugs or dyes purchased by the factory's agents needed to be of at least equal quality to the samples he carried.[17]

As the Court of Directors' instructions to Hoskins suggested, they were primarily interested in natural knowledge relating to medicines and dyes. Petiver reflected these priorities when he advised another South

Sea Company surgeon that "nothing can better or sooner recommend you to the South Sea Company's Favour or service than Communications" related to medicines and dyes. As evidence, he pointed to Burnet, whom he claimed owed his position in Portobelo to the collections he had made while a slave ship surgeon on the *Wiltshire*. According to Petiver, investigating Spanish American natural commodities could be a path to preferment and promotion within the South Sea Company. For the South Sea Company's Court of Directors, the value of natural historical investigations lay in the chance that they might discover new natural commodities and thereby improve the company's bottom line.[18]

Burnet's exchange of medicaments and natural curiosities with his British correspondents paralleled similar exchanges among medical men and naturalists throughout the early modern world. A few objects in his collection, however, were more directly tied to his role as a physician in the slave trade. Burnet's collection included human anatomical specimens, most likely from enslaved Africans for whose medical care he was responsible. While a slave ship surgeon on the *Wiltshire* in 1715, Burnet collected polyps that he removed from the hands of two Africans as well as what he described as "An Abortive Negroe." He also preserved "a worm of about 4 foot long ... taken out of the leg of a person in Guinea." A few months after Burnet's return to London, the physician Douglas displayed the worm at the Royal Society's meeting of 21 June 1716. There are no further details about the individuals from whom Burnet obtained these specimens, nor is there any indication as to how he obtained them. The historical record simply describes them as having come from individuals of African descent. However, Burnet's position as a slave ship surgeon suggests that they were likely from captive Africans for whose medical care he was responsible during the months that the *Wiltshire* was in West Africa and at sea.[19]

The human specimens in Burnet's collection can, in part, be understood in the context of his personal interest in medical knowledge, as well as the interest it held for many in early-eighteenth-century Britain. Beginning in the sixteenth century, anatomical specimens and human remains were often included in European cabinets of curiosities. Understandably, such objects were particularly common in collections belonging to medical men. By 1753, Sloane's museum included more than 750 "Humana" specimens. Skeletons, anatomical specimens, and human curiosities were also frequently displayed and discussed at meetings of the Royal Society. Fascination with anatomy and anatomical specimens in the early eighteenth century transcended the august circles of the

Royal Society and the Royal College of Physicians. Anita Guerrini has documented the popularity of anatomical lectures among Londoners who had no medical training, who sought them out as a form of entertainment. The inclusion of human anatomical specimens in Burnet's collection was therefore in keeping with this more generalized interest in anatomy and medical knowledge.[20]

However, it is also important to consider the specific context in which Burnet's specimens were gathered. In recent decades, scholars of early modern science and medicine have emphasized that the contingencies of place, including its social, cultural, and geographical contexts, influence the natural and medical knowledge produced in that place.[21] So if we take the networks of the transatlantic slave trade as a space of natural history, then, like all localities of science, its material and cultural contexts shaped and were shaped by the resulting natural knowledge.

An inherent part of the context in which Burnet gathered natural historical objects was the violence, coercion, and expropriation that characterized the transatlantic slave trade.[22] The inclusion of human remains in Burnet's collection reflects, in part, this context. As scholarship on medical museums in Antebellum America has argued, human anatomical specimens of enslaved Africans reflected and reinforced the inequalities of power and the exploitation of black bodies fundamental to the chattel slave system and to the transatlantic slave trade.[23] James Delbourgo has examined similar objects in Hans Sloane's museum. These included human specimens from enslaved Africans, objects related to the violence of slavery such as nooses and whips, and other objects associated with resistance to slavery. Delbourgo urged scholars to understand these objects in their early-eighteenth-century context, and in particular to resist the urge to look to them for a coherent ideology of race or empire. He reminds us that for Sloane and his contemporaries these objects were not "self-evident horrors" but, more likely, "morally and politically indeterminate" and best understood through the idea of curiosity. By definition, curious objects were miscellaneous, so that a curious collection such as Sloane's might contain human remains alongside Roman coins, mechanical marvels, stuffed birds, and pressed plants. Curiosity placed particular value on objects that were rare, surprising, or illicit. Delbourgo suggests that many of the objects associated with slavery in Sloane's museum were in this last category. Therefore, Sloane's collection of human remains and artefacts associated with slavery did not necessarily signal a stance on slavery, the slave trade, or colonialism.[24]

Even if these objects cannot be read for a coherent ideology of race or a moral stance on slavery, their very presence in European museums does testify to the exploitation, violence, and death that characterized the slave ship and to the powerful influence of global commerce on natural history. And if the meaning of such objects for Sloane and Burnet might have been morally ambiguous, it is hard to imagine that that would have been the case for the enslaved Africans onboard the *Wiltshire.*

Collecting the *Asiento*

The specific context of Burnet's collecting practices shaped his pursuit of natural history in other ways as well. The slave trade, specifically in this case the *asiento* trade, influenced where, as well as what, he collected. While Burnet and other Britons exploited the access to Spanish America provided by the slave trade, such access had its limits. The provenance of items Burnet collected suggests that his collecting efforts were confined to the immediate vicinity of the Cartagena and Portobelo factories where he worked; none of the objects were gathered farther afield. The specimens' provenance paralleled the circumscribed geography of British trade routes to Spanish America.

Another surgeon working for the South Sea Company, William Houstoun, similarly discovered the outer limits of his access to Spanish America when he tried to investigate the medicament jalap in 1730. The jalap root had long been a popular medicine in Britain, but no one was certain from which plant it was derived. Houstoun initially thought that since jalap was exported from Vera Cruz, he could determine its botanical identity during one of his trips to the port town as ship surgeon on the company's sloop delivering slaves from Jamaica. But to his disappointment, he discovered that he "could learn nothing" there about the botanical identity of the root. Undeterred, Houstoun vowed to visit the eponymous province where the root was grown the next time the *asiento* trade brought him to New Spain. However, the governor denied him permission to travel to the province. Ultimately, the ship surgeon hired a Native American to travel to the province on his behalf and gather seedlings of the plant. Houstoun smuggled these plants out of Vera Cruz and transplanted them into a garden belonging to a friend in Jamaica. Seeds from the transplanted jalap plants were eventually grown in the Chelsea Physic Garden and other British gardens. Although Houstoun found an alternative means of acquiring jalap plants, his inability to collect them himself reflected the geographical boundaries of British collecting in Spanish America under the cover of the slave trade.[25]

As much as on its geography, collectors such as Houstoun and Burnet relied upon the *asiento*'s commercial infrastructure to facilitate the transportation of their seeds, specimens, and observations back to Britain. They entrusted letters and specimens to various ship surgeons and captains working for the company. For example, during Burnet's first year as the factory surgeon at Cartagena, he acquired a female sloth and her offspring. Unfortunately, the animals died before the physician could arrange their transport across the Atlantic. Knowing that British naturalists would be almost as happy with a properly preserved specimen as a living one, Burnet stuffed the mother's skin and placed the juvenile sloth in a jar of spirits. He then packed the two specimens and directed the package to the attention of Daniel Westcomb, the South Sea Company's secretary in London. Burnet trusted that company agents, ship captains, and sailors who handled the package on its long journey from South America to Britain would take additional care with a package addressed to the influential company official. Burnet's faith in the infrastructure of the *asiento* trade paid off; with Westcomb acting as an intermediary, the two preserved sloths successfully reached Sloane, who added them to his growing museum.[26]

Like all of the specimens and letters Burnet sent to Britain, the sloths' travels included a stop in Jamaica. Within the commercial networks of the *asiento* trade, Jamaica played a uniquely central role. Three-quarters of the sixty thousand enslaved Africans whom the South Sea Company delivered to Spanish America were transshipped from the British Caribbean, rather than coming directly from Africa. Most of these slaves passed through the company's entrepôt in Jamaica. Jamaica's centrality to the South Sea Company's operations in the New World was also reflected in the company's internal hierarchies. The Jamaican agents were the company's top-ranking officials in the New World. Their senior position reflected the vital importance of Jamaica to the South Sea Company's operations in the Americas.[27]

Jamaica and the company's agents on the island played a similarly pivotal role facilitating the efforts of South Sea Company employees engaged in natural history. Burnet and Houstoun relied upon the company's agents in Jamaica to arrange transportation for their collections, and to forward the letters and packages sent in return by European naturalists. When his ship the *Assiento* returned to the British island, Houstoun entrusted his most recent collections to the safe keeping of

Jamaican colonists, including the South Sea Company's Jamaican agents. The ship surgeon often divided his Spanish American plants and seeds between acquaintances living in different parts of the island, hoping that the plants would thrive in at least one of Jamaica's microclimates. Burnet also relied upon the company's agents in Jamaica to arrange transportation for his collections as well as to undertake personal favours such as repairing his pistol. The agents who made such arrangements on Burnet's behalf were personal acquaintances rather than simply commercial contacts. Like most servants of the South Sea Company, the physician spent months on the island at numerous points in his career, usually waiting for the arrival of a company vessel that could convey him to Spanish America or one that would give him passage back to Britain. Burnet's collections indicate that he was not idle during such times. Over 20 per cent of his specimens came from the British Caribbean, and most of these were from Jamaica. Similarly, Jamaican plants represented a significant focus of Houstoun's botanical study. The ship surgeon observed over 40 per cent of the 661 plants described in his unpublished botanical text while in Jamaica. The South Sea Company's agents and factors, as much as its trade routes, facilitated the natural historical investigations of individuals such as Burnet and Houstoun.[28]

Conclusions

The seeds, sloths, and other specimens gathered by Britons in Spanish America bear traces of the *asiento* trade that made their collection possible. Dyes and drugs feature prominently among such collections, reflecting the shared interests of naturalists and the South Sea Company. The provenance of such specimens, collected in close proximity to South Sea Company slaving factories, and their transportation on company vessels with the assistance of company employees, reflected the geography and infrastructure of the *asiento* trade. The violence and exploitation of black bodies that lay at the heart of that trade was reflected in Burnet's collection, particularly in specimens such as the human remains he gathered while a slave ship surgeon on the *Wiltshire.*

During the fifteen years Burnet worked for the South Sea Company, he doggedly searched for ways to make his fortune. Exchanging scientific specimens and observations with prominent British naturalists can be understood as one strategy for achieving this goal. Well-connected friends in Britain such as Sloane could plead his case with the South Sea Company's Court of Directors for promotion or leniency. At multiple points in his career, Burnet asked to be promoted to the better-paid position of factor. Even with Sloane's lobbying on his behalf, he was told each time that company policy forbade a factory surgeon from becoming a factor. In 1722, shortly after arriving in Cartagena, the physician tried a different tack. He begged Sloane "would use your Interests with the Court of Directors for the enlarging my Salary or my advancement in their service, for it is thoroughing [throwing] away my time to serve for my present salary." The South Sea Company physician argued that the job of factory surgeon, if faithfully performed, was much more work than that of factor and that it was in the company's interest to compensate him accordingly. "The diligent discharge of a Physicians duty may save the life of seven or eight slaves in each Cargo which otherways might die & that being saved or lost farr exceeds his Sallary." Like his many requests for promotion to factor, Burnet's attempt to increase his compensation by appealing to the directors' sense of enslaved Africans as commodities failed.[29]

Despite Sloane's efforts, Burnet never received the increased salary or promotion to factor that he so desired. His ultimate decision to become a Spanish agent can be understood in light of his disappointed ambitions. In 1728, when he was part of the British delegation to the Congress of Soissons called to negotiate the end of the Anglo-Spanish War, Burnet began to secretly provide the Spanish government with evidence against the South Sea Company. The documents Burnet furnished, alongside his own testimony, helped prove the truth of Spanish allegations that the South Sea Company had consistently violated the *asiento* agreement through contraband trading, by bribing Spanish officials, and by allowing its employees to engage in private trading. The physician provided information about the company's illicit trading practices in exchange for a pension and a position as *médico de cámara* from the Spanish crown. Yet his new allegiance to Spain did not preclude his participation in the networks of British science. In the 1730s, Burnet continued to correspond with Sloane and the Royal Society of London, sending natural curiosities and reports on the latest scientific activities in his new home in Madrid.[30]

The *asiento* trade enabled a few South Sea Company employees such as Burnet to investigate first-hand the storied natural wonders of Spanish America. The specimens they collected and the observations they made shaped the production of natural knowledge about the region. Specimens and observations collected by Burnet, for example, were referenced in Sloane's natural history of Jamaica and were the basis of Douglas's essays on ipecacuanha (a medicament) and armadillos that he

presented to the Royal Society. In another instance, astronomical observations made by a Spanish American colonist and sent to the Royal Society by Burnet became the basis of Edmond Halley's calculation of the longitude of Cartagena, published in *Philosophical Transactions* in 1723. However, Burnet's role as an intermediary is absent from the published record, and at least through the 1720s, he seems to have been unaware that the observations even reached the Royal Society.[31]

Similarly, observations and specimens sent by Burnet were occasionally interpreted in ways quite different from what he intended. For example, Burnet sent Sloane drawings and botanical descriptions of a Portobellan plant known locally as the blood flower to support his contention that it was the true ipecacuanha. Sloane, however, used the observations and drawings he received from Burnet to prove the opposite. Armed with Burnet's drawing, along with descriptions of ipecacuanha published in herbals and his own specimens from Jamaica, Sloane convinced the censors of the College of Physicians and the wardens of the Society of Apothecaries that the blood flower was *not* the true ipecacuanha. Based on this evidence, both groups ordered their members "to condemn and destroy such a dangerous Root" whenever it was found.[32]

Burnet's collecting practices were part of a broader pattern by which European naturalists exploited the routes and personnel of the slave trade in order to add specimens to their museums and to facilitate their studies of the natural world. They also indicate the deep connections between science and the inhuman commerce of slaving that we have only begun to explore. In the British case, specimens were gathered on slave ships, at British slaving factories in West Africa, in British American ports where slaves were disembarked, and in the parts of Spanish America where the *asiento* extended the routes of British slaving. Many of the objects collected through the routes of the British slave trade in the early eighteenth century eventually became part of Sloane's museum. They thus became part of the founding collection of the British Museum after the naturalist's death, and in the late nineteenth century became part of the collections of the Natural History Museum in South Kensington. Some of these specimens, especially the more stable herbarium specimens, can be found there today, where they remain a valuable resource for those interested in taxonomy, biodiversity, and any number of related questions. Specimens gathered by Burnet, Houstoun, and other Britons employed in the British slave trade to Spanish America also became part of the collections belonging to other British scientific institutions, including the Oxford Herbarium, the Chelsea Physic Garden, and the

Royal Society. As such, they continued to contribute to the production of natural knowledge long after the *asiento* ended. Such legacies suggest we should count dozens of Vera Cruz plants, smuggled jalap roots, and stuffed armadillos among the profits of the *asiento* trade.[33]

ACKNOWLEDGMENTS

This chapter is based upon work supported by the National Science Foundation under Grant Number 1455679.

NOTES

1 James Petiver to James Douglas, 30 March 30, 1716, MS Hunter D513, University of Glasgow Special Collections; James Douglas, "The Description and Natural History of the Animal called Armadillo or the hog in armour from South America or the little American hog in Armour, by J.D.," MS Hunter D516, University of Glasgow Special Collections; *Voyages: The Trans-Atlantic Slave Trade Database*, http://slavevoyages.org (voyage ID 76318).

2 Petiver to Douglas, 30 March 30, 1716, MS Hunter D513, University of Glasgow Special Collections.

3 James Douglas, "The Description and Natural History of the…Armadillo"; 5 April 1716 and 21 June 1716, Journal Books of Scientific Meetings, Collections from the Royal Society, 1660–1800, vol. 11, 116, 131.

4 Jordan Kellman, "Nature, Networks, and Expert Testimony in the Colonial Atlantic: The Case of Cochineal," *Atlantic Studies* 7, no. 4 (December 2010): 383–6; Amy Butler Greenfield, *A Perfect Red: Empire, Espionage, and the Quest for the Color of Desire* (New York: Harper, 2005). Cochineal is made from the wingless females of the insect *Dactylopius coccus.*

5 "Account of Books," *Philosophical Transactions* 20, no. 240 (1698): 196–200; "Inquires for Suratte and Other Parts of the East-Indies," *Philosophical Transactions* 2, no. 23 (1666–67): 422; Phyllis Allen, "The Royal Society and Latin America as Reflected in the Philosophical Transactions, 1665–1730," *Isis* 37, nos. 3–4 (July 1947): 132–8.

6 In the Treaty of Tordesillas, Spain and Portugal, with the blessing of the papacy, drew a line dividing the world between them. Spain staked claim to the western side of the line, containing the newly discovered Americas, while Portugal claimed sovereignty over Africa and most of Asia.

7 Arthur S. Aiton, "The Asiento Treaty as Reflected in the Papers of Lord Shelburne," *Hispanic American Historical Review* 8, no. 2 (May 1928):

167–8; Colin A. Palmer, *Human Cargoes: The British Slave Trade to Spanish America, 1700–1739* (Urbana: University of Illinois Press, 1981), esp. 3–16; Nuala Zahedieh, "The Merchants of Port Royal, Jamaica, and the Spanish Contraband Trade, 1655–1692," *William and Mary Quarterly* 43, no. 4 (October 1986): 570–93.

8 Lewis Melville, *The South Sea Bubble* (1921; repr., New York, 1968), 14; Aiton, "The Asiento Treaty," 167–77; Elizabeth Donnan, "The Early Days of the South Sea Company, 1711–1718," *Journal of Economic and Business History* 2, no. 3 (May 1930): 419–50; Adrian Finucane, "The South Sea Company and Anglo-Spanish Connections, 1713–1739" (PhD diss., Harvard University, 2010); Palmer, *Human Cargoes*; Zahedieh, "The Merchants of Port Royal," 589–91; "MINUTES of the Court of Directors of the Governor and Company of Merchants of Great Britain Trading to the South Seas," 28 October 1713, South Sea Company Papers, vol. 1, Add. MS 25495, 189–90, British Library. Although the asiento was supposed to last until 1743, it ended with, and partly caused, the War of Jenkins' Ear in 1739.

9 Vera Lee Brown, "The South Sea Company and Contraband Trade," *American Historical Review* 31, no. 4 (July 1926): 662–78; Willem Klooster, "Inter-Imperial Smuggling in the Americas, 1600–1800," in *Soundings in Atlantic History: Latent Strutures and Intellectual Currents, 1500–1825*, ed. Bernard Bailyn and Patricia L. Denault (Cambridge, MA: Harvard University Press, 2009), 165–6, 169; George H. Nelson, "Contraband Trade under the Asiento, 1730–1739," *American Historical Review* 51, no. 1 (October 1945): 55–67; Gregory O'Malley, *Final Passages: The Intercolonial Slave Trade of British America, 1619–1807* (Chapel Hill: University of North Carolina Press, 2014), 240–1; Palmer, *Human Cargoes*, 9–11; Geoffrey J. Walker, *Spanish Politics and Imperial Trade, 1700–1789* (Bloomington: Indiana University Press, 1979), 68–72.

10 As a university-educated physician, Burnet had an unusually high level of education for a slave ship surgeon. Most surgeons employed in the slave trade were trained as surgeons, not physicians, and were generally considered by contemporaries to be poorly trained ones at that. Stephen D. Behrendt, "The Captains of the British Slave Trade, 1785–1807," *Transactions of the Historical Society of Lancashire and Cheshire* 40 (1991): 120n61.

11 Brown, "The South Sea Company," 670. For the impact of the War of the Quadruple Alliance on the asiento trade, see Finucane, "The South Sea Company," 95–7.

12 In cases where Burnet may have sent duplicates – for example, the "three sucking fishes" he collected in Guinea – I have counted the entire set as

one specimen. The objects collected by Burnet have been identified using the following sources: John Burnet to James Petiver, 26 December 26, 1716, Sloane MS 3322, f. 97; John Burnet to James Petiver, 16 April 1718, Sloane MS 4065, f. 285, British Library; John Burnet to Hans Sloane, 6 April 1722, Sloane MS 4046, f. 227r–228v, British Library; John Burnet to Hans Sloane, September 1722, Sloane MS 4046, f. 287–8, British Library; John Burnet to Hans Sloane, 6 August 1723, Sloane MS 4047, f. 29, British Library; John Burnet to unknown addressee, 14 May 1716, Sloane MS 4065, f.248r; Hans Sloane, *A Voyage to the Islands Madera, Barbados, Nieves, S. Christophers and JAMAICA, with the Natural History of the Herbs and Trees, Four-footed Beasts, …* vol. 2 (London, 1725); "List of plants received from John Burnett," Sloane MS 4072, f. 295r, British Library; Hans Sloane, Catalogue of Minerals, 3 vols., Palaeonotology Library, MSS SLO, Natural History Museum, London; Hans Sloane, Insects Catalogue, 2 vols., Entomology Library, Natural History Museum, London; Hans Sloane, Miscellanies Catalogue, Centre of Anthropology, Department of Africa, Oceania, and the Americas, British Museum; Hans Sloane, Vegetable and Vegetable Substances: being the original register of the plant collections of Sir Hans Sloane excluding the Herbarium, arranged in the order of their acquisition, 3 vols., Botany Library, Natural History Museum, London.

13 John Burnet to James Petiver, 26 December 1716, Sloane MS 3322, f. 97; John Burnet to Hans Sloane, 6 April 1722, Sloane MS 4046, f. 227r, British Library; Hans Sloane, Vegetable and Vegetable Substances, vol. 3, f. 797; "List of plants received from John Burnett," Sloane 4072, f. 295r, British Library.

14 For "scorpion," see Hans Sloane, "Insects Catalogue," vol. 2, 185, Entomology Library, Natural History Museum, London; Sloane, *A Voyage to the Islands,* vol. 2, 198.

15 Hans Sloane, Catalogue of Minerals, vol. 1, 160, Palaeonotology Library, MSS SLO, Natural History Museum, London; Hans Sloane, Catalogue of Minerals, vol. 2, 2, Palaeonotology Library, MSS SLO, Natural History Museum, London; Hans Sloane, Catalogue of Minerals, vol. 3a [unpaginated], Palaeonotology Library, MSS SLO, Natural History Museum, London. For "green gold," see Londa Schiebinger, *Plants and Empire: Colonial Bioprospecting in the Atlantic World* (Cambridge, MA: Harvard University Press, 2004), 7.

16 John Burnet to Hans Sloane, 6 April 1722, Sloane MS 4046, f. 227v, British Library.

17 "OFFICIAL copies of letters and instructions from the Court of Directors of the South Sea Company to their Factors abroad, persons in their

employ, and various public companies and officials," 12 July 1717, South Sea Company Papers, 7 vols., Add. MS 25563, vol. 2, f. 60v–61r, ("assist our Factory," 60v), British Library.

18 James Petiver to William Toller, 19 November 1716, Sloane MS 3340, f. 275v–276r, British Library.

19 "List of plants received from John Burnett," Sloane MS 4072, f. 295, British Library; John Burnet to [unknown addressee], 14 May 1716, Sloane MS 4065, f. 248r, British Library; Hans Sloane, "Insects Catalogue," vol. 2, 180, Entomology Library, Natural History Museum, London; 21 June 1716, Journal Books of Scientific Meetings, Collections from the Royal Society, 1660–1800, vol. 11, 131 ("a worm").

20 John H. Appleby, "Human Curiosities and the Royal Society, 1699–1751," *Notes and Records of the Royal Society of London* 50, no. 1 (January 1996): 13–27; Simon Chaplin, "Dissection and Display in Eighteenth-Century London," in *Anatomical Dissection in Enlightenment England and Beyond: Autopsy, Pathology, and Display*, ed. Piers Mitchell (Ashgate, 2012), 99; Simon Chaplin, "Nature Dissected, or Dissection Naturalized? The Case of John Hunter's Museum," *Museum and Society* 6, no. 2 (July 2008): 135–51; Anita Guerrini, "Anatomists and Entrepreneurs in Early Eighteenth-Century London," *Journal of the History of Medicine and Allied Sciences* 59, no. 2 (April 2004): 219–39. "Humana" specimens were "anatomical, pathological, or curious human specimens." Sloane's collection included 275 anatomical specimens and 41 fetuses. See Michael Day, "Humana: Anatomical, Pathological and Curious Human Specimens in Sloane's Museum," in *Sir Hans Sloane: Collector, Scientist, Antiquary, Founding Father of the British Museum*, ed. Arthur MacGregor (London: British Museum Press, 1994), 69–70.

21 See, for example, Paula Findlen, *Possessing Nature: Museums, Collecting, and Scientific Culture in Early Modern Italy* (Berkeley: University of California Press, 1994); Jan Golinski, *Making Natural Knowledge: Constructivism and the History of Science* (Cambridge: Cambridge University Press, 1998); Donna Haraway, "Situated Knowledges: The Science Question in Feminism and the Privilege of Partial Perspective," *Feminist Studies* 14 (1988): 575–99; David Livingston, *Putting Science in Its Place: Geographies of Scientific Knowledge* (Chicago: University of Chicago Press, 2003); Steven Shapin, "Placing the View from Nowhere: Historical and Sociological Problems in the Location of Science," *Transactions of the Institute of British Geographers* 23 (1998): 5–12; Charles W. Withers, *Placing the Enlightenment: Thinking Geographically about the Age of Reason* (Chicago: University of Chicago Press, 2007).

22 The literature on violence, terror, and coercion on the slave ship is vast. For a start see Sowande' Mustakeem, "'She Must Go Overboard & Shall Go

Overboard': Diseased Bodies and the Spectacle of Murder at Sea," *Atlantic Studies* 8, no. 3 (2011): 301–16; Marcus Rediker, *The Slave Ship: A Human History* (New York: Penguin, 2007); Rediker, "History from Below the Water Line: Sharks and the Atlantic Slave Trade," *Atlantic Studies* 5, no. 2 (August 2008): 285–97.

23 Todd Savitt, "The Use of Blacks for Medical Experimentation and Demonstration in the Old South," *Journal of Southern History* 48, no. 3 (1982): 331–48; Ann Fabian, *The Skull Collectors: Race, Science, and America's Unburied Dead* (Chicago: University of Chicago Press, 2010); Stephen C. Kenny, "The Development of Medical Museums in the Antebellum American South: Slave Bodies in Networks of Anatomical Exchange," *Bulletin of the History of Medicine* 87, no.1 (2013): 32–62.

24 James Delbourgo, "Slavery in the Cabinet of Curiosities: Hans Sloane's Atlantic World" (2007), www.britishmuseum.org/pdf/delbourgo%20 essay.pdf. See also Katie Whitaker, "The Culture of Curiosity," in *Cultures of Natural History*, ed. Lisa Jardine, J.A. Secord, and E.C. Spary (Cambridge: Cambridge University Press, 1996), 75–91.

25 William Houstoun to Hans Sloane, 9 December 1730, Sloane MS 4051, f. 141r, British Library; William Houstoun to Hans Sloane, 5 March 1731, Sloane MS 4052, f. 82r–82v, British Library; Philip Miller, *The Gardeners Dictionary; Containing the Methods of Cultivating and Improving All Sorts Of Trees, Plants, and Flowers*, 8th ed. (London, 1768), unpaginated; Bernard Romans, *A concise natural history of East and West Florida* (New York, 1775), 154. Unfortunately, the jalap plants that Houstoun introduced to Jamaica were destroyed by hogs when he was absent from the island.

26 John Burnet to Hans Sloane, 6 April 1722, Sloane MS 4046, f. 227v ("skin stuffed" f. 227v), British Library; John Burnet to Hans Sloane, September 1722, Sloane MS 4046, f. 287–8, British Library; John Burnet to Hans Sloane, 6 August 1723, Sloane MS 4047, f. 29r–29v, British Library.

27 O'Malley, *Final Passages*, 221, 232–6.

28 Ten of the forty-eight items in Burnet's collection for which the provenance is known came from the Caribbean. Seven of these came from Jamaica and three from unspecified locations in the British West Indies. Houstoun observed 293 of the 661 plants he described in his "Catalogus Plantarum" while in Jamaica. Some of these plants were likely collected between December 1732 and August 1733, when Houstoun was in the region as a traveling naturalist rather than as a slave ship surgeon. For Houstoun's collection see William Houstoun, "Catalogus Plantarum in America observatarum," in *Botanical manuscripts and drawings of plants collected in Central America, Jamaica and Cuba, c. 1730–33*, MSS Banks Coll Hou, Natural History Museum, London.

29 For "diligent discharge" see John Burnet to Hans Sloane, 6 April 1722, Sloane MS 4046, f. 228r–228v, British Library. For requests for a promotion or a raise see John Burnet to Hans Sloane, 30 November 1716, Sloane MS 4044, f. 250, British Library; "Official copies of letters and instructions from the Court of Directors of the South Sea Company to their Factors abroad," 30 April 1718, South Sea Company Papers, Add. MS 25,563, f. 164r, British Library; John Burnet to Hans Sloane, 6 August 1723, Sloane MS 4047, f. 29v, British Library; John Burnet to Hans Sloane, 24 February 1724, Sloane MS 4047, f. 323v–324r, British Library; John Burnet to Hans Sloane, 17 March 1725, Sloane MS 4047, f. 329r–330r, British Library; John Burnet to Hans Sloane, 4 February 1728, Sloane MS 4050 f. 54, British Library. For requests for leniency see "Official copies of letters and instructions from the Court of Directors of the South Sea Company to their Factors abroad," Dec. 12, 1723, South Sea Company Papers, Add. MS 25,564, f. 8v, British Library; John Burnet to Hans Sloane, 2 April [1724?], Sloane MS 4047, f. 164r, British Library; John Burnet to Hans Sloane, 7 April 1725, Sloane MS 4047, British Library, London, f. 333v; John Burnet to Hans Sloane, 5 January 1726, Sloane MS 4048, f. 120, British Library.

30 Brown, "South Sea Company," 662–78; John Burnet to Hans Sloane, 11 April 1733, Sloane MS 4052, f. 239, British Library; John Burnet to Hans Sloane, 30 October 1734, Sloane MS 4053, f. 363r–363r; John Burnet to Hans Sloane, 7 April 1736, Sloane MS 4055, f. 307, British Library; John Burnet to Hans Sloane, 10 October 1736, Sloane MS 4054, f. 314r–315v, British Library; John Burnet to Hans Sloane, 2 July 1736, Sloane MS 4054, f. 266, British Library; John Burnet to Hans Sloane, 10 October 1736, Sloane MS 4054, f. 314, British Library; John Burnet to Hans Sloane, 13 May 1737, Sloane MS 4055, f. 103, British Library; John Burnet to Hans Sloane, 8 July 1737, Sloane MS 4055, f. 129, British Library; John Burnet to Hans Sloane, 11 August 1737, Sloane MS 4055, f. 214, British Library; 8 July 1736, Journal Books of Scientific Meetings, Collections from the Royal Society, 1660–1800, vol. 15, 368.

31 Sloane, *A Voyage to the Islands*, vol. 2 (London, 1725); James Douglas, "A short account of the different kinds of Ipecacuanha," MS Hunter D422, University of Glasgow Special Collections; James Douglas, "Description and Natural History of the … Armadillo"; Edmond Halley, "The Longitude of Carthagena in America," *Philosophical Transactions* 32 (1722–23): 237–238; John Burnet to Hans Sloane, September 1722, Sloane MS 4046, f. 287–8, British Library; John Burnet to Hans Sloane, 6 August 1723, Sloane MS 4047, f. 29r–29v, British Library; John Burnet to Hans Sloane, 17 July 1725, Sloane MS 4048, f. 26, British Library; John Burnet to Hans Sloane, 5 January 1726, Sloane MS 4048, f. 120, British Library.

32 Sloane, *A Voyage to the Islands,* vol. 2, x–xii (quotation at xi). Eighteenth-century naturalists often preferred to work with images of flora and fauna rather than physical specimens. See James Delbourgo, "Sir Hans Sloane's Milk Chocolate and the Whole History of the Cacao," *Social Text* 29, no. 1 (Spring 2011): 82, 85–6.

33 C. Helen Brock, *Dr. James Douglas's Papers and Drawing in the Hunterian Collection, Glasgow University Library: A Handlist* (Glasgow, 1994); Raymond Phineas Stearns, *Science in the British Colonies* (Urbana: University of Illinois Press, 1970), 329; Miller, *The Gardeners Dictionary*; J.E. Dandy, *The Sloane Herbarium: An Annotated List of the* Horti Sicci *Composing it; with Biographical Accounts of the Principal Contributors* (London: British Museum, 1958), 88, 109–10, 139–40, 151, 165–8, 175–83, 230.

chapter six

From the Monumental to Minutiae: Serializing Polynesian Barkcloths in Eighteenth-Century Britain

BILLIE LYTHBERG

Fragile layers
so thin
the tapa is barely connected to its own self…
– Karlo Mila, "Paper Mulberry Secrets"[1]

The scholarship that maps the long eighteenth century's rich period of global maritime history is dominated by the British explorer Captain James Cook, not only because of his repeat visits to the Pacific and the publications that followed them but also because of his extensive, well-documented, and now widely dispersed collections. For many of the Pacific islands, the earliest extant examples of material culture are associated with the voyages of scientific exploration made by Cook and his crews in 1768–71 with *HMS Endeavour*; in 1772–75 with *HMS Resolution* and *HMS Adventure*; and in 1776–79 with *HMS Resolution* and *HMS Discovery*. For example, save a single barkcloth collected in Tahiti by Bougainville in 1768, Cook's are the first European voyages from which a corpus of Pacific barkcloths survive and can be identified.[2] This essay considers a series of sampler books made from Tahitian, Tongan, and Hawaiian barkcloths collected on Cook's voyages, which were first published in 1787 by a British bookseller named Alexander Shaw. Part catalogue, part collection, part technical document, Shaw's barkcloth books offer a fascinating window onto the rapid expansion of late-eighteenth-century British science to include Pacific territories, people, and "natural" and "artificial curiosities," all of which needed to be understood, categorized, and domesticated for a British (and wider European) audience. Published accounts and images made by explorers addressed this in part, drawing heavily on simile and metaphor to familiarize the unfamiliar.[3] The display of voyage artefacts in private cabinets and public exhibitions served as other means of knowledge circulation, materializing a "classic tenet of eighteenth-century thought": that artefacts bore authentic traces of those who had made and utilized them.[4] Shaw's innovation was that he bound actual voyage artefacts together with printed voyage accounts and a catalogue (promising and describing thirty-nine different barkcloth samples) in the easily distributed and intimate form offered by the book. With his serialization of Polynesian barkcloths, Shaw brought the very substance of South Seas encounter and exchange into the hands of eighteenth-century British society.

Beyond their significance as miniature collections of voyage artefacts designed for easy handling and circulation, these books offer a unique entrée to the collecting objectives of Cook and his crews and the gift prestation practices of the islanders they encountered. The potential to create barkcloth books emerged from the commercial concerns that shaped the behaviour of Cook and his men while in the field, as well as the subsequent distribution of their collections and written observations and the application of these to other ends. It was also predicated on a Polynesian propensity for gift exchange, which would be canonized in 1923 by the French anthropologist Marcel Mauss in his famous treatise *Essay sur le don* (1923–24; English translation: The *Gift: Forms and Functions of Exchange in Archaic Societies*, 1954), and which was engaged in by Cook, his predecessors, and successors as a means not only to build relationships and collections but also to secure the necessities of life on their lengthy voyages.

Shaw's books contain descriptions of some of these encounters, along with samples of cloth made from the inner bark of certain trees (often paper mulberry, *Broussonetia papyrifera*), which was soaked and beaten out into supple sheets and then felted or pasted together in single or multiple layers, and often decorated. In Tonga these are known as *ngatu*, in Hawai'i they are *kapa*, and in Tahiti they are *ahu*. In eighteenth-century Polynesia, barkcloth was the primary domestic textile and was also of great ceremonial significance. To barkcloth was attributed a particular propensity for managing and instantiating relationships (explained further below), and as such it was an essential part of formal gift exchanges by and between islanders. The varieties of barkcloth offered to Cook and his crew – and later incorporated into Shaw's barkcloth books – included fine gauzes from Tahiti, robust waterproof pieces from Tonga, and examples bearing patterns rather like the watermarks on British rag paper of the time, made with carved beaters from Hawai'i. Many of the books' samples are also decorated with washes and motifs applied using plant- and soil-based pigments.

For Shaw's book project, about 110 barkcloth specimens were cut into small rectangles or squares, mounted on rag paper pages, and assembled into quarto-sized volumes roughly 23 by 19 centimetres. According to a recent census,[5] at least sixty-six discrete versions survive of the books that Shaw caused to be called:

> *A catalogue of the different specimens of cloth collected in the three voyages of Captain Cook, to the southern hemisphere, with a particular account of the manner of the manufacturing the same in the various islands of the South Seas; partly extracted from Mr. Anderson and Reinhold Forster's observations, And the verbal Accounts of some of the most knowing of the Navigators: with some anecdotes that happened to them among the natives. Now properly arrainged and printed for Alexander Shaw, No. 379, Strand, London, MDCCLXXXVII.*

Some of their samples are as large as the pages they adhere to; others are barely larger than postage stamps. To the contemporary eye the decorated samples in particular resemble miniature and intact works of abstract art. Despite their diminution, the books are libraries of pristine examples of material culture, decorative arts, and design, which are today reinvigorating barkcloth and other textile making, inspiring contemporary artists, and providing grist for the mill of innovative textile creation, conservation, and performance and performativity projects.

The books first received scholarly attention in 1921 and since then have prompted research tracing their maker, the provenance of their contents, and the books themselves – many of which can be connected to well-known figures and collections – as well as comparing samples within and between volumes.[6] This essay frames Shaw's project of serialization as it emerged from Cook's collecting imperatives while in the Pacific, as well as the gift exchange practices of Polynesians that furnished barkcloth in sufficient quantities that a project like Shaw's became possible. Particular qualities of barkcloth and characteristics of their prestation are windows onto the worlds that Cook and his crews were being incorporated into and the ways in which barkcloths themselves helped shape relationships between the British and their hosts.

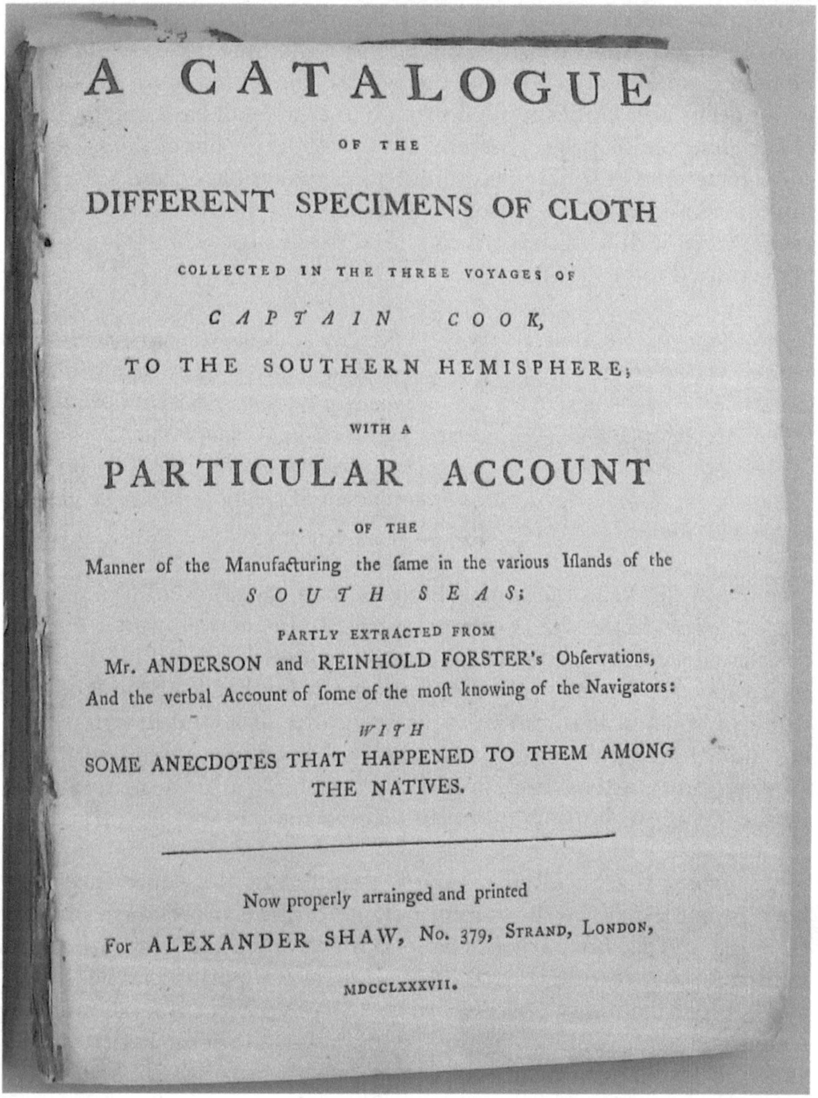

A CATALOGUE

OF THE

DIFFERENT SPECIMENS OF CLOTH

COLLECTED IN THE THREE VOYAGES OF

CAPTAIN COOK,

TO THE SOUTHERN HEMISPHERE;

WITH A

PARTICULAR ACCOUNT

OF THE

Manner of the Manufacturing the ſame in the various Iſlands of the

SOUTH SEAS;

PARTLY EXTRACTED FROM

Mr. ANDERSON and REINHOLD FORSTER's Obſervations,

And the verbal Account of ſome of the moſt knowing of the Navigators:

WITH

SOME ANECDOTES THAT HAPPENED TO THEM AMONG THE NATIVES.

Now properly arrainged and printed

For ALEXANDER SHAW, No. 379, STRAND, LONDON,

MDCCLXXXVII.

Figure 6.1 Title page, *A Catalogue of the Different Specimens of Cloth Collected in the Three Voyages of Captain Cook*, published by Alexander Shaw (1787). University of Pennsylvania Museum of Archaeology and Anthropology.

Alexander Shaw and His Barkcloth Books

Alexander Shaw was a London-based bookseller and "dealer in articles of natural history."[7] It is likely that he was an "amateur" in terms of his appreciation of Polynesian barkcloth. For years, Shaw was known to us only by the barkcloth books he published, his army records, and an advertisement he placed in the *London Chronicle* on 20–22 May 1783, in which he advertised his services as "an Agent for half pay" following his retirement after twenty-seven years' service as an army officer. He had joined the 60th Regiment as an ensign in 1756, and served Britain in the United States and Canada, fighting initially against the French and later against colonists during the American War of Independence; he became adjutant and lieutenant in the 4th Battalion in 1775, then captain in 1776. It is thought he may have sustained an injury during the defeat of the British forces in 1783, after which he returned to England.[8]

Shaw was clearly entrepreneurial: his *London Chronicle* advertisement notes that "[h]e further offers to buy, sell or exchange commissions." Thanks to the research of Erica Ryan and the digitization of eighteenth- and nineteenth-century newspaper and other resources, we now know him also as "Mr Alexander Shaw, bookseller, and dealer in articles of Natural History, late of the Strand, London" who died on 22 July 1807.[9] A sometime philanthropist who founded a school for orphans, Shaw ran various booksellers with his brother and in 1787 was trading from 379, The Strand. This is the address given in the final lines of his barkcloth books' printed pages, from which he wrote "may be had some fine specimens of the tree, with the bark."

The only extant documentation of Shaw's barkcloth book project, beyond the surviving books themselves, is this brief note:

> London the 24th
> May 1786.
>
> To go with the book of specemens of cloath.
>
> Sir, a full and Particular Account of this Cloath and the Manner of Manufacturing, is extracted from Capt[ain] Cook's voyages and other observations [...]m Be published and sent you I would [not det]ain this package, one day as I was v[ery anxi]o[u]s it should reach you soon I am with the Highest respect yours with [gra]titude. A Shaw.[10]

With this note, Shaw is announcing his assembly of a series of texts describing the manufacturing and use of barkcloths to accompany what we now know was his prototype barkcloth book. The note – handwritten, faded, stained and torn in places – survives because it was later pasted into the inside cover of a book, which we may infer is the very "book of specemens of cloath" his note announces. This book is now in the collection of Britain's Cambridge University Museum of Archaeology and Anthropology.[11] Quarto-sized and bound in unassuming board, the book itself seems a humble vessel for the treasures it contains: thirty-nine "specemens of cloath," cut from textiles made in the Pacific from beaten tree bark, purporting to have been collected on the then recent voyages of the British navigator Captain James Cook. The largest samples fit neatly onto one page; the smallest are mounted six to a page; some are barely larger than postage stamps. The book contains none of the textual accounts to which the note refers, but the description of them maps well onto the published title of the books proper. Shaw's note does not mention the catalogue his published series contain, and it may be that the possibility for this emerged later, perhaps from the note's recipient.

To whom did Shaw send his first compilation of cloth and associated texts? John Montrésor was a retired English military engineer who like Shaw had served in the 60th Regiment. Little more is known of their relationship, except for what we may intuit from Montrésor's signature inscribed in the upper left corner of the book now in Cambridge, the book to go with the note transcribed above, which it seems was addressed to him. Surely Montrésor was the first recipient of what Shaw later described in his published books' printed catalogue pages as "only select specimens for a few friends." We must assume that this prototype was met with enthusiasm, because the first instalment of his serializing project was published in 1787.

The publications themselves begin with the aforementioned wordy title page, with a dedication verso.[12] There follows "The Description": four pages offering "a particular account of the manner of the manufacturing the same in the various islands of the South Seas; partly extracted from Mr. Anderson and Reinhold Forster's observations, And the verbal Accounts of some of the most knowing of the Navigators: with some anecdotes that happened to them among the natives." This is followed by two pages of catalogue detailing thirty-nine samples: twenty from "Otaheite" (Tahiti);[13] fourteen from "The Sandwich Islands" (Hawaiian Islands), including two from the island of "Owyhee" (Hawai'i); four from "The Friendly Islands" (Tonga), including "New Amsterdam" (Tongatapu); and a single sample of lace bark from Jamaica "bought at the Duchess of Portland's sale."

For this printed component of his books, Shaw relied heavily on excerpts from works already published. He quotes liberally from William Anderson, whose ship journal was published in a single edition with those of James

Cook and James King.[14] Anderson had served on Cook's sloop the HMS *Resolution* as surgeon's mate on the second voyage, and as surgeon and naturalist on the third, before dying of consumption in 1778 while the *Resolution* was still in the Bering Sea. Further extracts were selected by Shaw from Johann Reinhold Forster's *Observations Made during a Voyage round the World* (1778), Forster having been one of Cook's naturalists aboard the *HMS Resolution* during the second voyage (see Heringman, this volume). Others Shaw claims to have received from unnamed "navigators." With this last claim, Shaw was inviting us to infer that he was well-connected and privy to information received either personally or via unpublished texts, possibly during the process of obtaining the barkcloths he sampled.[15]

Shaw's excerpts suggest that he was interested in compiling a technical document offering multiple accounts from different observers of the methods for manufacturing "cloth" in the "South Seas," including "Mr Anderson's account of the manner of making the cloth in the island of Tongataboo" (Tongatapu), and Atovi; Forster's more general account of barkcloth making in Polynesia with a focus on Tahiti; and an unnamed navigator's account of barkcloth making in "Huaheine" (Huahine, in French Polynesia). The last was presumably included because it referred to the lace trees of Jamaica – a lace-bark sample being the only specimen included in Shaw's books that is not from Polynesia. It is significant that with only minor differences in technique, Anderson's first account can still be applied to the contemporary procedures employed to make barkcloth from plant-based materials in Tonga;[16] whereas barkcloth making ceased in what we know now as French Polynesia and Hawai'i but is in a process of revival. Shaw's books provide the most easily accessible "survivors" of these artmaking complexes for contemporary makers.

Shaw ends his technical offerings with this advice:

> The reader is to observe, that many of the pieces aftermentioned, especially those of the coarser sort; measured above forty yards, and some had been seen to measure fifty; but these were few in number, as those of different colours seldom exceeded three or four: the breadth in general is various, from three to one and half yards.

Thereafter come the catalogue and samples. The catalogue entries are diverse: some offer scant detail, others offer detailed descriptions of the pieces' presentation to the British. Like the barkcloths that follow, they are fragments, some more diminutive than others. While these printed texts remain stable from book to book, the samples in only one of the sixty-six documented Shaw books (that one is now in the collection of the

Figure 6.2 Hawaiian *kapa* samples, from Shaw's barkcloth book (1787). University of Pennsylvania Museum of Archaeology and Anthropology. Photo by author.

State Library of New South Wales: DL 78/64) match precisely his printed list of contents. I have noted elsewhere that Shaw surely recognized when embarking on his assembly project the difficulty of matching so many small samples to his descriptions.[17] He seems to have made no attempt to number the specimens themselves, though in some books numbers have been added later. In most of the books the samples do not match either the order or the descriptions proposed by the catalogue, and in some, every sample has been inserted back to front. At the time these books were published, many volumes were sold as unbound blocks, to be bound by the purchaser – thus, a certain number of mishaps must have occurred with unpaginated pages. But the marbled paper boards used to bind so many of these suggest that at least some were bound prior to sale.[18] Presumably, Shaw did not work alone: a single book of samples bound in the same marble boards, but without his printed pages, suggests that an opportunistic apprentice compiled his own copy during the publication run.[19]

Perhaps we ought to imagine a bindery in some disarray, an assembly line in disorder, a tangle of European rag paper and Pacific barkcloth. Almost every Shaw book is unique and, in Ian Morrison's words, "located in a sort of no-man's land between cloth and paper – a European book, with its text printed on paper made from discarded clothing, containing samples of cloth-like paper made from the bark of trees."[20] As Shaw's catalogue informs us, some of these were themselves made from the very fabric of Tahitian underclothes – paper-clothing in collision with clothing-paper.

We might wonder what inspired Shaw to begin such a project. Was he aware of other "serialized" encounters: perhaps the sampler maps stitched by women depicting Cook's voyages around the globe,[21] including one made by Elizabeth Cook after her husband James's death, now in the collection of the National Maritime Museum in Sydney? These tame Cook's voyages for the delicate sensibilities of young women, bringing them into a domestic setting and scale. Might Shaw have held the same ambition? Or is it possible that he saw an earlier barkcloth compilation? Thanks to recent scholarly interest in the full spectrum of barkcloth samplers it is now possible to identify a forerunner to Shaw's publications – a sampler book of Tahitian barkcloth from the collection of the Duchess of Portland (from whom Shaw purports to have purchased his lacebark) made fifteen years before Shaw's, thus unsettling previously received wisdom about Shaw's primacy in this activity.[22]

Shedding light on the apparent disorder of the Shaw volumes, research has determined that three discrete issues make up Shaw's series, discernible by their differing arrays of barkcloths and watermarked paperstocks that help determine their time of manufacture.[23] Of these, one group corresponds roughly with Shaw's prototype book, which contains about half the specimens described in the catalogue, augmented by another set; a second group corresponds closely with the volume in the State Library of New South Wales; and a third contains a different set of specimens altogether. This suggests that the books, though all given a publication date of 1787 as printed on the title page, were assembled in three lots at different times. Did Shaw really intend to produce "only select specimens for a few friends," as his dedication states, but then make more on the strength of the books' popularity? Watermarks on the rag paper pages of one proposed "series" determine an assembly date post-1804,[24] possibly by Shaw's brother and business partner, Hary, after Shaw's death.[25] Furthermore, the catalogues appear to have been popular enough to prompt others to prepare their own. A possible series of four manuscript compilations thought to have been made after Shaw's, with hand-lettered title pages and similar contents, can be found in the British Museum, the Captain Cook Memorial Museum in Whitby, the National Library of Ireland, and the Mitchell Library of Australia. Research continues into whether or not these are a copycat "serialization."[26]

Other books suggest a barkcloth book version of "extra-illustration," also known as "grangerizing."[27] In 1958 the William L. Clements Library in Michigan acquired a particularly fascinating manuscript volume compiled by Thomas Pennant (1726–1798), a much-admired naturalist of the eighteenth century. Pennant's compilation comprises ninety-two barkcloth samples supplemented with rich ethnographic detail. It is believed that Pennant, inspired by Shaw's publication, compiled his own catalogue by obtaining barkcloth samples from every available source, including Shaw himself, and binding them together with a copy of Shaw's published essay – demonstrating perhaps that Shaw had a surplus of these samples to hand. Pennant then augmented this printed information with insights gleaned from several of Cook's crew and companions, noting in his own hand whence and from whom the samples were acquired and whatever information had been recorded about the use of the specimens by the "natives." Pennant's approach seems to demonstrate a carry-over from the fifteenth century, when the first printed books included hand-written and -wrought embellishments. Printed on vellum and decorated by hand, they replicated the look and feel of manuscripts.

Still more barkcloth books were compiled by enthusiasts, who snipped small pieces from Shaw's published volumes to create their own collections in miniature, or removed loose-leaf samples altogether. Whether presented as catalogues, incorporated into family albums, or kept as loose-leaf samples, these attest to the popularity of Shaw's books and the value of their samples; the late eighteenth century's affection for miniatures and extra-illustrated volumes; the fascination with the South Seas; and a desire to connect with "natives" in some way through the intimacy offered by cloth.

In later books such as the one at the Captain Cook Memorial Museum in Whitby – not a Shaw – samples clearly cut from the same cloth are attributed to geographically distinct locations, some of which did not have active barkcloth making at the time of Cook's visits. Moreover, the places to which they are assigned reflect the overlay of European names onto the great Pacific as well as nascent orthographies for the sounds of Polynesian languages. In these situations the samples are coerced into participation in a visual diary of a voyage – perhaps "proof" that the book's maker was there – rather than being representative of their actual places of origin.

Encountering the Pacific in the Eighteenth Century

When Cook first set sail from Plymouth in 1768, in what Anne Salmond has evocatively called "the wooden world of the *Endeavour*,"[28] he was embarking on an august scientific voyage as commander of the Royal Society expedition to observe the transit of Venus in Tahiti. He was also carrying "secret instructions" of a more territorial nature from the Admiralty (Royal Navy) for a mission to find the Great South Land, *Terra Australis* – the continent believed to exist if only as a counterweight to those in the Northern Hemisphere – and "with the Consent of the Natives to take possession of Convenient Situations in the Country in the Name of the King of Great Britain." The Admiralty perceived opportunities for economic expansion beyond land itself, and bestowed upon Cook the following imperative:

> You are also instructed to observe the Nature of the Soil, & the products thereof; the Beasts & Fowls that inhabit or Frequent it, the Fishes that are to be found in the Rivers or upon the coast & in what Plenty & in case you find any Mines, Minerals or valuable Stones, you are to bring home Specimens of each & also such Specimens of the Seeds of the Tree fruits & grains as you may be able to collect.[29]

Alongside these sealed and secret orders of the Admiralty, Cook received "hints" from the president of the Royal Society, James Douglas, 14th Earl of Morton (1702–1768), pertaining to the search for the mysterious southern continent and to the documentation of "valuable resources in the form of agricultural possibilities or minerals that might be evident," which should ideally include the vocabulary of names given by the indigenous inhabitants to their surroundings.[30] Medicinal plants and those used for dyes were also specifically requested. Morton described the appropriate treatment of the people that Cook and his crew might encounter, urging him to "exercise the utmost patience and forbearance" while among "the legal possessors of the several regions they inhabit."

Thus, we must imagine Cook embarking on a voyage with both overlapping and conflicting exploratory goals, steeped not only in the philosophical ideals of the Enlightenment exemplified by the Royal Society but also in the empire-building ambitions of the Admiralty. In service of both, he had clear instructions to describe, collect, and categorize all that he and his crew saw, experienced, and heard. All logbooks and journals resulting from the voyage were to be sealed and delivered to the Admiralty upon their return, and none of the crew were to speak of what they had experienced on the voyage until given permission (a directive contravened by some who instead published their own accounts from as early as 1771).[31]

Native plants and the "curiosities" made from them – such as barkcloth and the bast or inner bark of certain trees from which it is made – were of particular interest to the Royal Society, which had commissioned these voyages of scientific exploration with a view to economic exploitation. As Henare (Salmond) has explained, European expeditions to the Pacific were motivated by the potential for extraction of natural resources that could be used to make industrial commodities.[32] Based on a distinction contrived during the Renaissance, "when Europeans attempted to explain and so come to terms with the existence of a fourth continent – the New World – and decide on the significance of its inhabitants, flora, fauna and artificial curiosities," Cook and his companions were collecting and distinguishing between objects found in nature and objects crafted by people, which they called "artificial curiosities," even though a disciplinary distinction had yet to be drawn.

Their eye towards profit is reflected in their voyage accounts and inventories, in which they carefully listed, and described in detail, the different qualities of certain "types" of cloth, cord, and so on, in accordance with the mandate to identify potentially useful "manufactures." The expedition's agenda – at once economic and scientific – is manifest in the artefacts it acquired and in the status of these objects as "specimens" illustrating (among other things) various techniques of indigenous manufacture, often within a single object.

Cook's second and third expeditions to the Pacific would be similarly governed by two-part instructions. The Admiralty's sealed instructions called for a comprehensive exploration of the Pacific and Atlantic Oceans (including, on the third voyage, a search for the fabled Northwest Passage between the two). As with his first voyage, he was again required to "make scientific observations and collect natural specimens, and to show *every kind of civility and regard* to the natives, at the same time taking care not *to be surprised by them.*"[33] Notwithstanding his attempts to adhere to this advice, his third voyage was to be his final one, for he was killed in Hawai'i on 14 February 1779 during a skirmish that also claimed many Hawaiians' lives. His body could not be retrieved intact, but a portion of his thigh was eventually returned to his second-in-charge, Captain Clerke, wrapped in a piece of barkcloth. It was formally buried at sea in Kealakekua Bay, Hawai'i, a week after his death.[34] Thus, the shroud used to wrap his remains was precisely the sort of cloth on which Shaw's book project was based, offered in a ceremonial prestation and used in this way to contain Cook's *mana* or personal potency (further explained below).

A decade before his death, as Cook prepared to sail for the Pacific for the first time, a fellow of the Royal Society recorded that "[n]o people ever went to sea better fitted out for the purpose of Natural History."[35] As well as libraries, maps, scientific instruments, and all manner of devices for capturing and safely transporting natural specimens, Cook's ships carried cargoes of goods destined for trade with the people they would meet, to be exchanged for the foodstuffs and other supplies needed to keep their crews alive; this was in addition to "trifles" to exchange for natural and artificial curiosities. On Cook's second voyage – by which time, presumably, he had formed an idea of what might be most popular – the trade goods "to be exchanged for Refreshments with the Natives of such New discovered or unfrequented Countries as they may touch at, or to be distributed to them in presents towards obtaining their friendship, & winning them over to our Interest,"[36] included iron tools (adzes, axes, hatchets, chisels, saws, augers, hammers, knives, scissors, and tweezers), wire, nails, combs, beads, looking glasses, kettles and pots, grinding stones, cloth, old clothes, and sheets.[37] As they travelled they obtained goods that would prove even more valuable as exchange items, allowing them to engage in the trade of objects sourced from one group of islands with the inhabitants of others.[38] For example, fine white barkcloth sourced from Tahiti proved popular with the Māori inhabitants of what we now know as Aotearoa–New Zealand, where by the time of Cook's first visit in 1769 it was a scarce resource.

It has been suggested that a watercolour from this voyage – now known to have been painted by Tupaia, the navigator from Ra'iatea who joined the voyage – shows the "gentleman scholar" Joseph Banks exchanging a handkerchief-sized piece of barkcloth for a cooked lobster in New Zealand.[39] This painting has more to offer than a simple depiction of the exchange of goods: male members of the Tahitian religious sect known as *arioi*, to which Tupaia belonged, were often skilled in dyeing and decorating barkcloth, and an artistic exchange occurred whereby Tupaia was instructed in the use of watercolours and botanical illustrator and natural history artist Sydney Parkinson learned from him the names of Tahitian dyes and the plants from which they were made.[40] Some of the "watercolours" used by Tupaia may have been barkcloth dyes, demonstrating an artistic exchange beyond that already made apparent to us.[41] Thus the painting might be described as the seminal image of both gift and knowledge exchange between British and Polynesians.

Of course, Cook was not the first European to explore the Pacific and engage in exchanges with its inhabitants. Nearly 250 years prior, Ferdinand Magellan, a Portuguese navigator, had become the first documented European visitor to the Pacific; he made local contact at Puka-puka in the Tuamotu Archipelago in 1521. The first voyage from which accounts survive of meetings between Europeans and Polynesians was under the command of the Spanish navigator Alvaro de Mendaña de Neira, who arrived in what we now know as the Marquesas in 1595. Dutch navigators had sketched out the southern, western, and northern coasts of Australia, and Abel Tasman's 1642 voyage along the western coast of New Zealand had added an "enigmatic squiggle" to the maps Cook took with him.[42] Cook's own "findings" in the Pacific included an iron nail lashed by Tongans to a bone haft (now at the Pitt Rivers Museum, Oxford) and iron fragments in use as tools in Hawai'i.[43] The nail in the former artefact was believed to have been left in Tonga by Abel Tasman in 1643.[44] Through its return to the British, were Tongans demonstrating to their visitors the already *longue durée* of their relationship with Europe? As this volume's editors have noted in their introduction, European encounters on the global stage remained "sporadic and unpredictable" during this time – particularly, perhaps, for the islanders, whose gifting and exchange practices were predicated on an expectation of return, which could be delayed, both in terms of people returning to see them again and as gift reciprocation.

Through the prestation of ceremonial exchange goods, which often included barkcloth, Cook and his crews were being incorporated into worlds they could not have imagined. Shape was being given to relationships in particular ways, including through the exchange of clothing and cloth with cosmological associations.[45] As I have noted elsewhere, drawing on Anne D'Alleva[46] with regard to barkcloth prestations in Tahiti:

> Beginning with Wallis' visit to Tahiti in 1767, enduring *taio* friendships were instantiated by the exchange of names and garments; the first when Wallis' shipmaster George Robertson gave the "Great Woman" of Tahiti, Purea, a "Ruffeld shirt" and in return was dressed by her in a length of barkcloth. Thus shape was given to their relationship by clothing. Purea's actions recalled the shaping of Tahiti's formless god Tane by Ta'aroa, with various bark skins, and were invested with the *mana* she had as a direct descendant of the gods. Barkcloth in particular, and clothing more generally, was thus "an important nexus of social interaction" that "shaped relations of power between groups and individuals."[47]

When the *Endeavour* arrived in Tahiti, similar exchanges of barkcloth and European garments drew Cook and Joseph Banks into *taio* bonds with their hosts, and on subsequent voyages Cook's crew would experiment with the association materialized by Tahitian *ahu* and European bodies when they "bought some pieces of cloth of the country fabrick (*ahow's*), dressed in them, after the Taheitee fashion, to the infinite pleasure of the natives."[48]

Thus, it can be seen that the cosmological and relational power of barkcloth in a material sense relates to the intimacy of cloth with the body. This helps us understand why Cook's remains were returned wrapped in Hawaiian barkcloth prior to their burial at sea. When barkcloths from the Cook voyage reach Britain we see this same intimate connection between barkcloth and the body being explored through the adaptation of finely textured Tahitian barkcloths, those of which Banks remarked "nothing can be more soft or delicious to the feel."[49] A large piece of Tahitian *ahu* collected on Cook's second voyage was given by the voyage naturalist, George Forster, to the daughter of a Göttingen professor, who had a shepherdess outfit made from it to wear to a ball;[50] and Cook's wife is known to have made and embroidered a waistcoat from Tahitian barkcloth "soft as chamois" for him, during the third voyage, from which he did not return.[51]

Yet neither of these experimental uses of barkcloth warranted a mention by Shaw in the printed introduction preceding his catalogue, presumably because they either occurred outside his circle of knowledge or were thought too prosaic – perhaps too *familiar* – for his project. His catalogue also missed a quite singular opportunity to associate one of his barkcloth specimens with the first Polynesian to visit Britain. In many of Shaw's volumes, and in all four of the manuscript versions thought to be a copycat series, a sample of Tahitian cloth with bamboo-stamped circles (Figure 6.3) replicates the underlayer of barkcloth garments worn by Te Tupai Ma'i, known as Omai, in his 1774 portrait by Francesco Bartolozzi.[52] Shaw's catalogue of specimens does, however, describe a sample presented by a priest of "Owyhee" to James King; here the priest is described as a "very intelligent person," capable of handling shipboard instruments after seeing them in use only once, whom King thinks "would have been a far superior object to have brought to England than Omai." Travelling on the *Adventure* with Cook, from his home in Tahiti, Omai arrived in London in 1774 and spent two years there before returning to Tahiti on the *Resolution*; while in London, he enchanted high society and impressed people with his genteel behaviour and good humour.[53] He was presented at court to George III and was later celebrated in a play based on his life, "Omai; or a Trip Around the World," performed at the Theatre Royal,

Figure 6.3 Tahitian barkcloth sample (top) and Hawaiian sample, from Shaw's barkcloth book (1787). Tahitian cloth of the type seen worn by Te Tupai Ma'i (Omai) in his 1774 portrait by Francesco Bartolozzi. University of Pennsylvania Museum of Archaeology and Anthropology. Photo by author.

Covent Garden, in 1785, just two years prior to the publication of Shaw's books. Omai embodied the conflicting ideas of French philosopher Jean-Jacques Rousseau and his opponents; he appeared to be an "untainted noble savage" – Rousseau's romantic ideal – but simultaneously, his behaviour was apparently moderated by his participation in only the highest of society's circles. The publications that emerged from Cook's expeditions would go only some way towards moderating these opposing philosophical positions; Shaw's barkcloth books provide fodder for both.

Gifts from the Friendly Islands

When they first reached Tonga in 1773, Cook and his men were entertained by the local elites of the islands they visited, who hosted them with lavish feasts and elaborate gift exchanges. Cook and his crew were not the first Europeans to visit the Pacific, nor were they the first visitors to what they came to call "the Friendly Islands," based on their reception there. The Dutch explorers Willem Schouten and Jacob Le Maire had been the first Europeans to reach Tonga in 1616, followed by fellow Dutchman Abel Tasman in 1643 and the English navigator Samuel Wallis in 1767.

We have already encountered the European nail set in a bone handle, collected in Tonga by father-and-son naturalists George and Johann Forster on Cook's second voyage. Cook's first contact with Tongans off the northwest coast of 'Eua, a place Cook named "English Road," initiated the "return" via an exchange of further iron nails, a hatchet, and a large piece of red cloth; these were exchanged for Tongan fine mats and decorated barkcloth or *ngatu*, as well as *kava* (*Piper methysticum* – a drink with sedative properties). Both are at the heart of ceremonial events in Tonga.[54] Nails and hatchets were valued for their use as tools for fine work, and the colour red was associated with rank and chiefliness throughout Polynesia; thus high value was assigned to red items of European cloth and clothing.

Beyond the material value of the goods transferred, this and other exchanges were founded on Tongan concepts of managing relationships and power. It is likely that the *ngatu* gifted to Cook and his crew were given in part because of the power of *ngatu* to manage the *vā* or connective space between people, and to link people together in relationships of mutual support. A philosophical concept known by cognate terms throughout Polynesia, in Tonga *vā* "denotes the space between things or social space between people"; it is complemented by *tā*, which means "to beat, or to demarcate time through beats."[55] Both are manifest, or manipulated, in Tongan art practices such as barkcloth making as well as in gift prestations, the latter known as *tauhi vā*, literally the beating (*tā*) of space (*vā*). A person responsible for such manipulation of time and space, or "reorganizing socio-political relations," is known as a *tufunga fonua*, "an artisan of the land and its people."[56]

Tongan barkcloth played a crucial role in the managing and reorganizing of sociopolitical relationships during Cook's visits to Tonga, particularly where it was employed to contain the otherwise potentially dangerous *mana* (personal or scared power) of these European visitors. Barkcloths are creative technologies that manage transitions across thresholds. As Wonu Veys has observed, "[p]resenting female goods [such as barkcloth] is a means of relating to the stranger or the person who finds himself in a new situation. The new arrival must be incorporated, and whatever sacred powers he possesses must be domesticated."[57] One way to do so was to contain their *mana* with barkcloth, through their performative presentation and especially through their use as wrappings and ground coverings (a practice also observed in Tahiti and exemplified by the wrapping of Cook's remains in Hawaiian barkcloth).

Some of the qualities of Tongan barkcloth were uniquely suited to such a metaphysical task. The Tongan onomatipaoeic term that describes the sound of paper mulberry bark being beaten into *ngatu* cloth is also the word for time, *tā*. As it is made, *ngatu* absorbs time and makes it visible; as it is used, *ngatu* defines space or *vā* and materializes the collectivity of Tongan people. Describing the presentation of barkcloth in Polynesia, Nicholas Thomas explains:

> Tapa was presented not only in bundles that were wrapped around individuals, but also sometimes in long strips that were carried by dozens of individuals in line; and in some cases, long and wide strips were laid along the ground, especially for those of high rank to walk along. These uses of the material are significant because, in many parts of the Pacific, the metaphor of the path is fundamental to the imagining of relations of alliance and affinity. The long strip of cloth gives material form to the path, but does more than make a relationship visible: its presentation by a long line of people also makes their collective action, and their very collectivity, manifest.[58]

Moreover, some of the barkcloth prestations made by Tongans were surely intended to overwhelm Cook and his crew; these arrived in huge bales or were laid out as pathways; the longest piece observed was seventy-six yards long and seven and half wide.[59] Gifts on this scale conveyed both the giver's *tufunga fonua* prowess and the health of their village's economy. Yet these monumental cloths might later be cut into smaller sections. This practice, often applied to the *ngatu* used to line pathways for people to walk over or sit upon, was employed to safely distribute the *mana* that the *ngatu* had absorbed. We cannot be sure how many full-sized *ngatu* were received by Cook and his men, only that none of them survive intact today.[60]

Fragmentation

So, what happened to the huge barkcloths mobilized by Tongans – and other Polynesians – to receive and host Cook and his crews? And by what processes and for what purposes were some of these miniaturized and incorporated into the book-making projects of Shaw and other individuals?

Polynesian barkcloths were routinely cut down to size by the islanders themselves, for practical purposes – as spatial dividers and bedding; as clothing; as wrappers for newborn babies and the recently deceased; as shrouds for the interment of a baby's placenta or the dead – as well as metaphysical ones. It also seems that the process of carving up monumental barkcloths began – at least for some examples used as pathways – in Tonga itself, if only due to the need to safely distribute the *mana* of those who had been in contact with them. There is a discernible symmetry between Cook's voyages of scientific exploration, which aimed to domesticate and harness the potential of the natural resources of the Pacific, and the employment of the natural resources of the Pacific, in the form of barkcloth, to domesticate and harness the potential-as-potency of the European visitors to Tonga. Bark skins of Tongan trees, beaten into large bolts of *ngatu* and decorated with recurring geometric motifs, could absorb *mana*, and having absorbed it could be cut into smaller, "safer" portions or given whole to the person whose *mana* it now contained. These barkcloths, whether entire or already fragmented, would later be translated into "artificial curiosities" in the collections and documentation of what might prove valuable to the British Empire. Furthermore, as Shaw's book project demonstrates, they would continue to be fragmented and distributed in ways their donors could never have anticipated. Just as Cook and his crew were being incorporated into worlds they had not imagined, so was barkcloth, as it crossed beaches and entered the cramped holds of British ships.

Of the barkcloths that made their way back to London and into museum collections, some bear the telltale marks of having been "sampled": rectangles, clearly cut with scissors, are missing. Perhaps we might apportion some responsibility for this to Daniel Solander – the Swedish naturalist onboard the *Endeavour* as Joseph Banks's assistant – who was employed at the British Museum both before and after Cook's first voyage and who was eventually appointed its Keeper of Natural History. The barkcloths have had pieces cut from them that map perfectly onto the size of the Solander cases held at the British Museum: nine cases hold samples of barkcloths stuck to a cardboard substrate, permitting a quick overview of what was otherwise an unwieldy collection of large artefacts, difficult to handle and display. Solander's role in cataloguing the botanical specimens gathered on the voyage is well-documented, and in this time before ethnology or anthropology acquired disciplinary status of their own, the distinction between natural specimens and the things made from them remained porous. It would have been logical for Solander to take an active role in organizing the full range of collections he had helped assemble.

As Barbara Kirshenblatt-Gimblett has suggested, "disciplines make their own objects and in the process make themselves," which we might extrapolate to include the contribution that the collection- and typology-making actions of Cook and his men – including Solander – made to the development of anthropology and ethnology as disciplines. Moreover – and as if speaking about eighteenth-century barkcloth books – she proposes the term "ethnographic fragment" rather than object: that which might be removed from its intended spheres of use in a process requiring a considered excision of superfluous appendages to leave only the essential part(s) of the object itself, which can be packaged for display.[61] Samples in the Solander cases attest to the development of the disciplines of anthropology and ethnology – their object making or ethnographic fragmentation – and to what was considered essential for display and consultation. Barkcloths seem to have been particularly susceptible to being divided (without being destroyed or diminished) in ways that other ethnographic objects were not. Some appeared to be lengths of plain fabric awaiting use in much the same way as bolts of European cloth. The more elaborate pieces of Tongan *ngatu* and Hawaiian *kapa*, with their apparent "sections" of repeated motifs, would have appeared to be neatly divisible.

Beyond their instructive qualities – and the small roles they may have played in the development of social sciences – fragmented barkcloths are provocative because of how they reframe objects. Solander's cases and Shaw's barkcloth sampler books depended on fragmentation, but they also depended on the inference that the part resembled the whole – a kind of material metonymy. In doing so, they began a process of abstraction away from the entirety of the barkcloth itself and into transportable "abstract" art. For example, in the process of division, a single Hawaiian *kapa* might be cut into segments of different individual patterns, suggested by its maker's division by lines into framed squares and rectangles, thus making it possible to imply within Shaw's compilations that a number of barkcloths had been sampled – a technique that extended the number of artful singularities within each collection. Perhaps familiar with, or makers of, fabric sampler books, Shaw's audience may have thought that the part represented faithfully the whole.[62] We know it did not. There is thus a certain aesthetic fictionality within these books. The overall structure of each cloth has been broken down in the sampling process, causing both a reduction and a reframing of their visual qualities. These samples were not afforded art historical attention, which might have perceived them as whole works and preserved them as such, despite the voyagers themselves affording aesthetic evaluations to both the makers and manufactures of the Pacific. George Forster, for example, wrote about Tongans:

> Their progress in the arts, beyond other nations in the South Sea, and particularly their refinement in the music, serve to pass away their time agreeably, and give them taste to acknowledge and discern the beauties of their own exquisite forms, from whence one of the strongest ties of society is derived.[63]

Even the "everyday-ness" of the plainest pieces of barkcloth that Shaw's project fragmented still translates so completely as "exotic" (while at the same time becoming "familiarized" as a fabric sample) that it could indeed bear being fragmented, being made both singular and copious through this action.

Some tiny samples snipped from Shaw's books and grangerized into family albums and other volumes attest to the power of these textiles to conjure the whole in the minds of their viewers, to conjure, for their eighteenth-century audiences, distant places and people, "where sensations are always new, where art pours out of daily life, where everything exists in a dream of endless flow."[64] These words are Edmund de Waal's, describing the first imports of *Japonisme* to nineteenth-century Paris, yet they seem remarkably applicable to the century prior and to the appeal of barkcloth books. The very unobtainability and geographical remoteness of Polynesia creates the aura surrounding the books and their contents, accompanied by Shaw's extracted, first-hand descriptions. As well, to return to de Waal's understanding of *Japonisme* in Paris, there was "an exhilarating lack of connoisseurship, none of the enmeshed knowledge of art historians to confound your immediate responses, your intuitions."[65] He wonders, "What was it like to have something so alien in your hands for the first time … in a material that you had never encountered before and shift it around, finding its weight and balance?"[66] We might wonder the same of Shaw's barkcloth samples.

Within the Pages of Shaw's Barkcloth Books

I have encountered Shaw's books in library stacks; glass cases; and museum vaults and displays. Whether they are "book" or "artefact" remains unclear in these venues. I fill in the requisite paperwork and the book is retrieved and delivered, usually into a nest of soft supports. I don gloves – or not, as the institution demands – and open the delicate binding. Here is the title page; there are the library stamps, signatures, and insignias linking this book to famous collectors and important people; here are the printed pages, slightly brown at their edges. To the right of the final page of the catalogue, a guard page hides the first sample, yet is stained by its pigments. I turn to the samples, using soft weighted snakes, Perspex guards, or my own fingers to hold them flat. Here is the bleeding of Polynesian pigment onto British rag paper. I lift the pages slowly, carefully. Here is my favourite Hawaiian specimen, with its squat triangles of yellow and black; here is a Tahitian sample so fine that when lifted gently to the light I can see through it; there is the large decorated Tongan sample I enjoy because it has delaminated into its constituent layers and I feel like I can see right to the heart of it.

Beyond the visual satiation offered by creamy cloth stained yellow, red, brown, and black there is texture beneath my fingers, ranging from the finest Tahitian gauzes through Tongan cloth glazed lamp-black with the soot of candlenuts to the thick corrugations produced in Hawai'i. They are too small to produce the sound Tongans called *fakamakuku* – the bustling of someone dressed in *ngatu* – but tiny stitches in some and stretchy areas in others allude to the creation of garments. When the samples were fresh, they would also have given off various scents: the sweetness of perfumed dyes and coconut oils, and the fecundity of earth and plant-based materials and pigments.

I want to know: How did eighteenth-century viewers engage with these books – with their texts and samples? Did they inhale the fragrance of Polynesia? Did they assess the quality of these textiles, of these people, by testing the "hand of the cloth"?

I suspect that after the first glance at the specimens there would be a return to the printed pages of descriptions, and the attempted marrying of samples with the catalogue list. For seasonal ingenuity, viewers could marvel at specimen 1, "made to resist rain, by being smeared over with the juice of a glutenous herb or plant," and specimen 9, "wore by the people in fine weather it is made of the outer rind of the mulberry-tree." For domestic applications, specimen 6 was "used for bedding," specimen 17 had been "beat with a grooved piece of wood, and used as a mat," and 37 was deemed "common, but very durable." Is there something about the utilitarian value of these cloths that made these hybrid *objets* (print/cloth) also a hybridization of the exotic and the everyday?

The various uses outlined in the catalogue's explanations allowed readers in England to imagine the uses of the cloths and the lives of their makers. Adventurers must have been satisfied by specimen 32 "wore by the chiefs going to war," but may have paused at 15 "used at the human sacrifice." For the pious, 23 and 36 were "wore by the priests" and 14 was "used in the mourning dresses"; for the playful, 38 was "wore by the young dancers" and 28 "[u]sed as a sash, and under garments for the dancers at Otaheite." All of these descriptions employ the simile and metaphor required to afford familiarity, to circulate a form of knowledge within the capacity of its audience's knowing. What did their audiences make of the juxtaposition of several cloths on one page that might never have been brought together otherwise?

Finally – perhaps most significantly – Shaw included short narratives that spoke to the nature of the people of the South Seas, both supporting and challenging Rousseau's "noble savage" construct. For example:

> 18. The very finest of the inner coat of the mulberry; and wore by the chiefs of Otaheite.– Some of the seamen were sent ashore to bring fresh provisions on board; and not having an opportunity to return immediately, one of them wandered a little way up the country, where he saw some children at play, which to his surprize they all left, and surrounded him, making many antic gestures; at last a girl, about fourteen years of age, made a leap at him, at the same time endeavoured to seize a few red feathers which he had stuck in his cap, which he directly took out and presented her; upon which she made off with amazing swiftness, and the rest after her; he then returned to his companions, who were preparing to go on board. It was now the cool of the evening, when she came down to the waterside, and singling him out from the rest, presented him the piece of cloth from which this was cut. A true sign of gratitude in those people.

And:

> 34. From Otaheite, wore as garments by the ladies.– A number of the natives being on board of the Resolution, one of the chiefs took a particular liking to an old blunt iron, which lay upon one of the officer's chests, and taking hold of a boy about nine years of age, offered him in exchange, pointing to the iron. The gentleman, although he knew he could not keep the youth, yet willing to see if he would willingly stay; or if any of the rest would claim him, took the child and gave the savage the iron; upon which a woman, who appeared rather young for the mother, sprung from the other side of the

> ship, and with the highest emotions of grief seemed to bewail the loss of the infant: but the lieutenant, with a true British spirit, took him by the hand and presented him to her, upon which, after putting her hands twice upon her head, she unbound the roll of cloth which was round her body, and from which this specimen was cut, and having spread it before him, seized the boy, and jumping into the sea both swam ashore, nor could he ever learn whether she was the mother, sister, or relation, and this he lamented the more, as such affection was very seldom seen among those people.

The barkcloths attributed to these events are their tactile, tangible survivors, linking us to these dramas. Never mind that the cloths to which these descriptions are ascribed differed from book to book, with only two of those extant containing the same samples inserted in the same order.[67] Never mind that in some examples, every sample has been inserted back to front. These barkcloths retain their allure, their traces of the people who made and used them, even when misattributed; the texts convey a curated knowledge of Polynesia even without appropriate samples to instantiate their teachings; and through the ongoing excision of samples and addition of notes and marginalia, every book remains a work in progress.

Conclusion

Shaw's book series, and its possible precursor and its derivatives, are hybrid volumes that bring actual voyage artefacts together with typeset excerpts from shipboard journals and/or handwritten descriptions, attributing samples to people and places – often incorrectly – and the encounters they instantiate. Where published accounts of Cook's voyages offered both officially sanctioned and surreptitious narratives for public consumption, the barkcloth books offered instead innovative, tactile, and unstable compositions for imagining their encounters at an intimate scale. More than an illustration of Cook's voyages, and impacted by both the insufficiency of their texts and their tendency to be further sampled from or grangerized, they continue to invite our speculation: What had these textiles and their exchanges meant to their makers and donors? What they had been witness to? What might they have been intended to offer to the transformation of European knowledge of the world? And to what extent does the barkcloth they contain – in the words of Tongan poet Karlo Mila that opened this chapter – remain connected to its own self?

As Igor Kopytoff has explained, "an eventful biography of a thing becomes the story of the various singularizations of it, of classifications in an uncertain world of categories whose importance shifts with every minor change in context."[68] Every time an object changes hands it gains and loses parts of its "cultural biography," becoming "partial" and fragmented,[69] and simultaneously augmented or overlaid. Shaw's barkcloth books, and those that would follow, are examples of the first attempts to tame the textiles intimately associated with the peoples of the South Seas, to overlay them with textual reference and British authority. These were the projects of amateurs, not art historians; projects born out of wonderment as well as products of the Enlightenment; pages of abstracted art as well as catalogues of commercial possibility. Despite their fragmentation and confinement, these barkcloths remain port-keys to eighteenth-century encounters, with all their potential and potency.

These books are puzzles and shape-shifters, and the surge of scholarly interest in them in the past decade is surely partly to do with the sophistication of databases and digital collections that allow us to look at and compare various books from our desktops. Just as Alexander Shaw has taken more detailed form through projects of digitization, so his barkcloth books are increasingly available to view through the websites of institutional websites, assisting in projects focused on academic, artistic, and cultural revitalization. The legacy of the exchanges that supplied the cloths cut to size by Shaw can be seen in the continued interest in Cook voyage collections and accounts, in the new discoveries still being made within these, and in the possibilities they afford for reframing historical interactions and collaborations between Europeans and Polynesians. It is all there, in "the hand of the cloth."

NOTES

1 Karlo Mila, "Paper Mulberry Secrets," *A Well Written Body* (Wellington: Huia Press, 2008), 29.

2 Bougainville's barkcloth is now in the Muséum d'histoire naturelle in La Rochelle. I am grateful to Wonu Veys for this information.

3 Amira Henare [Salmond], *Museums, Anthropology, and Imperial Exchange* (Cambridge: Cambridge University Press, 2005), 40.

4 Ibid.

5 Donald Kerr, "Census of Alexander Shaw's Tapa Cloth Book, 1787." Online pdf version, University of Otago, Dunedin, New Zealand, 2015, https://ourarchive.otago.ac.nz/handle/10523/4573, accessed 25 March 2018.

6 Henry Usher Hall, "A Book of Tapa," *Museum Journal* 12, no. 1 (1921): 8–29; Wonu Veys, "Les livres tapa d'Alexander Shaw: le marriage captivant de l'objet et du texte," in *Tapa: Southeast Asia to Eastern Polynesia,* ed. Michel Charleux (Papeete and Paris: Aux Vent des Îsles, 2017), 465–72.
7 Erica Ryan, "The Mysterious Alexander H. Shaw: Bookseller, and Dealer in Articles of Natural History in Aberdeen and London," National Library of Australia blog, 3 July 2015, https://www.nla.gov.au/blogs/behind-the-scenes/2015/06/09/mr-alexander-shaw-no-379-strand-london, accessed 25 March 2018.
8 Maryanne Larkin, "Tales and Textiles from Cook's Pacific Voyages," *Bulletin of the Bibliographical Society of Australia and New Zealand* 28 (2004): 26.
9 Ryan, "The Mysterious Alexander H. Shaw."
10 Author's reconstruction.
11 This book was conserved in April 1995 at the University Library. Its samples were removed and remounted in their original positions in a new book made to the dimensions of its predecessor. The old book, now empty, is still kept with the new, and its eighteenth-century rag paper pages are stained with barkcloth dyes that echo the samples removed from it. Billie Lythberg, "A Fascination for Barkcloth: The First Eighteenth-Century Barkcloth Book," in *Artefacts of Encounter: Cook's Voyages, Colonial Collecting. and Museum Histories,* ed. Nicholas Thomas et al. (Dunedin: Otago University Press; Honolulu: University of Hawai'i Press, 2016), 186–9.
12 It is not clear to whom Shaw dedicated these volumes, but suggestions include Montresor or Warren Hastings.
13 Otaheite would later become a catch-all name for the islands of the Pacific, but at this time we can be confident that it refers to Tahiti.
14 James King served under James Cook on his last voyage around the world and assumed command following Cook's death.
15 It is thought Shaw secured barkcloths from London dealer George Humphrey, who had purchased them from the 1781 sale of the collection of David Samwell (surgeon's mate on Cook's third voyage) and from Reinhold and George Forster. Wonu Veys has suggested he also obtained not only Jamaican lacebark but also "South Seas" barkcloths from the Duchess of Portland sale in 1786. See Veys, "Les livres tapa d'Alexander Shaw."
16 Phyllis Herda, "The Changing Texture of Textiles in Tonga," *Journal of the Polynesian Society* 108, no. 2 (1999): 149–67. Cf. Billie Lythberg, "Polyvocal Tongan Barkcloths: Contemporary Ngatu and Nomenclature at the Museum of New Zealand Te Papa Tongarewa," *Tuhinga* 24 (2013): 85–104.
17 Lythberg, "A Fascination for Barkcloth," 186–9.

18 Robert MacLean, "Alexander Shaw's Curious Cloth Catalogue," University of Glasgow Library blog, 26 November 2016, https://universityofglasgowlibrary.wordpress.com/2015/11/26/alexander-shaws-curious-cloth-catalogue, accessed 25 March 2018.

19 Billie Lythberg, "Captain Cook's Barkcloth Books," *Expedition: The Magazine of the Pennsylvania Museum* of *Archaeology and Anthropology* 59, no. 1: 30–7.

20 Ian Morrison, "The Cloth, the Catalogue, and the Collectors," *Bibliographical Society of Australia and New Zealand Bulletin* 27 (2003): 52.

21 Vivien Caughley, "Cook Map Samplers: Women's Endeavours," *Records of the Auckland Museum* 50 (2015): 1–14.

22 Nicholas Thomas, "'Specimens of Bark Cloth, 1769': The Travels of Textiles Collected on Cook's First Voyage," *Journal of the History of Collections*, https://doi.org/10.1093/jhc/fhy009, published June 2018.

23 Based on close examination of extant books, Maryanne Larkin ("Tales and Textiles from Cook's Pacific Voyages," 20–33) posits three versions or archetypes; but cf. Rick Watson, who suggests two "issues" released in 1787 and 1805–6 respectively. See Kerr, "Census of Alexander Shaw's Tapa Cloth Book."

24 Larkin, "Tales and Textiles," 28.

25 Erica Ryan, "Alexander's Roup: An Auction Thickens the Plot," National Library of Australia blog, 14 October 2016, https://www.nla.gov.au/blogs/behind-the-scenes/2016/09/23/alexanders-roup-ra-p-scottish, accessed 22 March 2018.

26 Rachel Hand at Cambridge MAA is comparing volumes at the Mitchell Library, Sydney (C523); the National Library of Ireland (Joly 9); the British Museum (Oc.1989, Q.2); Whitby (no number). Adrienne Kaeppler suggests that three similar manuscript volumes, one of them the Whitby volume, may have been compiled at the Leverian Museum, each containing bunches of feathers, strips of fibre, and strands of shells as well as barkcloth. See Kaeppler, *"Artificial Curiosities": An Exposition of Native Manufacture Collected on the Three Pacific Voyages of Captain James Cook, R.N.* (Honolulu: Bishop Museum Press, 1978), 118. It now seems likely there is a set of four, but the connection to the Leverian Museum requires further investigation.

27 Luisa Calè, "Extra-Illustrations: The Order of the Book and the Fantasia of the Library," in *The Material Culture of Enlightenment Arts and Sciences*, ed. Adrian Craciun and Simon Schaffer (London: Palgrave Macmillan, 2016), 235–55.

28 Anne Salmond, *The Trial of the Cannibal Dog: Captain Cook in the South Seas* (Auckland: Penguin, 2003), 25.

29 "Secret Instructions, Cook's voyage 1768–1771: Copies of Correspondence, etc. 1768–1771," National Library of Australia MS 2, http://nla.gov.au/nla.obj-229102048/view, accessed 25 March 2018.

30 James Douglas, Earl of Morton, *Hints Offered to the Consideration of Captain Cooke, Mr Bankes, Doctor Solander and the Other Gentlemen who go upon the Expedition on board the* Endeavour, 10 August 1768, Papers of Sir Joseph Banks, 1745–1923, National Library of Australia, Manuscripts Collection, MS 9, http://nla.gov.au/nla.ms-ms9-113, accessed 25 March 2018.

31 Salmond, *The Trial of the Cannibal Dog,* 32. For a discussion of the Admiralty's assertion of control over published accounts, see Heringman, in this volume.

32 Henare, *Museums, Anthropology, and Imperial Exchange,* 82.

33 Stephen Thompson, Migration Heritage Centre website, December 2005, updated 2011. Thompson's full text and facsimilies of Cook's secret instructions can be read here: http://www.migrationheritage.nsw.gov.au/exhibition/objectsthroughtime/secret.

34 Many scholars have explored the reasons for Cook's death. A bibliography of the more substantial writing on Cook's voyages, as well as links to the National Library of Australia's considerable holdings relating to this topic, can be found here: https://www.nla.gov.au/selected-library-collections/james-cook-and-his-voyages.

35 John C. Beaglehole, ed., *The Journals of Captain James Cook on His Voyages of Discovery,* vol. 1: *The Voyage of the* Endeavour *1768–1771* (Cambridge: Cambridge University Press for the Hakluyt Society, 1955), cxxxvi; Salmond, *The Trial of the Cannibal Dog,* 31.

36 Anne Salmond, *Between Worlds: Early Exchanges Between Māori and Europeans 1773–1815* (Auckland: Penguin, 1997), 39.

37 Henare, *Museums, Anthropology, and Imperial Exchange,* 34.

38 See Jennifer Newell, "Irresistible Objects: Collecting in the Pacific and Australia in the Reign of George III," in *Enlightenment: Collecting the World in the Eighteenth Century,* ed. K. Sloan et al. (London: British Museum Press, 2003), 246–57; Jennifer Newell, "Exotic Possessions: Polynesians and Their Eighteenth-Century Collecting," *Journal of Museum Ethnography* 17 (2004): 75–88.

39 Tupaia, 1769, "Maori bartering a crayfish." British Library, Add. MS 15508, f. 11. For a description of the painting, see Anne Salmond, "Back to the Future: First Encounters in Te Tai Rawhiti," *Journal of the Royal Society of New Zealand* 42, no. 2 (2012): 71.

40 Salmond, *The Trial of the Cannibal Dog,* 76–7; 456n40.

41 Ibid., 456n41.

42 Ibid., 25.

43 Adrienne Kaeppler, "Tonga – Entry into Complex Hierarchies," in *James Cook: Gifts and Treasures from the South Seas,* ed. Brigitta Hauser-Schaublin

et al. (New York: Prestel-Verlag, 1998), 195. Kaeppler cites John C. Beaglehole, ed. *The Journals of Captain James Cook*, vol. 3: *The Voyage of the* Resolution *and the* Discovery *1776–1780* (Cambridge: Cambridge University Press for the Hakluyt Society, 1967), 162.

44 Johann Reinhold Forster, *Observations made during a voyage round the world [in H.M.S. Resolution] on physical geography, natural history, and ethic philosophy, especially on 1. The Earth and its Strata, 2. Water and the Ocean, 3. The Atmosphere, 4. The Changes of the Globe, 5. Organic Bodies, and 6. The Human Species.* (London: G. Robinson, 1778), 368. https://archive.org/details/NHM6732, accessed 25 March 2018.

45 Billie Lythberg, Maia Nuku, and Amiria Salmond, "Relating to, and through, Polynesian Collections," in *Artefacts of Encounter*, ed. N. Thomas et al., 43–55.

46 Anne D'Alleva, 'Elite Clothing and the Social Fabric of Pre-Colonial Tahiti," in *The Art of Clothing: A Pacific Experience*, ed. S. Küchler and G. Were (London: UCL Press, 2005), 48–50.

47 Billie Lythberg "'Fine Fancy and Delicate Taste' – The Queen of Ra'iatea's Royal Robe," in *Artefacts of Encounter*, ed. N. Thomas et al., 207–9.

48 George Forster, *A Voyage Round the* World, ed. Nicholas Thomas and Oliver Berghof, vol. 1 (Honolulu: University of Hawai'i Press, 2000), 164.

49 Wendy Arbeit, "The 'Curious Manufacture' of Cloth from the Bark of Trees," in *Made in Oceania*, ed. Peter Mesenhöller and Oliver Lueb (Köln: Rautenstrauch-Joest-Museum Kulturen der Welt, 2013), 27. Arbeit cites John C. Beaglehole, ed. *The Endeavour Journal of Joseph Banks 1768–1771* (Sydney: Trustees of the Public Library of New South Wales, 1962), 355.

50 Adrienne Kaeppler, "Culture, Conservation, and Creativity: Two Centuries of Polynesian Barkcloth," in *Made in Oceania: Proceedings of the International Symposium on Social and Cultural Meanings and Presentation of Oceanic Tapa Cologne, 16–17 January 2014*, ed. Peter Mesenhöller and Annemarie Stauffer (Newcastle: Cambridge Scholars, 2015), 2.

51 Ibid., 3. The waistcoat survives in the Mitchell Library in Sydney, inv. No. R198.

52 Francesco Bartolozzi, *Portrait of Omai, a Native of Huahine* (1774). Engraved by Nathanial Dance (1775). British Library Add. Ms. 23921 f. 45.

53 Anne Salmond, *Aphrodite's Island* (Auckland: Penguin Books, 2009), 393.

54 Salmond, *The Trial of the Cannibal Dog*, 215.

55 Tēvita Ka'ili (2005), "Tauhi vā: Nurturing Tongan Sociospatial Ties in Maui and Beyond," *Contemporary Pacific* 17, no. 1: 83–114.

56 Ibid.

57 Wonu Veys, "Materialising the King: The Royal Funeral of King Taufa'ahau Tupou IV of Tonga," *Australian Journal of Anthropology* 20 (2009): 152.

58 Nicholas Thomas, *Oceanic Art* (London: Thames and Hudson, 1995), 143.

59 Arbeit, "The 'Curious Manufacture,'" 25.

60 In October 2017 it was determined that Etnografiska Museet, Stockholm, Sweden, holds the largest piece of barkcloth with a Cook voyage provenance: a Tongan *ngatu* 15 x 2.5 metres (1848.1.13). Possibly acquired by the Forsters during Cook's second voyage, it entered the collections of Joseph Banks who gave it to the Stockholm naturalists, the Alstromers. I am grateful to Nicholas Thomas for this information. The only intact eighteenth-century Tongan barkcloth is in the Museo de America in Madrid, where it is known as "Malaspina's carpet," in reference to the Italian navigator Allessandro Malaspina, who explored the Pacific in the service of Spain. A journal entry from 25 May 1793, made while he was in the Tongan archipelago of Vava'u, describes the Spanish crew's bearing arms to escort their host Vuna ashore to attend a session of entertainment, which caused their Tongan host some anxiety. "Shortly afterwards, we attributed to this same dread, the new civility which he showed us by spreading out one large carpet ['una largo alfombra'] from the water's edge to the *cava* house," honouring his guests with a barkcloth pathway while simultaneously containing their dangerous potency. (Translated by Phyllis Herda from the Spanish.) Herda, "A Translation and Annotation of the Journals of the Malaspina Expedition during Their Stay on Vava'u, Tonga, 1793" (MA thesis, University of Auckland, 1983), 70.

61 Barbara Kirshenblatt-Gimblett, *Destination Culture: Tourism, Museums, and Heritage* (Berkeley: University of California Press, 1998), 18.

62 See the Victoria and Albert Museum's holdings for examples, such as http://collections.vam.ac.uk/item/O140029/album-unknown, accessed 25 March 2018.

63 George Forster, *A Voyage Round the World*, vol. 2 (London, 1777), 190.

64 Edmund de Waal, *The Hare with Amber Eyes* (London: Chatto and Windus, 2011), 64.

65 Ibid., 59.

66 Ibid., 56–7.

67 Two copies in the Dixson Library in New South Wales (DL78/64 & DL78/65) have the same samples, arranged in the same order, and all of approximately the same size. DL78/65 has lost its lacebark sample, only a tuft remains glued to the page. Larkin, "Tales and Textiles," 21.

68 Igor Kopytoff, "The Cultural Biography of Things: Commoditization as Process," in *The Social Life of Things: Commodities in Cultural Perspective*, ed. Arjun Appadurai (Cambridge: Cambridge University Press, 1986), 180.

69 Ibid., 64–91.

chapter seven

Formal Encounters: Education, Evangelization, and the Reproduction of Custom in Seventeenth-Century Peru

MATTHEW GOLDMARK

In the Papal Bull *Inter Caetera* (1493) that divided the New World between Iberian powers, Pope Alexander VI presented an evangelical mandate. Monarchs were obliged to "indoctrinate said native peoples and inhabitants in the Catholic faith and instill them with good customs."[1] This duty to evangelize served as a justification for the colonial mission that was deployed by monarchs, friars, and conquistadors alike.[2] However, it must be emphasized that this Papal Bull provided two parts to evangelization: "faith" (*fide*) and "morals" or "customs" (*moribus*). Instruction had to be given in both for the missionary project to be considered a success. In various colonial tracts, these two terms intertwined as the end goal of evangelization, according to which indigenous peoples' deviant religious practices had to be reshaped into proper Christian mores. Friars and colonial administrators argued that without this reformation of indigenous customs – in particular those considered diabolical inversions of Christian practice, such as sacrifice, idolatry, and polygamy – faith could not take root and flourish in indigenous soil.[3]

Yet in the Spanish imperial context, lineage presented a seemingly insurmountable problem. One prevalent strain of Spanish religious ideology in Iberia stated that only those who could be designated Old Christians (persons without Jewish, Muslim, apostate, or newly converted forefathers) could reliably maintain true faith and its good customs. The "tainted blood" of New Christians amounted to an indelible stain that corrupted these converts and that was passed to their children. Regarding the Spanish Americas, María Elena Martínez has noted that jurists and friars initially remained undecided regarding indigenous peoples' Old or New Christian status, given that New World subjects had no prior knowledge of Christianity. This uncertainty defined matters of evangelization. The recency of indigenous peoples' exposure to faith challenged their designation as New Christians; at the same time, their customs – especially by the late sixteenth century – were increasingly considered ingrained by lineage.[4] Imperial officials thus began to see evangelization as an eternal task, for they viewed indigenous customs as a deviant inheritance that defined New World populations.[5]

Here, I argue that claims to Christian faith and, in particular, to good customs were not always determined by lineage in the late sixteenth and early seventeenth centuries. A claim to possess good customs could also be made through self-presentation according to a regulated form. By form, I am referring to the bureaucratic procedures of documentation to which imperial subjects were beholden. Before they could acquire professional positions dependent on religious and political quality or *calidad*, vassals had to demonstrate their good customs, and this in turn required the textual encounter of witness testimonies and their translation into the standardized shape of a fixed document. Through this textual encounter, one defined by regulated form, indigenous subjects could claim to possess good customs, regardless of lineage.

To illustrate how regulated form could enable the assertion of good customs, I begin with two bodies of documentation from sixteenth- and seventeenth-century Peru. First, I look at petitions submitted by potential instructors of Christian doctrine and literacy housed in the Archbishop's Archive of Lima.[6] These petitions argue that proper instruction depends on the exemplary customs that a teacher presents to his pupils. As proof, he must be shown to present a standard and unvaried example in his words and deeds. However, to prove one's uniform self-presentation in the classroom, the petitioner had to accumulate witness testimonies and cast this evidence in uniform language on the page.[7] Proof of proper practice and good customs depended on their composition in regulated language repeated across testimonies. Second, I engage evangelical tracts that emerged during the Viceroyalty of Peru's Third Lima Council (1582–83). There, gathered friars blamed the supposed intransigence of indigenous customs on the spread of inconsistent versions of doctrine and the fickle and often detrimental behaviours of parish friars.[8] As a solution, religious treatises commanded priests to disseminate an invariable model of Christianity in word and deed – in a "single form" – to indigenous neophytes.[9]

These two bodies of text thus posit that the presentation of a standardized form enabled the transfer of good customs to others. In turn, it was through this reproduction and in regulated form that indigenous subjects could claim to possess these same customs. To illustrate this political possibility, I conclude with a petition submitted by an indigenous instructor who employs this bureaucratic language to show that he can embody and impart good customs to other indigenous neophytes.[10] By emphasizing how identities are composed according to the regulated rules of form, I show that indigenous subjects could lay claim to good customs by reproducing the very terms of imperialism that supposedly excluded them.

Good Customs, Good Examples

The Archbishop's Archive of Lima houses a series of petitions submitted by Spanish solicitors throughout the seventeenth century, requesting approval from ecclesiastical authorities to instruct youth of unspecified background in Christian dogma and first letters in the Viceroyalty of Peru. Some petitioners are identified as native-born inhabitants of the city of Lima; others are recent transplants.[11] Despite these differences in terms of their life circumstances, all confirm that they are able to serve as "maestros de niños" by virtue of their identical qualifications. Each claims to possess good customs and the ability to serve as a good example.

As with so many bureaucratic documents that fill regional and central archives throughout the former Spanish empire, petitioners had to draw together notaries, witnesses, and other interlocutors to confirm their statements and certify their claims. Their possession of "good customs" would be proven – and made – in the accumulation of standardized text. Petitioners such as Baltasar Pérez de Atocha in 1642 presented testimony from witnesses who promised to tell the truth, swearing by God and the cross as required by law.[12] Despite this oath, or perhaps as a consequence of the guiding hand of a notary, each testimonial offers similar details regarding Pérez de Atocha's character and qualifications. Some witness testimonies do mention Pérez de Atocha's experience as a teacher; all of them refer to the quality of his life and customs. The witness Manuel Pérez's testimony affirms that he had "seen [Pérez de Atocha] teach Christian doctrine to children as well as to write, read, and count" and states that Pérez de Atocha is a "virtuous good Christian of good life and example."[13] Another witness, Cristóbal Vásquez, also confirms that the petitioner is "a virtuous man of good life and customs."[14] The last witness, Tomás de Lumbreras, also says that Pérez de Atocha is "a virtuous person of good life and custom."[15] In this gathered testimony, the petitioner's traits take their place as a set of pre-established terms: Pérez de Atocha is repeatedly asserted to be a "good example" and a "virtuous person" who leads a "good life." The repetition of these attributes across documents proves his appropriate Christian "customs"; indeed, it makes them true.

This standardization may frustrate those who study these traits, but in fact, their interlocking arrangement is what determines their meaning. These character traits signify because they align; their definition rests in their syntactical conjunction. That is, an uncontested and unmarked alignment between the good life, good customs, and good example emerges in the conjunction "and." Therefore, though this testimony notes exchanges between witnesses and petitioner (Manuel Pérez's testimony states that "[Pérez] has had cordial conversation and interaction" with Pérez de Atocha), the terms of these meetings are reduced to boilerplate language.[16] The bureaucratic form determines the information needed from a physical encounter, reducing the complexity and excising details that such interactions surely entail. The only qualities that matter are those that correspond to the rhetorical and syntactical rules of the form.

Some nineteen petitions housed in the Archbishop's Archive of Lima follow this structure. They include a general summary submitted by the potential teacher followed by testimony from members of the community. This testimony includes how long each witness has known the petitioner and where, the witness's opinion of the petitioner's customs, life, and example, and a final affirmation that his testimony is accurate. Each petition concludes with a decision from the Dean of the Cathedral. Testimonies do not record the prompts that motivate witness responses, though a final signature by a notary does indicate that an authorizing hand had witnessed and documented the procedure. Implicitly, we can assume that this notary converted possibly meandering testimony into the regulated structure of bureaucratic proof.[17] Like witnesses, the notary thus becomes an integral author in this process of a petitioner's "self-presentation"; he applies a standard rubric that determines the shape a petitioner's identity will take. The petitioner himself and the traits that define him must be composed according to a set textual form – a predetermined exemplar with its model phrases and mandatory details – to ensure a rubber stamp from colonial administrators. With the bureaucratic form, each petitioner is made, as Rolena Adorno writes in a gloss of exemplarity, "in the space that exists between history and precept, between the novelistic episode and the maxims that assimilate the biography to the didactic system."[18] In these petitions, each individual petitioner is remade according to the standard model dictated by the bureaucratic form in order to certify his customs and receive approval from ecclesiastical authorities.

Ultimately, the presentation of this petitioner in the standard form of bureaucratic procedure serves its purpose. The Vicar General of the Archbishopric of Lima Don Martín de Velasco y Molina orders that a permit be given to Pérez de Atocha. Velasco y Molina adds that the instructor must teach children Christian doctrine, the catechism, and to read, write, and count, all while "giving them a good example."[19]

This command to *give* a good example echoes throughout witness testimony. Lumbreras's statement notes that Pérez de Atocha had previously taught children with much care, "without drawing attention to himself or providing a bad example of his person for having behaved very well."[20] Along these lines, testimony given by the witness Pérez concludes with a pithy assertion: "it is very important for this profession ... virtue and exemplary life."[21] Though no definition is given for "good example," these petitions leave no doubt as to its centrality for the execution of instruction. Exemplarity identifies a theory of reproduction whereby the customs of an instructor are modelled for and given to his pupil – for better or worse. That is, if a good example can be given, then a bad one can be transmitted as well. This premise illustrates the stakes of a regulated exemplar standardized in word and deed. Only through uniform practice could authorities ensure the uniform education and preservation of pupils' good customs.

Circulating Exemplars

The theory that the example would mould pupils and neophytes proved central to the evangelical project of the sixteenth and seventeenth centuries. As John Charles has noted, "the Church's evangelizing mission drew from the conviction that standards of civility and goodness would find their maximum expression through the Indians' exposure to Spanish and written texts."[22] Contact with the right models would encourage the transformation of indigenous customs. However, as the sixteenth century progressed, religious authorities began to regulate the "example" to which neophytes could – and should – be exposed. In the 1580s, a period that opened what Juan Carlos Estenssoro Fuchs terms the second phase of Peruvian evangelization, friars began to question the efficacy of the previous evangelical approach that had allowed priestly examples to adjust to local circumstance.[23]

Thus, by the 1580s, friars attributed the failures of evangelization to a lack of standardized doctrinal practice. Under the leadership of José de Acosta and the recently arrived Jesuits (1568), the assembled religious authorities of the Third Lima Council (1582–83) argued that a single doctrinal text must be imposed and disseminated across dioceses and missions. They emphasized the promise of print; the creation of a single exemplar, they argued, would eliminate the deviations prevalent in manuscript copies. As one such catechism states in its royal provision: "One of the most important items addressed by the Provincial Council was to order that the doctrine of the natives … be *uniform*, without making a difference in even a single syllable for the great damage that has resulted from not having done so in the past."[24] However, while print promised to disseminate precise textual language, the acts themselves insinuated that regulation had to move beyond the written word. The presentation of "the *same form* of a *single* doctrine" also referred to a friar's embodied actions.[25]

As the acts note: "If no one who knows [the language] appears, the parish, however, shall not be left without a priest, as long as he does not have bad customs since it is preferable to send a parish priest who lives correctly over one who speaks well, if one had to choose, because life edifies much more than language."[26] This passage names the pedagogical approach identified in the petitions where the presentation of customs serves as a strategy of edification and transformation. But in the process, this statement undermines the primacy of text by placing the regulation of a body and its performance of customs (*moribus*) above verbal doctrine (*linguae*). Indeed, this need to standardize embodied behaviour evinces the realities of evangelization: working across the multiple languages that persisted in the Viceroyalty made the transmission of doctrine in a single language impossible.[27] As a solution, these writers emphasize the force of the good example. The absence of verbal understanding need not impede the instruction of Christian practice; the body will still teach.

Instruction by a body's example means that the performance of custom must be equally regulated since the "example" is a template that will be followed and reproduced by malleable pupils. To justify this evangelical strategy of presenting doctrine and custom in deed, the acts point to the church fathers and their methods of evangelization:

> With reason our elders teach that there is nothing that moves others more towards piety and the cult of God than the *life and example* of those who dedicate themselves to the divine ministry, since, given that these have been

elevated from our terrain to a higher place, the others naturally turn their eyes to them like a mirror from which they take that which they should imitate.[28]

This passage focuses on the life and example of a priest as a model that will be reproduced. Followers will "look" to the qualities presented by the exemplar and perform these customs with their own bodies.[29] The passage notes that this example is not a simple verbal presentation. It continues:

> It is best that clerics called to the divine ministry organize their *lives* and *all their customs* so that they do not do anything that is not respectful in their habit, their gesture, their movements, discourse, or any other thing. Just as they must also avoid those small errors that in them would be grave, so that their actions produce the veneration of all.[30]

In emphasizing the cleric's way of life, this passage does not point to the standardized words of doctrine, but rather to the regulated customs and behaviour of a body: gestures, movements, habits, and gait. The friar must do more than speak Christian doctrine. He must model it in body, dress, and comportment, that is, in his customs. If the Third Lima Council seeks to ensure that doctrine does not vary in text, it also codifies its circulating performance in the body. Friars cannot stray from a regulated template if they hope to instil good customs and Christian practice in others. Thus, the phrase "small errors" as a deviation in appearance provides a corporeal mirror for the condemnation of differences by "a single syllable" in textual doctrine. Both body and text must be regulated and presented in an unvarying form to ensure the proper edification of neophytes.

Formal Reproduction

This repeated stress on the need for a regulated standard illustrates the belief in exemplarity as a means of reshaping pupils' or neophytes' customs. Insistent calls to control an instructor's behaviour indicate the threat that an unregulated example would pose. Richard Kagan has attributed this scrutiny to the Protestant Reformation and fears of heresy, which together had led to an "educational revolution" in the sixteenth and seventeenth centuries.[31] He notes that Spanish intellectuals and jurists believed children to be especially open to damaging influence, particularly from subjects who might be engaging in suspicious religious practices. To "protect" these young subjects, jurists legislated blood purity requirements for instructors in the Old and New Worlds. For instance, a 1573 royal decree forbade *conversos* and those of "bad blood" from teaching.[32] However, even though these prohibitions assumed that New Christians possessed corrupt customs, they ironically insinuated the force of an example and the malleability of Old Christians. Regardless of their lineage and blood purity, children could be perverted as a result of the example they followed. If the bad example of New Christians could pervert Old ones, then lineage alone could not guarantee the inheritance of good customs.[33] In contrast, customs would depend upon the provided model.

Lineage does appear in various petitions submitted by potential instructors in the Viceroyalty of Peru, indicating that anxieties over the relationship between lineage and customs infused these documents as well. Case files often remarked on the petitioner's purity of blood when asserting his eligibility as an instructor. Francisco de Sosa's 1658 petition, for instance, seeks witnesses to attest to the petitioner's "life and customs" as well as to the fact that he is the "child of Old Christian parents."[34] Likewise, in the file submitted by Antonio Jurado Toralba in 1658, witnesses address the petitioner's Old Christian status. Pablo de Noguera states that he knows Jurado Toralba to be the child of Francisco Ruiz Jurado and Francisca Ramos, both of whom are "Old Christians clean of the bad race of the Jews, Moors, or the newly converted."[35] Witness Juan Zeberino also notes that Jurado Toralba is an "Old Christian clean of the bad race of the Moors, Jews, and the newly converted" and confirms that Jurado Toralba's parents are known to be the same.[36] And the witness Alonso Pacheco affirms, as well, that he has not "seen, known, heard, or understood anything in contrary" to Jurado Toralba's stated religious lineage.[37]

While these boilerplate phrases would serve to confirm Jurado Toralba's status as an Old Christian, they make their case through the absence – not presence – of proof otherwise. Jurado Toralba's lineage is not a stable fact, but rather the accumulation of properly experienced and documented impressions from several community members. While his lineage may be "true," the reliance on multiple witnesses illustrates that the truth of Old Christian heritage remains inextricable from bureaucratic procedure.[38] Truth is made in the collation of documents and the proper arrangement of terms.

The role of bureaucratic practice in the composition of an instructor's lineage, custom, and thus qualification appears most clearly in the case of the 1649 petition submitted by the Spanish solicitor Cristóbal de Siles. In testimony for this petition, the witness Pedro de Carmona affirms that he had always seen Siles "live honestly and discreetly as a good Christian, fearful of God and, in his opinion, giving a very good example in his actions and comportment."[39] However, the witness testimonies provided to confirm Siles's qualifications make no mention of his parentage or lineage based on personal experience. Instead, they note that Siles is a "chapetón," a recent arrival who relocated from Spain and passed through Panama before settling in the Viceroyalty of Peru. Given that they may not have known his parentage or past, witnesses place their faith in documentation. Carmona's testimony states that he can confirm Siles's qualifications because he has seen textual evidence. His document states that Siles has "always given a very good account of his person and [the witness] knows this *because of the papers he has seen* as well as by that which had been said by people who saw and met [Siles] in said profession."[40] By citing these papers and "reliable" hearsay, Carmona shows that documentation is an important site of encounter between petitioner and witness where customs are seen and known. Bureaucratic form becomes not only a place for witnesses to support the petitioner, but also a witness in itself. The circularity of this procedure demonstrates that customs do not exist in lineage alone. Rather, good customs could be made true by being properly registered in form.

The Same Form

As the example of Siles indicates, identities confirmed in textual form served as their own proof. By reproducing the exigencies of form, a petitioner's qualities would be held and certified as genuine. This possibility of asserting good customs through documentation created political possibility for subjects who did not meet the assumed requirements of lineage that seemed a precondition for the possession and performance of good customs. To illustrate this point, I conclude with a 1685 document housed in the National Archive of Peru where an indigenous solicitor employs this same formal procedure to claim his own status as a subject with good customs capable of giving a good example.[41] The petition begins with a request of payment for services rendered by Juan Mateo González, a teacher who claims to have educated poor indigenous people without payment for six months of service.[42] In a *memorial* (history) included in this file, several residents of the city – Francisco Velázquez, Mateo de Carvajal, Tomás de Bermudez, Diego Flores, and

Felipe Santiago – write in support of González in the name of the community's "indios vecinos." They explain that a licence had been issued previously to the friar don Juan Núñez Vela de Rivera to mount a school for the "instruction and education of the poor native Indians of this city."[43] That instructor, however, did not appear for eight months, and in response these residents recurred to Juan Mateo González, "*indio ladino* in the Spanish tongue and of good customs."[44]

The language employed to describe González responds to a pre-established form; it repeats the conventional rhetoric of similar petitions that had confirmed the qualifications of Old Christian instructors. Like those documents, González's presents no contradictions among the various characteristics that describe a petitioner. This text defines its subject via the conjunction "and." That is, indio and good customs join and make truth through uncontested accrual and juxtaposition, just as the sequential presentation of "custom," "life," and "example" had in the case of the petitions discussed above. The strength of this conjunction does not appear solely in the testimony of indigenous community members; this formal correspondence between identifying terms is repeated by Spanish officials who posit González's "costumbres" as qualification. For instance, after the superior of the Church of Desamparados tests González, his testimony names the teacher "suitable for the instruction of the children for being an indio of good customs."[45]

The text does insinuate that González's status as *indio* will facilitate his instruction of indigenous pupils, a fact that may seem to diminish his commensurability with other instructors identified as Old Christians in possession of good customs. However, it is in the standardized, formal presentation of customs that the document identifies a notable equivalence between González and his Old Christian counterparts. In the licence issued to González, one that instructs him to teach Spanish letters, doctrine, the Castilian language, and Christian mores to his pupils, González is commanded to instruct children "in the *same form* and manner as all other school teachers."[46] While González's pupils will be indigenous, this emphasis on form is an important one. It states that he can present customs to students just as would his Old Christian counterparts. In asserting this equivalence in/as form, the approval suggests that González's status as an *indio ladino* does not foreclose his possession of good customs, nor does it his capacity to serve as a good example who can reproduce these customs in others.[47] This approval thus intertwines the theories of pedagogical transfer named in both the petitions and the documents of the Third Lima Council. However, unlike those two bodies of text, González's petition indicates that customs can traverse the vertical lines of lineage and reproduce themselves in indigenous peoples via regulated encounters of bodies both in classrooms and on a page. The claim to good customs made in the execution of standard forms bridges the distance between indigenous and Spanish subjects since both groups are qualified based on their proper presentation under a set rubric.

In sum, if the Christian mission depended upon the good example that could edify and transform indigenous customs, this undertaking often contained a limit: lineage defined the indigenous subject's customs and placed a permanent obstruction in his or her path to Christianity. However, when composed in the standard form of colonial bureaucracy, the customs of indigenous and Spanish interlocutors alike depended upon their successful articulation according to a pre-established mould. Both groups faced the scrutiny of a bureaucracy that would confirm or reject their claims. Thus, when scholars consider the possession of customs as a matter of lineage alone, they ignore how colonial subjects challenged their marginalization from authority by producing official encounters sanctioned by the forms of colonial bureaucracy. In their codification of imperial customs, bureaucratic forms did not simply produce difference. They also made political possibility.

NOTES

1 Antonio Flavio Sanctis, ed., *Bullarum Privilegiorum ac Diplomatum Romanorum Pontificum Amplissima Collectio Cui Accessere Pontificum Omnium Vitae, Notae, & Indices Opportuni* (Roma: Typis, et Sumptibus Hieronymi Mainardi, 1743), 234. "Ad instruendum incolas & habitatores praefatos in fide Catholica, & bonis moribus imbuendum destinare debeatis." Cited in Monique Alaperrine-Bouyer, *La educación de las elites indígenas en el Perú colonial* (Lima: Institut français d'études andines, 2007), 13. "Adoctrinar a los indígenas y habitantes dichos en la fe católica e imponerlos en las buenas costumbres." The language of "good customs" was reiterated in Charles V's edicts of 1540 and 1563. See Alcira Dueñas, *Indians and Mestizos in the "Lettered City": Reshaping Justice, Social Hierarchy, and Political Culture in Colonial Peru* (Boulder: University Press of Colorado, 2010), 27.

2 See Robert Ricard's canonical text, *The Spiritual Conquest of Mexico: An Essay on the Apostolate and the Evangelizing Methods of the Mendicant Orders in New Spain, 1523–1572,* trans. Lesley Byrd Simpson (Berkeley: University of California Press, 1966).

3 See Fernando Cervantes, *The Devil in the New World: The Impact of Diabolism in New Spain* (New Haven: Yale University Press, 1994); and Sabine MacCormack, "Gods, Demons, and Idols in the Andes," *Journal of the History of Ideas* 67 (2006): 623–47.

4 María Elena Martínez highlights the rhetoric of Mexico's Third Provincial Council (1585) where the friars of New Spain designated indigenous peoples as "tender plants in the faith." As she notes: "This claim enabled the exclusion of native people from the priesthood and from certain religious offices and institutions without necessarily contradicting the official discourse regarding their 'purity of blood.' In other words, it allowed for their construction as not quite 'impure,' but also as not quite 'Old Christians.'" Martínez, *Genealogical Fictions: Limpieza de Sangre, Religion, and Gender in Colonial Mexico* (Stanford: Stanford University Press, 2008), 103.

5 Along these lines, Carolyn Dean notes that the Jesuits José de Acosta and Bernabé Cobo in sixteenth-century Peru employed infantilizing rhetoric to describe indigenous peoples. She also points to similar language used by the seventeenth-century extirpator of idolatries, Pablo José de Arriaga. Dean, "Familiarizando el catolicismo en el Cuzco colonial," in *Incas e indios cristianos: elites indígenas e identidades cristianas en los Andes coloniales*, ed. Jean-Jacques Decoster (Lima: Institut français d'études andines, 2002), 170.

6 I have consulted the nineteen petitions submitted by potential instructors housed in the Archbishop's Archive of Lima (hereafter AAL). The earliest petition dates to 1605 (AAL, Papeles Importantes, legajo 5, expediente 9), and the last remits to 1698 (AAL, Papeles Importantes, legajo 16, expediente 19).

7 See Dean, "Beyond Prescription: Notarial Doodles and Other Marks," *Word and Image* 25 (2009): 294–5; and Burns, "Notaries, Truth, and Consequences," *American Historical Review* 110 (2005): 352. For a detailed account of Peruvian notarial practices see Burns, *Into the Archive: Writing and Power in Colonial Peru* (Durham: Duke University Press, 2010); and Burns, "Dentro de la ciudad letrada: La producción de la escritura pública en el Perú colonial," *Histórica* 29 (2005): 43–68. For an introduction to the genres and formal exigencies of colonial textual production in general, see Walter Mignolo, "Cartas, crónicas y relaciones del descubrimiento y la conquista," in *Historia de la literatura hispanoamericana. Época colonial*, vol. 1, ed. Luis Iñigo Madrigal (Madrid: Cátedra, 1982), 57–116.

8 For a summary of the regulations of doctrine produced by the Third Lima Council, see John Charles, *Allies at Odds: The Andean Church and Its Indigenous Agents, 1583–1671* (Albuquerque: University of New Mexico Press, 2010); Alan Durston, *Pastoral Quechua: The History of Christian Translation in Colonial Peru, 1550–1650* (Notre Dame: University of Notre Dame Press, 2007); and

Juan Carlos Estenssoro Fuchs, *Del paganismo a la santidad. La incorporación de los indios del Perú al catolicismo, 1532–1750* (Lima: Institut français d'études andines, 2003).

9 Religious and pedagogical exemplarity evoke the religious (and, in turn, classical) tradition of modelling oneself after the holy family and other saints. For a discussion of New World saints, see Ronald J. Morgan, *Spanish American Saints and the Rhetoric of Identity, 1600–1800* (Tucson: University of Arizona Press, 2002); and Antonio Rubial Garcia, *La santidad controvertida. Hagiografía y conciencia criolla alrededor de los venerables no canonizados de Nueva España* (México: Universidad Nacional Autónoma de México, 1999).

10 I thus build upon the work of scholars such as Rolena Adorno, Charles, and Kenneth Mills who have attended to indigenous subjects' use of bureaucratic procedure to contest their marginalization from colonial authority and the codification of their difference. See Charles, "Felipe Guaman Poma de Ayala en los foros de la justicia eclesiástica," in *Justicia y población indígena en la América virreinal*, ed. Ana de Zaballa Beascoechea (Madrid: Iberoamericana, 2011), 203–22; Charles, *Allies at Odds;* Charles, "More *Ladino* Than Necessary: Indigenous Litigants and the Language Policy Debate in Mid-Colonial Peru," *Colonial Latin American Review* 16 (2007): 23–47; Mills, *Idolatry and Its Enemies: Colonial Andean Religion and Extirpation, 1640–1750* (Princeton: Princeton University Press, 1997); Mills, "Bad Christians in Colonial Peru," *Colonial Latin American Review* 5 (1996): 183–218; Mills, "The Limits of Religious Coercion in Mid-Colonial Peru," *Past and Present* 145 (1994): 84–121; Adorno, "Images of *Indios Ladinos* in Early Colonial Peru," in *Transatlantic Encounters: Europeans and Andeans in the Sixteenth Century*, ed. Kenneth J. Andrien and Rolena Adorno (Berkeley: University of California Press, 1991), 232–70.

11 See, for instance, the case of Francisco Ruiz de Pineda, natural of Lima, in AAL, Papeles Importantes, legajo 5, expediente 10 (1642) and the case of Bartolomé de Aramburú, natural of Guipúzcoa, in AAL, Papeles Importantes, legajo 5, expediente 12 (1646). An analysis of the ages, professions, origins, and citizen statuses of petitioners and witnesses lies outside the scope of this essay. I have, however, included such details in footnotes when they appear in the petitions. While I have modernized spellings of names in the body of this article, I respect orthography in my transcriptions included in the footnotes. For a discussion of the different terminologies that defined the political status of community members in early modern Spain and the colonial Spanish Americas, see Tamar Herzog, *Defining Nations: Immigrants and Citizens in Early Modern Spain and Spanish America* (New Haven: Yale University Press, 2011).

12 AAL, Papeles Importantes, legajo 5, expediente 9 (1642). Pérez de Atocha is documented as a "natural de Lima." Solicitors' ages are frequently not listed in the petitions.

13 Ibid., 2r. "Persona buen christiano virtuoso de buena vida y exemplo por lo qual le a visto exercitarse en enseñar la doctrina christiana a los niños y a leer escrivir y contar." The notary records Manuel Pérez to be a resident of the city, more or less fifty years old, and family of the inquisitor don Antonio de Castro.

14 Ibid., 2v. "Hombre virtuoso y de buena vida y costumbres." According to the text, Vásquez is the "ayudante de las compañías de los pardos" or a ranking officer in the company of the *pardo* militia, and forty years old.

15 Ibid., 3r. "Persona virtuosa de buena vida y costumbres." The notary lists Lumbreras as a "natural" and "morador" (inhabitant) of the city and more than fifty years old.

16 Ibid. 2r. "Le a tratado y comunicado familiarmente."

17 See footnote 7.

18 Adorno, *Guaman Poma: Writing and Resistance in Colonial Peru* (Austin: University of Texas Press, 1986), 52.

19 AAL, Papeles Importantes, legajo 5, expediente 9 (1642), 3v. "Dandoles buen exemplo."

20 Ibid., 3r. "Sin dar nota ni mal exemplo de su persona por auer procedido muy bien."

21 Ibid., 2r. "Es muy importante para el dicho exercisio ... virtud y vida exemplar."

22 Charles, *Allies at Odds*, 20.

23 Estenssoro Fuchs, *Del paganismo a la santidad*, 94–114.

24 José Toribio Medina, ed., *La imprenta en Lima (1584—1824)* (Lima, 1904), 28. [Original title and imprint: *Tercero cathecismo y exposicion de la Doctrina Christiana, por sermones, para que los curacas y otros ministros prediquen y enseñen a los yndios y a las demas personas conforme a lo que en el Sancto Concilio Provincial de Lima se proveyo* (Lima: Antonio Ricardo, 1585.] "[U]na de las cosas de mayor substancia que se trató en el Concilio Provincial...fue dar orden que la doctrina de los naturales ... fuese uniforme, sin hacer diferencia ni aun en solo una sílaba por el gran daño que ha resultado de no haberse hecho assi en lo pasado." Durston quotes a Catechism published the previous year that employs the same language, 331.

25 Francisco Leonardo Lisi, ed., *El Tercer Concilio Limense y la aculturación de los indígenas sudamericanos. Estudio crítico con edición, traducción y comentario de las actas del concilio provincial celebrado en Lima entre 1582–1583* (Salamanca: Universidad de Salamanca, 1990), 125. "La misma forma de una única

doctrina." For accessibility, I cite Lisi's Spanish translations of the original Latin. English translations are my own. Friars were concerned with the standardization of conversion during the First Lima Council (1551–52) as well, arguing that "porque como los naturales destas partes es gente de poco entendimiento" it is necessary to teach them "una misma cosa y en un mismo estilo y lengua." Rubén Vargas Ugarte, ed., *Concilios Limenses (1551–1772)*, vol. 1 (Lima: Arzobispo de Lima, 1951), 7. "Because the natives of these parts are of little understanding"; "the same thing in a same style and language."

26 *Tercer Concilio Limense*, 155. "Si no apareciere ninguno que la sepa, no ha de dejar de proveerse sin embargo la parroquia con un sacerdote cualquiera, mientras no sea de malas costumbres, pues es preferible enviar un párroco que viva correctamente a uno que hable bien, si hubiera que elegir uno, porque la vida edifica mucho más que la lengua."

27 Larissa Brewer-García has addressed the continued need for translators in the instruction of doctrine, despite their official exclusion as legislated by the Third Lima Council. See Brewer-García, "Bodies, Texts, and Translators: Indigenous Breast Milk and the Jesuit Exclusion of Mestizos in Late Sixteenth-Century Peru," *Colonial Latin American Review* 21 (2012): 365–90.

28 *Tercer Concilio Limense*, 175. "Pues con razón nuestros mayores enseñan que no hay nada que mueva más a la piedad y al culto de Dios al resto que la vida y ejemplo de aquellos que se dedicaron al divino ministerio, pues, como se ve que han sido elevados del siglo a un puesto superior, naturalmente los otros vuelven sus ojos a ellos como a un espejo de donde toman lo que imitar ..."

29 The idea of imitation does not only appear in religious texts that address indigenous difference. In Francisco de Sosa's 1658 petition, the witness Joseph Santos testifies that he has "seen [Sosa's parents] raise and nourish" their son and, in turn, seen their son "imitate his Christian parents." AAL, Papeles Importantes, legajo 5, expediente 19 (1658), 2v–3r. Santos is identified as a *vecino* of the city and is forty-four years old. "Los vido criar y alimentar"; "hijo de tales y tan cristianos padres imitándoles."

30 *Tercer Concilio Limense*, 175–7. "Por ello, conviene que los clérigos convocados al dominio del señor compongan su vida y todas sus costumbres de tal modo que ni en su hábito, ni en su gesto, ni en el modo de andar, el discurso o cualquier otra cosa hagan nada que no sea grave, moderado y lleno de religión, así como también que eviten los delitos leves que en ellos serían gravísimos, para que sus acciones produzcan veneración a todos."

31 Richard Kagan, *Students and Society in Early Modern Spain* (Baltimore: Johns Hopkins University Press, 1974), xvii. See also Charles, *Allies at Odds*, 203.

32 Ibid., 11–12.

33 See Mills, "Bad Christians."

34 AAL, Papeles Importantes, legajo 5, expediente 19 (1658), 1r. "vida y costumbres, y de como es hijo de padres christianos viejos."

35 AAL, Papeles Importantes, legajo 5, expediente 18 (1658), 2r. "Cristiano viejo y limpio de toda mala raza de judíos ni moros ni de los nuevamente convertidos." Pablo de Noguera is listed as "español," a "vecino" of the city, and seventy years old.

36 Ibid., 3r. "Christiano viejo limpio de toda mala raça de moros y judios y de los nuebamente conbertidos." Zeberino is identified as a "natural" of the city, a master carpenter, and forty-four years old.

37 Ibid., 4r. "Visto sabido oydo ni entendido cossa en contrario." Pacheco is identified as a "vecino" of the city and fifty-four years old.

38 See Henry Kamen, *The Spanish Inquisition: A Historical Revision* (New Haven: Yale University Press, 1997), esp. 137–73.

39 AAL, Papeles Importantes, legajo 5, expediente 13 (1649), 3r. "Proceder mui honesta y rrecoxidamente como buen xptiano temeroso de Dios y de su conciencia dando mui buen exemplo en sus acciones y proceder." Carmona is listed as a "maestro de escuela" and sixty years old.

40 Ibid., 3v. "Siempre a dado mui buena quenta de su persona savelo assi por los papeles que a visto como por averselo dicho personas que le vieron y conocieron en el dho ministerio."

41 Archivo General de la Nación, Gobierno 2, caja 868, legajo 92 (1685), 5f. This document has been mentioned by Alaperrine-Bouyer, *La educación de las élites*, 146–7; and Rubén Vargas Ugarte, "La instrucción primaria en el Perú virreinal," *Fénix. Revista de la Biblioteca Nacional* 22 (1972): 162–8.

42 Alaperrine-Bouyer suggests that Mateo González could be one of the indigenous students educated at the Colegio del Príncipe, one of the first schools for the indigenous elite founded in the Viceroyalty of Peru in 1618. She notes that a Juan González appears on the list of students in 1657. *Educacción de las elites*, 146–7.

43 AGN, Gobierno 2, caja 868, legajo 92 (1685), 2r. "Enseñanza y educación de los yndios pobres naturales de esta ciudad."

44 Ibid., 2v. "Indio ladino en lengua española y de buenas costumbres." While the category *ladino* indicated familiarity with the Spanish language, *indios ladinos* could have varying degrees of proficiency in Spanish language, reading, and writing. Their status as translators, religious intermediaries, and often litigants made them polemical figures in the colonial landscape. See note 10 for scholarship on the category and the range of subjects that fit into it.

45 Ibid., 3r. “A propósito para la enseñanza de los muchachos por ser yndio de buenas costumbres.”

46 Ibid., 4r. “De la misma forma y manera que lo hacen los demas mros de escuela.”

47 Charles notes that the seventeenth-century Viceroys Martín Enríqeuz de Alamanza and Pedro de Toledo y Leiva established provisions allowing priests to use the most “ladino” or lettered indigenous subjects to teach children up to fourteen the Castilian language, reading, and writing. Charles, *Allies at Odds*, 20.

chapter eight

Stadial Environmental History in the Voyage Narratives of George and John Reinhold Forster

NOAH HERINGMAN

John Reinhold Forster's *Observations Made During a Voyage Round the World* was published in 1778, the same year as the comte de Buffon's *Epochs of Nature*, which developed by far the longest detailed geological time scale offered by a naturalist up to that time. George Forster had published his more copious narrative, *Voyage Round the World*, the previous year, anticipating his father's more focused treatment of natural history. Both Forsters employed and corrected Buffon's earlier work, as well as the mineralogical fieldwork of Johann Jakob Ferber and several others, in their study of volcanic phenomena throughout the voyage of the *Resolution* from 1772 to 1775. They brought the question of how Pacific islands formed to bear on the question of human origins and migrations. In so doing, they established experimental points of contact and divergence between recorded human time, on the one hand, and deep time with its associated geological terms, including "primitive rocks," on the other. Buffon made some use of heterodox antiquarian scholarship in his attempt to incorporate the history of peoples into the history of nature, and some conjectural historians, such as Lord Kames, made an effort to engage with natural history in their "Histories of Mankind." The Forsters, however, made especially vivid use of cultural evidence to explore geological time, and vice versa: their contact with Pacific peoples revealed areas of uncertainty common to both and allowed them to revise and transform the conjectural model of "stages" in the history of the species.

The Forsters, somewhat like Buffon in *Epochs of Nature*, elaborated a deep human past by adapting the geological term "primitive." "Savage" was primarily used by all three to designate non-European peoples, and their differing uses of both terms shed light on important differences in approach to the unsettling intimation of human marginality in relation to geological time. Buffon makes generalized use of "savages" as they appear in travel narratives to "form an idea of [man's] ancient condition," only to deduce that humanity itself is very modern indeed (*encore bien moderne*) compared to the geological "revolutions anterior to the memory of man" and even to the species produced by Nature "in her primitive vigour."[1] In a review of *Epochs of Nature*, Reinhold Forster rejected Buffon's arguments for the antiquity of the earth, inspired at least in part by what he had observed in the Pacific. Voyaging with Cook, the Forsters learned to identify atolls and recent volcanic islands, which seemed to support a more orthodox "young earth" view, and they made copious observations in the field concerning "the history of mankind [in] various stages," which led Reinhold in particular to regard only a very limited subset of human groups as "savages, removed but in the first degree from absolute animality."[2] In the *Observations*, he challenges purely philosophical (or "closet") histories of the species on principle, for lacking field evidence. George Forster offered the same rebuff to Immanuel Kant in his polemic, "And Another Thing about the Human Races." By insisting on natural history as the framework for their ethnography, the Forsters gained access to a vocabulary shared with other naturalists, including the key term "primitive," used strictly in its then-current geological sense of "unaltered"; without excusing their Eurocentrism, the earlier, more neutral sense of the term promotes an understanding of Pacific peoples in relation to their environmental histories rather than as "early" in relation to a scheme of universal history.

Appropriating his experience of first contact as a "great branch of the study of nature" (*OM* 145), Reinhold Forster argues that Pacific "arts and sciences" represented a creative response to the natural setting of the islands, but both Forsters' estimates for the length of these processes vary wildly from generations to unspecified "ages." These contradictions support their claim to be testing philosophical conjectures experimentally in the field, but they also reflect the ambivalence inherent in the discourse of primitivism itself. Empirical study of customs and artefacts readily unsettled the orderly sequence of four stages of society partly because the theorists of those stages themselves suspected or recognized that the sequence was not orderly. Nicholas Thomas points out that although both Forsters readily invoke the ancient/primitive analogy to explain violence among the Māori, their response is ultimately ambivalent, mirroring the ambivalence already inherent in stadial histories such as that of John Millar. Thomas notes that Millar made "liberty" characteristic of both early and late stages of civil society and argues that Reinhold shared Millar's anxiety about the slippage from "liberty" to "licence" in both stages.

Nostalgia for "savage" liberty casts doubt on the celebration of commerce and progress in the Forsters as in Millar and even in more conservative theorists such as Adam Ferguson. Harriet Guest argues that Reinhold "was concerned to develop these theories" – Millar's in particular – "and adapt them to his novel experiences." In a similar vein, but emphasizing the Forsters' use of European climate theory, David Bindman points out that "experience made things complex and unstable, challenging the formulae of climate and social life that had dominated views of the 'savage' world."[3] Richard Lansdown expands this broader European frame of reference by tracing the "bipolar vision" of "cultural" and "chronological" primitivism from classical antiquity down to the Enlightenment, emphasizing "the depth of Rousseau's ambivalence" as a major influence on the voyagers. Thus both new empirical evidence and instability in the theories themselves made it far from a "simple matter," as Thomas rightly suggests, "for Europeans to apply their prior notions of savage or primitive life" to Pacific peoples.[4] All these interpretations reinforce Reinhold Forster's own distinction between armchair theorizing and ethnographic fieldwork.

Theories of the earth further complicated the Forsters' fieldwork, and vice versa, because they too carried particular investments in the shape of the primitive world. For the Forsters, taking a naturalist's view means attending to the geology of the islands and its implications for the prehistory of a population. The advanced civilization on Tahiti presupposes the "long existence and fertility" of the island (*OM* 41), measured in relative terms by its apparently long-dormant volcanoes and abundant "fat" volcanic soils. Easter Island, on the other hand, appears to have been devastated recently by a "terrible revolution," as George puts it.[5] Re-establishing the ancient civilization seemingly implied by the monuments there would have to be a "work of ages" (*OM* 198). The Forsters exploit the double sense of "revolution" – a commonplace in theories of the earth – as a social or natural phenomenon to posit a wide range of dates for the formation and the settlement, respectively, of the various islands. Reinhold in particular insists that lands can become "habitable" and "inhabited" at widely different times (*OM* 105).

Both Forsters emphasize the ubiquity of volcanoes and volcanic islands all across the Pacific. Volcanic eruptions, and the formation of volcanic islands in particular, presented a geogony in miniature, as Darwin later noted enthusiastically of the Galápagos. Volcanic rock could not be primitive by definition, but it constituted a suggestive middle ground between stratified and unstratified materials.[6] George takes the active volcano on Malekula as a proof of the island's fertility (*RW* 679) and explains

Figure 8.1 *Cascade Cove, Dusky Bay*, by William Hodges (1775). Oil on canvas. Image in the public domain. https://commons.wikimedia.org/wiki/File:Hodges_dusky-bay.jpg.

the apparent contrast between the islanders' intelligence and their lack of "conveniences" by conjecturing that they have arrived on the island only recently, since the geology stabilized (699). By contrast, Reinhold places great emphasis on the geologically primitive state of New Zealand at Dusky Sound. His influential distinction between civil Polynesians and savage Māori depends on the geological rate of improvement: "The tropical isles have all the appearance of a long existence and fertility. But the southernmost parts … are still unimproved, and in that rude state in which they sprung up from the first chaos" (*O* 41). On the South Island of New Zealand, "Nature has just begun her great work," while the South Atlantic island of Ascension provides evidence of a recent eruption initiating the long, slow alteration of "primogenial" land for the better (110).

For the Forsters, human prehistory came into view as a part of geological succession, and recently established populations afforded a glimpse of prehistory in real time. As Thomas has noted, William Hodges's painting of Dusky Sound (Figure 8.1) seems to capture the "undomesticated strength" that the artists and naturalists on board the *Resolution* perceived holistically as the natural state of the place, surrounded by forests unchanged since the Flood (as George claims) and teeming with previously unknown genera and even families (which Reinhold celebrates). In their narratives, the Forsters struggle to map a scale of human values onto an increasingly long and unsettled time scale and onto the complex geographic itinerary of their voyage. They ultimately produce a conjectural history of the present, a history animated by their heterodox notions of progress and incorporating not only time's arrow but also time's cycle as illustrated by the geological environment. To chart the progress of their voyage, as well as the "progress" of populations and ecosystems they encountered, they continually revised and amended their criteria and scale of analysis by establishing new correlations – between or among populations and geological features as well as plants and animals in a given climate. In this way, deep time emerged from human time, and evolutionary time (to use modern terms) could be inferred from phenomena on the "eco-devo" scale of ecology and development.

Recognizing the social-natural character of "revolutions" such as volcanic eruptions, the Forsters also developed a limited receptivity to indigenous knowledge on these subjects. Concluding his "Remarks on the Changes of Our Globe," Reinhold enters somewhat self-consciously "into the land of fables and mythology" to suggest that "the inhabitants themselves have some idea of a great revolution, which happened to their isles" (*OM* 112). The story of the god Maui "dragging a great land from west to east through the ocean" indicates that perhaps some of the Society Islands were not raised from the sea by volcanoes, but "were only dismembered by the sinking of the intermediate parts." In *Epochs of Nature*, Buffon claims that "the first men were witnesses of the convulsive motions of the earth, which were then frequent and terrible," and that the fear of earthquakes is their enduring legacy.[7] The Tahitian myth similarly recalls an earlier state of humanity for Forster and may provide evidence of geological upheaval in the prehuman past. For both Forsters, however, the presence of "young" civilizations on "young" islands provided viable grounds for conjectures about origins, and at least in this analogical sense volcanic revolutions brought human prehistory into contact with primitive geology. When native people on Tanna (Vanuatu/New Hebrides) denied them access to the one active volcano they had the opportunity to study, this mountain, Yasur, became a "mediator," in Bruno Latour's sense, displacing geological into ethnographic inquiry and making indigenous knowledge more visible.[8]

Navigating Pacific Time

This chapter follows a Pacific itinerary – from Dusky Sound to Tanna to New Caledonia and back to New Zealand (Queen Charlotte Sound) – to illustrate the interplay between the varying scales of time revealed by environmental history. When considering interactions such as the Tannese refusal to allow a geological investigation of Yasur, I will be asking what happened when the encounter with this culture, instead of being merely an obstacle, itself became a scientific pursuit for the Forsters in this context. How did their study of the volcanic soil and its vegetable and animal "productions" inform this pursuit, and vice versa? The chapter first takes up these kinds of questions for all three sites in a broad ecological context and then turns more specifically towards ethnography. George celebrates the eruption of Yasur as a "wonderful phaenomenon," and such aesthetic categories help establish a holistic ecological view of each place on this abbreviated itinerary – each of which is also a site of first contact.[9]

Hodges's painting of Dusky Sound provides a visual index of the convergence of aesthetic conventions and novel experiences in the field that produced this "savage place." I borrow Coleridge's description of the "romantic chasm" that traverses his response to exotic travel narrative, "Kubla Khan," to indicate the influence of the Gothic and picturesque traditions – besides the ethnographic tradition of "savages" – on the Forsters' construction of New Zealand as the primitive foundation of their social stratigraphy. They draw attention to these influences themselves. The epithet "savage," so often attached to the paintings of Salvator Rosa in picturesque theory, moved Reinhold to wish for him in Dusky Sound: "Some of these cascades with their neighboring scenery, require the pencil and genius of a Salvator Rosa to do them justice: however the ingenious artist [Hodges], who went with us on this expedition has great merit, in having executed some of these romantic landscapes in a masterly manner" (*OM* 51–2). George begins his chapter on Dusky Sound with a similar aesthetic response, declaring that "this landscape is entirely in that artist's [Rosa's] taste" because of its cliffs, waterfalls, and "forests that seem to date back before the Flood" (*RW* 137). The family depicted here by Hodges thus belongs to a time at least as old as sacred history. The Forsters treat them accordingly as a first family of humans – though, as Thomas points out, it is far from clear in George's narrative, and even less so in the painting, what sort of family this is or whether it is a nuclear family at all. The posture and costume of these figures, the dense "primeval" forest, the foaming cascade, and the snow-covered "primitive" peaks evoke an environmental history of human society that adapts and revises the stadial theory (i.e., the theory, primarily Scottish and French, of civilizational "stages") that Hodges as well as the Forsters brought to bear on the encounter.[10]

The Forsters' approach to the study of peoples and climate made biogeography more than crust-deep by incorporating geological questions. Incorporating not only rocks, but also flora and fauna, along with more immediate intellectual influences such as Linnaeus and Buffon, the Forsters came into their own as environmental historians of the species at Dusky Sound. They rendered this spot on New Zealand's South Island a "savage place" by taking the most comprehensive view of nature, classifying and correlating flora, fauna, and human populations previously unknown to Europeans with climate and geology. George's narrative celebrates the diversity of new plants and animals at Dusky Sound: "there was hardly a genus that corresponded to the known genera, and some could not even be classed among the known families" (*RW* 138). Early in the narrative he had expressed anxiety that they would not have the same opportunities that Joseph Banks and Sydney Parkinson had on the *Endeavour* to make discoveries (92), but here (as later on Tanna and New Caledonia) he claims a kind of Adamic priority, giving names to things with an enthusiasm inspired by the "patriarchal" family of humans in Dusky Sound. Martin Guntau identifies the Forsters' "holistic concept of nature" as typical for the "bourgeois Enlightenment worldview"; it is also invoked by Alexander von Humboldt as a precedent for his encyclopedic view of global nature.[11] My point here is that environmental history generates new metrics by which to gauge the state or "stage" of a society, as Reinhold and George both insist on a correlation between a comparatively smaller number of unknown species and a "higher state of civilization" associated with agriculture (*OM* 114). Hence the contrast between New Zealand with its estimated four to five hundred new plant species and Tahiti, where the scarcity of new species attests to that island's "high culture" (*RW* 263).

Thus all the human and natural features of Dusky Sound help establish one pole of a binary that eventually structures both narratives: the Society Islands are cultured and beautiful, while New Zealand is savage, primeval, and by turns sublime or picturesque. It also happens to be the first significant stage (for the Forsters as naturalists) of the *Resolution*'s itinerary. The cascades of Dusky Sound were "astonished" to see themselves "so correctly imitated" on Hodges's easel, but although the arts and sciences seemed to flower there during the ship's time at anchor, George anticipates that all their traces will soon "sink back into the original, chaotic state of this country" (*RW* 180–1). The younger Forster's predilection for literary *topoi* such as recognition and reversal is apparent here; his narrative is more sceptical and ambivalent about progress than his father's, in both its style and its philosophical content. Nevertheless, the polarity of "savage" higher latitudes versus "cultured" tropics and the framework that follows from it – the developmental spectrum of island societies, the scale of time and values mapped onto the ship's geographic itinerary – together often structure George's narrative, while in Reinhold's *Observations* this framework becomes the burden of the argument.

Reinhold Forster offers a stadial environmental history that, although comprehensive and revisionist, leaves little doubt about the ultimate progress of human and non-human nature. His chapters on mineralogy, botany, and zoology present a series of nested progress narratives that begin either with Dusky Sound or with the even more "degenerated" southernmost lands of the Western Hemisphere. While George worries that their conversion of Dusky Sound from a "wild and desolate spot" to a "living country" might prove to be only temporary (*RW* 179), Reinhold assures us that here "nature has just begun her great work" (*OM* 41). If the forests of Dusky Sound are left to rot a while longer, the island is merely "hoarding up a precious quantity of the richest mould, for a future generation of men," a matrix that in the meantime has the power to "rescue new animated parts of the creation from their inactive, chaotic state" (43). In their notes to the *Observations*, Thomas, Guest, and Dettelbach credit Reinhold with extending to the plant and animal kingdoms Lord Kames's "polarity" of "torpid" or stagnant versus "roused" or progressive civilizations (416n2), exemplified for Reinhold in the contrast between New Zealand and Tahiti. He not only encompasses non-human nature – even the mineral kingdom, if one looks closely – within a dualism of extreme versus moderate climates (which probably owes as much to Montesquieu as to Kames's *Sketches of the History of Man*), but also insists, in colonial fashion, that "the lord of the creation" is a necessary part of this economy; non-human nature can only become degenerated or "deformed by being left to itself" (99).

In surveying all the kingdoms of nature, including "the human species," the *Observations* amasses the evidence needed to flesh out the savage/civilized binary so that it forms a complex progress from one environmental stage to the next. Moving from the mineral into the plant kingdom,

Reinhold seems to identify four stages along the continuum from rude to cultured environments:

> We have observed how much the least attractive of these tropical countries, surpasses the ruder scenery of New-Zeeland: how much more discouraging than this, are the extremities of America; and lastly, how dreadful the southern coasts appear, which we discovered [South Georgia]. In the same manner, the plants that inhabit these lands, will be found to differ in number, stature, beauty, and use. (113)

Because of its retrospective form, the *Observations* incorporates all of these stages more fully than George's journal. In the chapter on "organic bodies," Reinhold tends to reverse the order of the ship's itinerary in 1773 from Antarctic waters to New Zealand to Tahiti. By starting with Tahiti and the tropical islands which he views as the cradle of humanity (342), Reinhold constructs an "implied history of gradual migratory degeneration" (417n2), as Thomas aptly puts it. His zoological observations further elaborate this structure: "In the same manner the animal world, from being beautiful, rich, enchanting, between the tropics; falls into deformity, poverty, and disgustfulness in the Southern coasts" (128). Reinhold glosses this particularly succinct (and inverted) version of the progress narrative with illustrations ranging from the delicious hogs of the Society Islands to the "degenerated" dogs of New Zealand (130) and finally the "monstrous" seals of Tierra del Fuego (129). This scheme of classification even allows paradoxically for the degeneration of *in*animate nature, for Reinhold claims that by contrast to the North Island of New Zealand, which has some fertile ground, the South Island "still degenerates into rude rocks" (117).

Because it follows the itinerary of the voyage more closely, George's narrative shows more clearly how both Forsters gradually revised their itinerary of environmental stages and modified their accounts of places and peoples to accommodate the diversity they found. At first, the encounter on Dusky Sound conditions his assessment of New Zealand as a whole, figured as the savage home of what he imagines as the first family. Since the *Resolution* next visited the more populous region of Queen Charlotte Sound (at the north end of the same island), and anchored there twice more in the course of the voyage, George had ample opportunities to correct his first impression – both by comparing the two populations (*RW*882), much as Reinhold compares the two environments above, and by revising upward his estimate of the islands' biodiversity (904). At first, however, the small population at Dusky Sound seemed to both Forsters to correspond at most to the "small band" level of organization familiar both from Buffon and from conjectural history. Reinhold presents his revision in retrospect by situating the "barbarism" of the Māori, considered as "one of the steps" towards "a better state of happiness" (*OM* 210), ahead of the "stupid indolence" of the Fuegians (214), whom the *Resolution* actually encountered twenty-one months later. He places the Fuegians, by contrast, in the same situation as "all the nations found by the first European discovery ... of America," that of "savages, just one degree removed from animality" (205), using the same language that appears in his preface (9) to signal his expansion and revision of stadial history.[12]

The use of animal products offers another environmental standard for assessing the movement of peoples in both directions along this expanded continuum. On Tahiti, Reinhold finds luxury articles made of "bone, shark's teeth, &c." together with "delicate ... victuals"; in New Zealand, some "conveniences," together with palatable food; and in Tierra del Fuego only the "bare necessaries of life," "bit[s] of seal skin" for clothing and meat that he (like Darwin after him) considers "putrid" and "disgustful" (140–1). Thomas, Guest, and Dettelbach again seek to derive this metric from Kames's *Sketches*, observing that this derivation would be "more clearly articulated" if the *Resolution* had encountered a pastoral society in the Pacific (419n11). In fact, the Scottish Enlightenment model could only have been of limited usefulness for a paradigm that was built on natural history rather than political economy and that responded dynamically to the information provided by each new encounter. Environmental conditions were, for Reinhold Forster, "the true cause" both of civilizational progress and of "debasement and degeneration among savages" (207). The Forsters' conjectural history of the ethnographic present thus unfolds in the course of the ship's itinerary – a spatial movement correlated in shifting and unpredictable ways with distance in time.

First Contact and the Revision of Progress

In June 1773 the *Resolution* proceeded to the Society and Friendly Isles before returning to Queen Charlotte Sound and then making a second, much longer circuit to the south and east that took in a number of new island groups including the New Hebrides (July–August 1774). While these were not the *Resolution*'s only experiences of first contact, Reinhold's and particularly George's narratives make much of the insights gleaned from newly encountered peoples in Vanuatu / New Hebrides, especially Tanna, and afterward in New Caledonia. This stage of the voyage revolutionized the Forsters' stadial environmental history, complicating the binary scheme of "savage" and "cultivated" that had been reinforced by repeated visits to New Zealand and Tahiti and by the Forsters' extensive use of earlier voyage narratives. On Tanna, the active volcano Yasur opened a new time dimension for the correlation of social and natural "improvement." The encounters with human and non-human populations during this phase of the voyage transformed the Forsters' understanding of the *topos* of travelling into the past and focused attention on ongoing processes of adaptation. The environmental histories of Malekula, Tanna, and New Caledonia were less intelligible by analogy to the ancient past and instead made clear how much of this past, including the quantity of time elapsed, remained unknown.

The encounter on Tanna stands out for its novelty – that is, for its abundance of new natural phenomena as well as for the sociability that mediated the Forsters' knowledge of these phenomena and prompted their rich but inconclusive analysis of the "stage" or state of the environment as a whole. The island offered their first opportunity to study an active volcano as well as especially intriguing flora, such as the wild coconut palm – which, as George notes, they encountered nowhere else – and wild nutmeg. Their keen interest in the latter led to a complex engagement with the bird and human populations that used this seed. Their adventure with the nutmeg began the morning after they abandoned their effort to ascend the volcano, Yasur, having met again with strong resistance from the Tannese on their third and final attempt. In the event, the Forsters (Reinhold particularly) were frustrated again in their efforts to find the source – the nutmeg tree in this case – and it may be that frustration with the attempt on the volcano spilled over into this encounter. Searching the forest for specimens, George shot a variety of pigeon that he thought he remembered from the Friendly Islands (actually the Tannese ground dove, now extinct), calling it "the most valuable find" of the day (*RW* 785). After making the beautiful watercolour sketch now held by the Natural History Museum, he and his father dissected the bird and found two fresh nutmegs in its crop, noting the intact mace surrounding the seeds and even their bitter taste. It was presumably due to the money value of the spice that the Forsters doggedly, but unsuccessfully, sought to persuade (and even intimidate) the Tannese to show them the tree. Michael Hoare calls the whole episode a "comedy of errors" because their first informant took them to be requesting information about the dove instead of the tree and was then accused of deliberately misleading them.[13] They had already discovered that the Tannese coconut palm plantations contained improved varieties of the endemic wild species, and they surely wanted to know if the nutmeg (probably *Myristica inutilis*) was a cultivar as well. Any stadial assessment of this island's ecology as a whole depended on the answers to such questions.

The role of indigenous people as both abettors of and impediments to discovery (only rarely acknowledged by the Forsters elsewhere) renders the savage/cultivated binary moot.[14] On the one hand, the presence of an active volcano signifies ongoing improvement of the land and perhaps a recent "revolution," as I suggested above. Similarly, the presence of wild coconut palms alongside the cultivars suggested an active process of improvement, probably in its early stages, but impossible to date either in absolute or in relative terms (808). On the other hand, George notes customs as well as physical characteristics suggesting that the main outlines of Tannese culture may predate the migration of this group or groups (three different languages were spoken) to the island (807). In the effort to identify a metric for their civilization (*Maaß der Civilisation*), George articulates a comparative ethnography, noting the presence of certain features (music, respect for property) and the absence of others (dress, trade) before concluding tentatively that the Tannese have advanced beyond the Māori and are approaching the degree of gentility (*Grade von Sanftmuth*) exhibited by the Tahitians (812). The long chapter on Tanna presents a mass of observed detail but also acknowledges many contradictions. The Forsters were delighted with the hospitality of the local people, who rewarded them for desisting from their volcanic expedition with prolonged and repeated exchanges of gifts and song (Figure 8.2). But islanders' resistance to the European knowledge project made it difficult to gauge the state of their (and their island's) "improvement" – and must have struck the Forsters on some level as a mark of sophistication in its own right. Their unwillingness to trade for food accounts in part for the explorers relatively short stay of two weeks, which also limited the opportunity for knowledge-gathering; in this case, George seems naively certain that scarcity of food – hence lack of cultivation – must be the cause. Throughout his chapters on Vanuatu / New Hebrides and New Caledonia, George emphasizes how much of their history must remain unknown and recognizes that the lapse of time required for the natural and social processes he observes cannot be measured or even guessed at.

Figure 8.2 "View in the Island of Tanna," engraving by William Woollett from a drawing by William Hodges. *James Cook, Voyage towards the South Pole*, 2nd ed. (London, 1777), vol. 2, plate XXIX. Courtesy of Linda Hall Library of Science, Engineering, and Technology, Kansas City, MO.

The attempt to correlate climate and culture on New Caledonia met with even greater difficulties. The very large main island of this group (Grand Terre) was the only island on the voyage that showed no evidence of volcanism, or "even of any volcanic products," as George notes with some surprise (823). Volcanic activity in the remote or recent past provided a rough measure of "improvement" elsewhere, but here the existence of a complex agricultural society in a rugged and seemingly barren environment posed a new kind of challenge. This difficulty, and the apparent lack of any anatomical or linguistic kinship with either the Vanuatuans or the Māori, led him to declare the New Caledonians "a race of men very distinct from all we had hitherto seen" (*VRW* II.588) and to increase his emphasis on the uncertainty of Pacific history (*RW* 823, cf. 835, 861).[15] Their small plantations, surrounded by large tracts of desert or "heath," appear to George so unproductive that he ranks the whole agro-ecosystem only "just above" that of Easter Island; every other tropical island has boasted "an abundance of fruits" (831). Instead of volcanic or humus-rich soils, he notices extensive outcrops of what is now known as ultrabasic igneous rock – George, following Ferber, uses the German term *Gestellstein* (833n). Once again, Cook and his men are unable to trade for food, and here George bases his inference of scarcity on the soil, which "only scantily" rewards the local farmers' labour (836). Although neither Forster offers an explicit correlation between the land and the people, it stands to reason that this "primogenial" earth carries a strong association with the deep geological past, a time predating even the volcanoes.[16]

George Forster glosses Cook's choice of the name New Caledonia by explaining that, like Scotland, it is a barren land inhabited by a hospitable people (*RW* 846). It is at least a suggestive coincidence that these "New Caledonians" – the Kanak – occasion some of the Forsters' most refined revisions of the stadial theory associated with the Scottish Enlightenment. While retaining the paradigm of stadial progression, they recognize that progression is non-linear and identify "microstages" of social development, as I will call them, by comparing many different local populations. On Tanna, George had already noted that a truly barbarous "stage" is out of the question where there are no game animals (808), and on New Caledonia he imagines that introducing goats on the island might compensate the islanders for having missed the pastoral stage and "forward civilization among them" (*VRW* II.593). Since the Kanak have no experience of quadrupeds, they assume that the sailors eating salt beef must be cannibals. Their horror at this sight implies a degree of civilization that renders them, in George's view, "farther advanced" than "their more opulent neighbors" on Tanna, who still practise cannibalism (592). He adds, however, that they are "not [yet] sufficiently enlightened to remove the unjust contempt shewn to the fair sex" (cf. *RW* 862). In these analyses, civilization is decoupled from political economy, or "opulence," and the recognized stages of progress become disordered, fragmented, and ambivalent.

The sheer difficulty of ethnographic classification does at times prompt broad generalizations in *Voyage Round the World*, and even more frequently in Reinhold Forster's *Observations*. George reports, for example, that "perhaps each family" on New Caledonia "forms a little kingdom of its own, which is directed by its patriarch, as must be the case in all infant states" (*VRW* II.593); thus he attempts to subsume his finer distinctions under a purported Pacific universal. The idea of "patriarchal" hospitality occurs frequently in the first chapter on Tahiti (*RW* 262, 271, 278), where Reinhold also argues that "the beginning of their civil society ... is of the patriarchal kind" (*OM* 223). The term in this sense seems to allude to the

Biblical patriarchs; at the end of their first long stay on Tahiti (*RW* 331), and again at Tanna (791), George also uses the term "patriarchal" in a more ethnographic sense, to refer to a form of social organization that is gradually being superseded. The Forsters' repeated use of this category may provide evidence that a homogenizing idea of primitive peoples is beginning to emerge out of the contradictions between the stadial model and observed local differences. This idea of an aboriginal Pacific population in a generally "infant state" remains in tension with the Forsters' more sophisticated idea of highly differentiated populations resulting from migrations and differing environmental histories.

Some criteria for distinguishing populations evolved as metrics for gauging the "level" of civilization on a given island and became increasingly refined in the latter stages of the voyage. These metrics include refinement of "conveniences" and mechanical arts; complexity of diet; music; sexual mores; and aggression as reflected in practices such as misogyny and cannibalism, which are explicitly paired in George's New Caledonian narrative. In one of his most moving descriptions of contact on the island, George describes his repeated attempts to observe three women at work, who communicated by signs that they would be strangled if they were caught with him (*VRW* II.577). "Considering these humiliations and cruel oppressions of the sex," he then reflects, "we have sometimes the greatest reason to admire, that the human race has perpetuated itself" (583). In his detailed description of the incident of supposed cannibalism, he achieves something like a reversal of the gaze, contemplating the sailors gnawing on a beef bone from what he takes to be an indigenous perspective. Here too a larger generalization in the mode of conjectural history follows: "men seem to have had recourse to animal food by necessity at first, as the depriving any creature of life is an act of violence" (586). Misogyny provokes an unfavourable comparison between the Society Islanders and Tannese, who are "not yet as civilized" on this score (*RW* 753); because the latter also practise cannibalism out of an instinctive thirst for vengeance – so George conjectures – they "still belong" to the "class" of vengeful peoples exemplified by the Māori (773; cf. *VRW* II.533). The binary opposition between this "class" and the more peaceable stage represented by Polynesia is consolidated in another cannibalism episode, when the *Resolution*'s Raiatean passenger, Maheine, is horrified by evidence of cannibalism during their second visit to New Zealand (*RW* 445). On their third visit, however, two new factors complicated this binary: first, they had now visited the New Hebrides and New Caledonia, where they had experienced a wider range of attitudes towards cannibalism; second, they gathered evidence that crew members from their companion vessel, the *Adventure*, might have been killed (and eaten, as they learned later) at Grass Cove, near Queen Charlotte Sound, in 1773 after the two ships were separated.[17]

A New Comparative Method

Music and chastity also come into play in the complex four-way comparison among Polynesia, Tanna, New Caledonia, and New Zealand that develops in George's account of this third and final sojourn in Queen Charlotte Sound. Returning to the issue of misogyny at the end of his chapter on Tanna, George finally decided that the Tannese were "gradually advanc[ing]" towards the Polynesian standard after all, because "less unjust to their women" than the Māori (*VRW* II.556). The new evidence of large-scale cannibalism among the Māori tended to support that view. At the same time, however, these two populations both had music that sounded relatively complex and pleasing to the European ear. George and the Forsters' assistant naturalist, Anders Sparrman, spent long afternoons exchanging songs with the inhabitants of a Tannese village, who were especially delighted with Sparrman's Swedish songs (534). George in turn credits their songs as harmonically richer and rhythmically more complex than anything they had heard in the Society and Friendly Islands. Recounting these events in sequence, rather than presenting a synthetic judgment, George begins at this moment to reconsider his emphasis on the "vengeful" nature of the Tannese and to credit them with "benevolence" and hospitality (535). The highly emotive songs of the Māori fall between this complex Tannese music and the "wretched humming of the Taheitian" on the scale of "genius" (615). Here George draws on the observations of James Burney, who recorded Polynesian and Māori songs in detail on the *Adventure*, to upend the usual hierarchy of value. This superior "taste for music" among the Māori, he concludes, is one of the "stronger proofs in favour of their heart" (616). Even the cannibalistic attack on the *Adventure*'s boat in 1773 can be justified as an expression of the "right of retaliating injuries" consistent with savage liberty (610). When it comes to chastity, however, Tanna and New Caledonia – the scenes of first contact – set the highest standard, while the Māori, the Polynesians, and the Europeans themselves all fall short.

As concerned as he is to do justice to the native genius and the savage liberty of the Māori, and to refine his naive initial account of the "first family" at Dusky Sound, George is unsparing with his disgust when narrating the sexual traffic between Māori women and the ship's company. On the positive side, their instinctive sense of justice and their lack of duplicity provide additional "proofs in favour of their heart," besides their musical sensibility. As Thomas has argued, George was already inclined at Dusky Sound to defend Māori characteristics that seemed to him to express an idea of liberty that was both consistent with the values of an advanced commercial society and harder to attain in "civilized" circumstances. Thomas's juxtaposition of "liberty and license" also provides an effective lens for analysing the final episode at Queen Charlotte Sound, where the Forsters gathered new evidence of both and of the complexity of the dynamic between them. Music and revenge (or resistance to oppression) become aligned with "liberty" in this episode, while sexual traffic becomes associated with the "license" that George had earlier noted as the cause of extreme and violent misogyny at Dusky Sound.[18] The sensibility of the Maori heart, which he holds up as a rebuke to "philosophers in their cabinets," possibly Rousseau in particular (616), helps explain in some measure the Māori leader's "puzzling" refusal to sail with them to England even though "he felt the superiority of our knowledge ... and mode of living" (615). That superiority is, however, very much in question when George slips from a description of the "inconvenience" of domestic life among the Māori into an invective on the "grovelling appetites" of those shipmates (both officers and men) who entered their smoke-filled houses "in order to receive the caresses of the filthy female inhabitants" (612). He praises the natives of the New Hebrides and New Caledonia for "having very wisely declined every indecent familiarity with their guests," unlike both the Māori and the Polynesians, and in his New Caledonian narrative he specifically praises the women's skill at eluding the sailors' advances (577–8).

The problem of chastity, and the behaviour of sailors more generally, provides an opportunity for both Forsters to explore the degeneration of Europeans, a provocative theme briefly mentioned in the Introduction to Reinhold's *Observations.* There, Reinhold pointedly sets his "History of Mankind" apart from "systems formed in the closet or at least in the bosom of a nation highly civilized, and therefore in many respects degenerated from its original simplicity" (*OM* 9). This is not quite the "gradual migratory degeneration" (417n2) caused by movement away from the tropics. In the penultimate stage of the voyage, on Tierra del Fuego, this scheme becomes a pretext for highly pejorative racist representations apparently more indebted to Buffon's view of the Americas. George Forster claims that here even the sailors are disgusted by the native women (*VRW* II.631). Much earlier in the voyage, at Dusky Sound, there is the sense that the Māori there have degenerated only a little from the "original simplicity" of the species, and in a different direction from the Europeans. The environment may be seen to "degenerate into rude rocks," yet the human population at this microstage appears to have retained something of the "original system," which seems threatened or obscured – as George comes to feel on Tahiti – by increasing refinement.

At Dusky Sound, too, the savagery of the sailors is represented in a more positive light. This chapter makes a very artful transition from "savages" to savage landscapes to the rigours of exploration: after an attempt by the Māori patriarch to anoint the captain with "odoriferous" seal oil, Cook and the Forsters take their longboat up into a rocky fjord, where they proceed to sleep rough. These conditions, writes George, "soon taught us to overcome the ideas of indelicacy" attached by "civilized nations" to eating with one's fingers, to sleeping in a "wigwam," or even to the "droll" antics of common sailors (I.99). Later on he frames the character of the sailors in terms that also resemble Thomas's dynamic of "liberty and license," underscoring the slippage from "civilized" to "savage": "Though they are members of a civilized society, they may in some measure be looked upon as a body of uncivilized men, rough, passionate, revengeful, but likewise brave, sincere, and true to each other" (290). In Reinhold's preface, the term "degeneration" seems instead to refer to European refinement or luxury, and George echoes this sense in his first, more idealistic narrative of Queen Charlotte Sound, where he attributes the appearance of prostitution to previous European contact (*RW* 209).

The Forsters' innovative use of conjectural history as a form enables highly nuanced, empirically grounded ethnographic comparison but also requires some commitment to human universals and an overarching chronology. Though it shows him at his most prejudiced, George's reflection on the sexual disgust he feels on Tierra del Fuego illustrates the two aspects of this innovation particularly well. Although the Fuegians present "the most loathsome picture of misery and wretchedness," he notes that they nevertheless wear paint and jewellery, and concludes that "ideas of ornament are of more ancient date with mankind, than those of shame and modesty" (*VRW* II.628). The reflection implies that the Fuegians are in fact more "ancient," and not, as Reinhold more consistently argues, degenerated from a better ancestral condition. The Forsters' complex awareness of environmental factors and cultural differences does not always cancel the demand for linear progression and universals inherited from conjectural history. In his early chapters, George is especially apt to lapse from the study of customs and manners into generalizations about human antiquity, as when he notes that the Māori observe the custom of presenting white flags (or green branches) as tokens of peace. The universal recognition of these symbols, he writes, implies a "general agreement ... anterior to the universal dispersion of the human species" (100). David Bindman argues that in such moments, George "speculates that a folk memory of the original state of humanity might remain with the peoples he encounters."[19] In the case of the unfastidious and "keen appetite" that he shares with the sailors at Dusky Sound, or even the impulse towards contact and trust that seemed to be felt on both sides of the beach, these universals extend to Europeans as well.

The stadially oriented comparison of societies also at times implies a universal human trajectory that populations follow (or diverge from) at differing rates. At the end of his first long chapter on Tahiti, George omits his usual detailed overview of customs and manners, deferring to existing accounts, and instead offers a particularly sweeping history of civil society (*RW* 328). He specifies the stage of Tahitian politics, in the manner of conjectural history, as incipiently "feudal" with some "patriarchal" qualities remaining (330–1). Although the forms of feudal despotism vary somewhat on Tonga, George argues that Tahiti and Tonga share "primitive concepts" from a common source (416) – perhaps the mother country on the Asian mainland that putatively "colonized" both, or perhaps even an original, pre-"dispersion" society. (Reinhold Forster remains committed to this monogenist view of human origins, but George eventually takes a more polygenist view in *Noch etwas über die Menschenrassen.*) Six months later on the Marquesas Islands, George is more inclined to contrast Tahiti as a scene of luxury against what seems to him the simpler and happier state of the Marquesans, who are prevented by no refinement from "obeying nature's voice" (*VRW* I.341). Still later on Tanna, he stresses instead the redeeming features of "abundance" as the economic precondition for women's rights. Making an appeal to political economy that recalls Adam Smith, George argues that Tanna (unlike Tahiti) lacks the population and the advanced division of labour required for "refined sentiment in the commerce of the sexes" (II.537). He goes on to note, however, that even "the crudest savage" (*der roheste Wilde*) is "capable of tenderness," which he then illustrates with the local instance of a Tannese man's attachment to his young daughter. Elsewhere the "savagery" of the Tannese is mitigated by "the custom of making friendship by reciprocal exchange of names" (519), which the Forsters seem to regard as a Pacific universal. As their field of comparisons expands, they modify the vocabulary of conjectural history, marking local differences as well as introducing new universals, ranging from customs such as this one to entirely new stages – such as agriculture in the absence of a prior hunting or pastoral stage, a pattern they first recognize on Tanna (554).

I have argued that the Forsters' innovations in the history of the species depend on their practice of natural history – a science of secondary importance to most other historians of civil society in this period. It is at least a suggestive coincidence that Buffon himself returned to the "natural history of man" in the 1770s and published *Epochs of Nature*, with its seventh "epoch" devoted to the ascendancy of the human species on the planet, at the same time that the Forsters' narratives appeared. For all his commitment to Linnaean natural history, clearly explicated by Dettelbach (*OM* lx), Reinhold Forster felt it was a mistake for naturalists to abandon the comprehensive, philosophical view of nature that Buffon offered, as he made clear in his otherwise mixed review of Buffon's *Epochs* (1779). A similar logic motivates George Forster's insistence on the philosophical history of humankind as a priority for the naturalist. In the preface he defends their work as a "philosophical history" of "human nature" (*VRW* I.5–6), and he later insists in a crucial passage that "observations on men and manners ... ought to be the ultimate purpose of every philosophical traveler" (423).[20] This transitional passage introduces the final year of the voyage, which "teem[ed] in new discoveries" – prior to July 1774 the *Resolution* had mostly landed in places where Bougainville, Cook himself, or others had landed before. Though their work in the first two years was still worthwhile because "men and manners" had been neglected by their "unphilosophical" predecessors – as George reflects somewhat ungenerously – the final year was invaluable above all because of the research on human populations enabled by its multiple, sustained experiences of first contact.

Ethnography itself was very much a pre-paradigm science (to use Kuhnian terms) in the late eighteenth century. George Forster's 1786 debate with Immanuel Kant on the subject of race helps clarify the stakes of joining ethnography and natural history. In his polemical reply to Kant's anthropology, Forster points to the philosopher's geographically specific misreading of "Indian" in Pacific travel narratives as evidence that the "natural history of man" has not yet reached the stage of an established discipline, also noting that even established disciplines are eventually transformed.[21] The field evidence that Kant marginalizes is precisely what is needed to give the history of humankind a disciplinary foundation. In the latter one-third of the *Voyage*, George increasingly uses the more established branches of natural history as an alibi or pretext for investigating human varieties in the field. The pretext does not always work, however: he notes ruefully that even though they gestured to botanical specimens they had already gathered, he and his father were turned back from the interior of the island by the native people on Malekula (*RW* 689). Initially, the same thing happens on Tanna. Then, in the case of the volcano, a derailed attempt to study the natural world becomes an opportunity for ethnographic work. In this context, botany, zoology, and mineralogy become subordinate to the study of cultures and peripheral to the narrative (though George's notes often refer readers to his father's *Nova Genera Plantarum* for details). Thus the Forsters insisted on a naturalistic context for stadial and other forms of conjectural history, mapping a generative area of uncertainty between geological and species time at a moment when the distinction between "human" and "natural" time, as Johannes Fabian would later term it, was far from clear.

NOTES

1 Buffon, *Natural History, General and Particular*, trans. William Smellie, 9 vols., second ed. (London: Cadell, 1785), vol. 9, 258–410, at 286, 303.

2 Forster, *Observations Made During a Voyage Round the World*, eds. Nicholas Thomas, Harriet Guest, and Michael Dettelbach (Honolulu: University of Hawai'i Press, 1996), 9–10. Hereafter cited parenthetically as *OM*.

3 Thomas, *In Oceania: Visions, Artifacts, Histories* (Durham: Duke University Press, 1997), 86; Guest, *Empire, Barbarism, and Civilisation: James Cook, William Hodges, and the Return to the Pacific* (Cambridge: Cambridge University Press, 2007), 56; Bindman, *Ape to Apollo: Aesthetics and the Idea of Race in the Eighteenth Century* (Ithaca: Cornell University Press, 2002), 149–50.

4 Lansdown, ed., *Strangers in the South Seas: The Idea of the Pacific in Western Thought* (Honolulu: University of Hawai'i Press, 2006), 69–70; Thomas, *In Oceania*, 71. In his general introduction, Lansdown discusses the classical legacy (*Strangers* 11–12) and introduces his concept of bipolar vision (16); he develops his distinction between cultural and chronological primitivism and his reading of Rousseau in a subsequent discussion of the "noble savage" (65). Bindman and Lansdown offer a larger European framework for understanding the voyages, which is just as important – especially in the case of continental intellectuals such as the Forsters – as the Scottish Enlightenment framework emphasized by Thomas and Guest.

5 In many cases I cite the more complete German version of George Forster's text, *Reise um die Welt*, ed. Gerhard Steiner (Frankfurt: Insel, 1967), here at 505. Hereafter cited parenthetically as *RW*.

6 See further Robert Siegfried and Robert H. Dott, eds., *Humphry Davy on Geology: The 1805 Lectures for the General Audience* (Madison: University of Wisconsin Press, 1980), 130–5, 96.

7 Buffon, *Natural History, General and Particular*, vol. 9, 381. Unlike Ferber's, Buffon's natural history was also an important source on human nature for the Forsters, and both of them cite him frequently – not always critically – on matters of ethnicity and the geographic distribution of human populations. On Buffon's importance for the Forsters, see also John Gascoigne, "The German Enlightenment and the Pacific," in *The Anthropology of the Enlightenment*, ed. Larry Wolff and Marco Cipolloni (Stanford: Stanford University Press, 2007), 141–71, at 147–8.

8 Bruno Latour, *Reassembling the Social: An Introduction to Actor-Network Theory* (Oxford: Oxford University Press, 2005), 79–80.

9 George Forster, *A Voyage Round the World*, ed. Nicholas Thomas and Oliver Berghof, 2 vols. (Honolulu: University of Hawai'i Press, 2000), vol. 2, 510. Hereafter cited parenthetically as *VRW*.

10 See further Thomas, *In Oceania*, ch. 3; and Guest, *Empire, Barbarism, and Civilisation*, ch. 2.

11 Guntau, *Die Genesis der Geologie als Wissenschaft* (Berlin: Akademie Verlag, 1984), 22; in Humboldt, see, for example, his preface to Humboldt and Aimé Bonpland, *Essay on the Geography of Plants*, trans. Sylvie Romanowski (Chicago: University of Chicago Press, 2008), 61.

12 See also *OM* 214. Forster did read and cite Kames (cf. *OM* 416n2), but not until after the voyage, since *Sketches* was published in 1774.

13 Michael Hoare, ed., *The* Resolution *Journal of Johann Reinhold Forster*, 3 vols. (London: Hakluyt Society, 1982), vol. 3, 66.

14 Margaret Jolly analyses the implications of this dynamic for race and racism during the encounter on Tanna (ni-Vanuatu) in "'Ill-Natured Comparisons': Racism and Relativism in European Representations of ni-Vanuatu from Cook's Second Voyage," *History and Anthropology* 5 (1992): 331–64.

15 On the ethnographic difficulties posed by these encounters with the Kanak and the Vanuatuans, see Bronwen Douglas, "Art as Ethno-Historical Text: Science, Representation, and Indigenous Presence in Eighteenth- and Nineteenth-Century Oceanic Voyage Literature," in *Double Vision: Art Histories and Colonial Histories in the Pacific*, ed. Nicholas Thomas and Diane Losche (Cambridge: Cambridge University Press, 1999), 65–99, esp. 70–3.

16 On "primogenial," Reinhold's alternative to "primitive" rock, see *OM* 34, 35n, as well as his earlier *Introduction to Mineralogy* (London: Joseph Johnson, 1768), 58. Hodges's finished painting of 1778, *View of the Island of New Caledonia* (National Maritime Museum), captures something of this ruggedness.

17 Confirmation of this incident of cannibalism did not come until after their departure from New Zealand (*VRW* II.606–11). See further Anne Salmond, *The Trial of the Cannibal Dog* (New Haven: Yale University Press, 2003), 228–30.

18 The German text introduces the idea of resistance to oppression (*RW* 812). See further Guest, "Looking at Women: Forster's Observations in the South Pacific" (*OM* xli–liv).

19 Bindman, *Ape to Apollo* 129; Bindman also notes that the Forsters differ from Bougainville on this point.

20 I have interpolated my own translation of Forster's German version for the second half of this quotation, because his language in the German is stronger and makes the connection more explicit: "Menschen und Sitten als … der vornehmste Endzweck eines jeden philosophischen Reisenden" (*RW* 675). See also Gascoigne, "The German Enlightenment," 147–8.

21 Forster, "Noch etwas über die Menschenrassen," *Werke in Vier Bänden*, ed. Gerhard Steiner (Frankfurt: Insel, 1970), vol. 2, 78, 75.

Contributors

Michael Bravo is University Senior Lecturer and Fellow of Downing College at Cambridge University, where he convenes the Circumpolar History and Public Policy Research group at the Scott Polar Research Institute. He has published widely on the history of science, exploration, and empire and has worked closely with Inuit communities in Canada's High Arctic. His published work includes such titles as *The Accuracy of Ethnoscience* (1996), *Narrating the Arctic* (2002), *Arctic Geopolitics and Autonomy* (2010), *The Pan-Inuit Trails Atlas* (http://paninuittrails.org, 2014), and the forthcoming *North Pole: Nature and Culture* (2018).

Adriana Craciun is Emma MacLachlan Metcalf Chair of Humanities and Professor of English at Boston University. Her most recent books are *Writing Arctic Disaster: Authorship and Exploration* (Cambridge UP, 2016) and *The Material Cultures of Enlightenment Arts and Sciences*, co-edited with Simon Schaffer (Palgrave, 2016). In 2014–15, she served as Clark Professor at UCLA (with Mary Terrall).

Markman Ellis is Professor of Eighteenth-Century Studies in the School of English and Drama at Queen Mary University of London. He is the author of *The Politics of Sensibility: Race, Gender, and Commerce in the Sentimental Novel* (1996), *The History of Gothic Fiction* (2000), and *The Coffee House: A Cultural History* (2004), and co-author of *Empire of Tea* (2015). He was the general editor of *Eighteenth-Century Coffee-House Culture* (4 vols., 2006) and *Tea and the Tea-Table in Eighteenth-Century England* (4 vols., 2010). He has also published on the history of natural history, georgic poetry, slavery and empire, literary coteries, and library history.

Matthew Goldmark is Assistant Professor of Spanish at Florida State University where he specializes in colonial Latin American studies with an emphasis on Iberian empire, Indigenous cultural productions, and gender and sexuality studies. In 2014–15 he was an Ahmanson–Getty Postdoctoral Fellow at UCLA's Center for Seventeenth- and Eighteenth-Century Studies for the core program "Explorations, Encounters, and the Circulation of Knowledge." His current book project, *Formal Attachments: Compositions of Kinship in Colonial Spanish America,* demonstrates how the regulated practices of imperial documentation created intimate, but not biological, ties that organized and extended empire.

Noah Heringman teaches English at the University of Missouri. His publications include two monographs, *Romantic Rocks, Aesthetic Geology* (2004) and *Sciences of Antiquity: Romantic Antiquarianism, Natural History, and Knowledge Work* (2013), as well as two edited volumes and numerous articles on topics ranging from Romantic poetry to Anthropocene popular culture. He is currently working on a monograph, *Deep Time and the Prehistoric Turn,* and an edition of *Vetusta Monumenta.*

Donna Landry is Professor of English and American Literature at the University of Kent and a Fellow of the Royal Asiatic Society. The author of essays on Anglo-Ottoman exchanges and of *Noble Brutes: How Eastern Horses Transformed English Culture* (Johns Hopkins University Press, 2009), *The Invention of the Countryside: Hunting, Walking, and Ecology in English Literature, 1671–1831* (Palgrave, 2001), and *The Muses of Resistance: Labouring-Class Women's Poetry in Britain, 1739–1796* (Cambridge University Press, 1990; 2005), she co-edited with Gerald MacLean *Travelling in Anatolia, the Ottoman Empire, and the Republic of Turkey,* a special issue of *Studies in Travel Writing* 16, no. 4 (December 2012), *The Country and the City Revisited: England and the Politics of Culture, 1550–1850,* with MacLean and Joseph P. Ward (Cambridge University Press, 1999; 2006), and *The Spivak Reader,* with MacLean and Gayatri Chakravorty Spivak (Routledge, 1996). Landry is a founder-member of the Evliya Çelebi Way Project, a team of scholars and equestrians who rode across western Anatolia on horseback following the great Ottoman travel writer Evliya Çelebi, establishing a UNESCO Cultural Route. Project website: http://www.kent.ac.uk/english/evliya/index.html.

Billie Lythberg is an interdisciplinary researcher working at the junction of economics, anthropology, and history. Her research interests include

Oceanic sciences, arts, and oral histories; cross-cultural theories of value, valuables, and valuation; sustainability and environmental management; and social innovation. She is co-author of *Artefacts of Encounter: Cook's Voyages, Colonial Collecting, and Museum Histories* (University of Otago Press, 2016).

Kathleen S. Murphy is Associate Professor of History at the California Polytechnic State University, San Luis Obispo. Her current research examines the intertwined histories of science and the slave trade in the eighteenth-century British Atlantic world.

Miles Ogborn is Professor of Geography at Queen Mary University of London. He is the author of *Spaces of Modernity: London's Geographies, 1680–1780* (1998), *Indian Ink: Script and Print in the Making of the English East India Company* (2007), and *Global Lives: Britain and the World, 1550–1800* (2008). He is currently writing a book on the historical geographies of speech and slavery in Barbados and Jamaica.

Victoria Pickering is a Postdoctoral Researcher at the British Museum. She is part of a Leverhulme Trust–funded project that explores the intellectual structures of Hans Sloane's manuscript catalogues of his collection. Her PhD research at Queen Mary University of London and the Natural History Museum, London, focused on part of Sloane's botanical collection, the "Vegetable Substances," and its role in early-eighteenth-century natural knowledge.

Mary Terrall is Professor of History at UCLA. She is the author of *The Man Who Flattened the Earth: Maupertuis and the Sciences in the Enlightenment* (2002) and *Catching Nature in the Act: Réaumur and the Practice of Natural History in the Eighteenth Century* (2014). She has served twice as Clark Professor at UCLA: in 2005–6 with Helen Deutsch (resulting in the University of Toronto Press volume *Vital Matters: Eighteenth-Century Views of Conception, Life, and Death* (2012)), and in 2014–15 with Adriana Craciun. Her current research focuses on natural history in the European encounter with West Africa in the eighteenth century.

Index

Page references in *italics* refer to illustrations.

THE UCLA CLARK MEMORIAL LIBRARY SERIES

1. *Wilde Writings: Contextual Conditions*, edited by Joseph Bristow
2. *Enchanted Ground: Reimagining John Dryden*, edited by Jayne Lewis and Maximillian E. Novak
3. *Culture and Authority in the Baroque*, edited by Massimo Ciavolella and Patrick Coleman
4. *Ritual, Routine, and Regime: Repetition in Early Modern British and European Cultures*, edited by Lorna Clymer
5. *Momigliano and Antiquarianism: Foundations of the Modern Cultural Sciences*, edited by Peter N. Miller
6. *Monarchisms in the Age of Enlightenment: Liberty, Patriotism, and the Common Good*, edited by Hans Blom, John Christian Laursen, and Luisa Simonetti
7. *Thinking Impossibilities: The Intellectual Legacy of Amos Funkenstein*, edited by Robert S. Westman and David Biale
8. *Discourses of Tolerance and Intolerance in the European Enlightenment*, edited by Hans Erich Bödeker, Clorinda Donato, and Peter Hanns Reill
9. *The Age of Projects*, edited by Maximillian E. Novak
10. *Acculturation and Its Discontents: The Italian Jewish Experience between Exclusion and Inclusion*, edited by David N. Myers, Massimo Ciavolella, Peter H. Reill, and Geoffrey Symcox
11. *Defoe's Footprints: Essays in Honour of Maximillian E. Novak*, edited by Robert M. Maniquis and Carl Fisher
12. *Women, Religion, and the Atlantic World (1600–1800)*, edited by Daniella Kostroun and Lisa Vollendorf
13. *Braudel Revisited: The Mediterranean World, 1600–1800*, edited by Gabriel Piterberg, Teofilo F. Ruiz, and Geoffrey Symcox
14. *Structures of Feeling in Seventeenth-Century Cultural Expression*, edited by Susan McClary
15. *Godwinian Moments*, edited by Robert M. Maniquis and Victoria Myers
16. *Vital Matters: Eighteenth-Century Views of Conception, Life, and Death*, edited by Helen Deutsch and Mary Terrall
17. *Redrawing the Map of Early Modern English Catholicism*, edited by Lowell Gallagher
18. *Space and Self in Early Modern European Cultures*, edited by David Warren Sabean and Malina Stefanovska
19. *Wilde Discoveries: Traditions, Histories, Archives*, edited by Joseph Bristow
20. *Jesuit Accounts of the Colonial Americas: Intercultural Transfers, Intellectual Disputes, and Textualities*, edited by Marc André Bernier, Clorinda Donato, and Hans-Jürgen Lüsebrink

21. *Skepticism and Political Thought in the Seventeenth and Eighteenth Centuries,* edited by John Christian Laursen and Gianni Paganini
22. *Representing Imperial Rivalry in the Early Modern Mediterranean,* edited by Barbara Fuchs and Emily Weissbourd
23. *Imagining the British Atlantic after the American Revolution,* edited by Michael Meranze and Saree Makdisi
24. *Life Forms in the Thinking of the Long Eighteenth Century,* edited by Keith Michael Baker and Jenna M. Gibbs
25. *Cultures of Communication: Theologies of Media in Early Modern Europe and Beyond,* edited by Helmut Puff, Ulrike Strasser, and Christopher Wild
26. *Curious Encounters: Voyaging, Collecting, and Making Knowledge in the Long Eighteenth Century,* edited by Adriana Craciun and Mary Terrall

www.ingramcontent.com/pod-product-compliance
Lightning Source LLC
LaVergne TN
LVHW041114090826
844660LV00062B/906/J
9781487503673